The Indo-Aryan Races

A Study of
The Origin of Indo-Aryan People and Institutions

THE INDO-ARYAN RACES:

A Study of
The Origin of Indo-Aryan People and Institutions

BY

RAMAPRASAD CHANDA, B.A.

Honorary Secretary, Varendra Research Society, Rajshahi.

GYAN

Published by

GYAN

Gyan Publishing House
5, Ansari Road
Daryaganj, New Delhi-110002
Phone: 011-47034999, 9811692060
E-mail: books@gyanbooks.com

Distribution Network
gyanbooks.com
India, USA, Canada, UK, Australia, France

ISBN : 978-81-212-2278-5 (HB)
First Published, 1916

2nd Impression 2021

Printed at: Gyan Press, Delhi.

The Indo-Aryan Races
A Study of The Origin of Indo-Aryan People and Institutions
Author: Ramaprasad Chanda

The Indo-Aryan Races:

A Study of
The Origin of Indo-Aryan People and Institutions.

BY

RAMĀPRASĀD CHANDA, B.A.,
Honorary Secretary, Varendra Research Society, Rajshahi.

RAJSHAHI:
PUBLISHED BY THE VARENDRA RESEARCH SOCIETY.

1916.

TO

THE SACRED MEMORY OF MY PARENTS

KĀLĪPRASĀD CHANDA AND SONĀTĀRĀ CHANDA.

FOREWORD.

In the second session of the Bengal Literary Conference held at Rajshahi in February, 1909, it was resolved to cause enquiries to be made and publish a monograph on the origin of the Bengali people. On behalf of the organisers of the Conference I requested my learned friend, Mr. Ramāprasād Chanda, who read a paper on this subject in the Conference, to undertake the work. It was originally contemplated that the monograph should be published in the Bengali language; but as Mr. Chanda was for writing out the results of his investigations in English for submitting them to the scrutiny of all scholars interested in the subject, I agreed to the proposal with the approval of my revered teacher and friend, Principal Ramendra Sundar Trivedi, who had moved the resolution in the Conference.

The delay in the publication is due partly to the many disadvantages under which the author had to work and partly to his natural diffidence. Meanwhile the Varendra Research Society was established and I placed funds at its disposal for the publication of this work.

I have now great pleasure in introducing this very interesting work to the public and hope it will stimulate further research in this new line.

SARAT KUMAR RAY
of Dighapatiya.

DAYĀRĀMPUR, RAJSHAHI,
June, 1916.

PREFACE.

These notes owe their publication to my esteemed friend Kumār Sarat Kumār Ray, M.A., M.R.A.S., of Dighapatiya, who has been pressing me to bring out a monograph on Bengali origins for the last seven years. The encouragement given by him as president of the Varendra Research Society and by my other colleagues, Mr. Akṣay Kumār Maitra, the Director of the Society, and Messrs Rādhāgavinda Basāk, M.A., and Upendranāth Ghosāl, M.A., has sustained me in my investigations and emboldened me to submit the first instalment of the results to the public.

Chapter I is the outgrowth of a paper entitled *India and Babylonia* published in *East and West* of Bombay of 1905, and Chapter II of another paper published in the same magazine in 1907. The latter chapter in its present form was read in a public meeting held at Darjeeling in June, 1913, under the presidency of His Excellency Lord Carmichael, Governor of Bengal. In Chapter III I have failed to notice a very learned work on Vaiṣṇavism, Professor Brajendranāth Seal's monograph submitted to the International Congress of Orientalists held in Rome in 1899. In this work the author mainly deals with the influence of Christianity on latter-day Vaiṣṇavism, but he recognises in Kṛṣṇa the historical founder of the religion. In Professor Seal's opinion Vāsudeva, Samkarṣaṇa, Pradyumna and Aniruddha were originally hero-gods, and Śāṇḍilya derived the root ideas of the Bhāgavata philosophy from Vedic sources.

The anthropometric data embodied in the appendix are the results of measurements taken in 1909 and 1910. In 1909 Mr. Śaśadhar Ray, the well-known Bengali writer, and myself, took measurements of the head form of living subjects belonging to different sections of the Brāhman caste. In this work we were helped by Mr. Surya Kumār Guha, M.A., then Deputy Superintendent of Police, Rajshahi, Mr. Hem Chandra Ganguly, M.A., of the Rajshahi College, and other friends. In 1910 the Government of Eastern Bengal and Assam placed me on special duty for ethnological researches for three months on the recommendation of the Hon'ble Mr. H. Sharp, M.A., then Director of Public Instruction. In taking measurements with instruments lent by the Ethnographical Survey of India during this period of deputation I was greatly assisted by Mahārāja Sir Girijānāth Ray Bahadur, K.C.I.E., of Dinajpur, the Hon'ble Mahārāja Sir Manindra Chandra Nandī, K.C.I.E., of Kāśīmbāzār, Mahāśay Tārak Chandra Ghose of Bhagalpur, Paṇḍit Binodvihari Vidyābinod of Bhātpāḍā, Dr. Mohini Mohan Ghosh of Champanagar, Bhagalpur, Principal Rāmendra Sundar Trivedī of Calcutta, and Mr. Rākhāldās Banerji of the Calcutta Museum, to all of whom I gratefully acknowledge my indebtedness.

My thanks are also due to Professor Srish Chandra Śāstrī who drew my attention to some of the passages of the *Mahābhāṣya* quoted in the text and helped me in explaining their meaning, and to Mr. Akṣay Kumar Maitra and Professors Upendra Nath Ghosal and Ramesh Chandra Mazumdar who have rendered me occasional help in correcting the proofs.

The system of transliteration adopted is that recommended by the Council of the Royal Asiatic Society with the exception of *ṃ* for *ṁ*. Owing to a large number of quotations it has not been possible to follow the system consistently. Unfortunately a considerable number of mistakes also have escaped my notice.

RAMĀPRASĀD CHANDA.

VARENDRA RESEARCH SOCIETY,
Rajshahi, June, 1916.

CONTENTS.

CHAPTER I.

The Āryas and the Anaryas of Vedic India.

PAGE

Ārya and Dāsa—Origin of Śūdras—Niṣādas—Modern hill tribes—Austro-Asiatic race—Ṛṣi families formed a hereditary priesthood—Office of Brahman priest a monopoly of the Vasiṣṭha family—Direct divine origin claimed by the Ṛṣi families—Kuśikas and Kaṇvas—Conflict of Vasiṣṭha and Viśvāmitra—White Ṛṣi and dark Ṛṣi—Warrior tribes, Yadus and Turvaśas—Early Indian home of the Yadus—Aryans in Syria and Upper Mesopotamia—Origin of Caste 1-36

CHAPTER II.

Indo-Aryans of the Outer Countries.

Boundaries of Vedic Aryandom—Vedic Āryas hostile to the nations of the Outer Countries—Different types of social organisations—Inner and Outer groups of Indo-Aryan languages—Vedic Midland—Kośalas, Kaśis, Videhas—Early history of Northern India—Magadhan Empire—Khasas—Head form as a test of racial affinity—Risley's Scytho-Dravidian type—Risley's Mongola-Dravidian type—*Homo-Alpinus* type in Central Asia—Coming of the *Homo-Alpinus* 37-78

CHAPTER III.

Race and Cult—Vaiṣṇavism.

Primitive culture of the Outlandic Indo-Aryans—Weber's theory of the Christian origin of the cult of child Kṛṣṇa—Sir R. G. Bhandarkar's arguments—Kṛṣṇa legend in Bhāsa's drama—Antiquity of the cults of Rāma and child Kṛṣṇa—Is *Kaṁśabadha* a nature-myth—Origin of Pāñcarātra—Pāñcaratra originally un-Vedic—Kṛṣṇa a religious reformer—Destruction of the Yādava tribe—Vāsudeva, Samkarṣaṇa, Pradyumna and Aniruddha

PAGE

deified by the Saurāṣtras and the Ābhiras—Pāñcarātra systematised by Śāṇḍilya—Nārāyaṇīya section of the Mahābhārata—Cult of the *Avatāras* of Viṣṇu—Rāma as *Avatāra*—The cult of the *Vyūhas* superseded by the cult of the *Avatāras* 79–121

CHAPTER IV.

Race and Cult—Śāktism.

Female deities in the Vedas—Epic conception of Durgā—Durgā as Śavarī or Kiratī—Dakṣa's sacrifice and the Pāśupata cult—Devī in the Devī-māhātmya—Durgā as the vegetation spirit or corn-mother—The nine plants—Durgā as war-goddess—Durgā as Annadā—The *kula* trees—Kāl , the all-destroying time—Tārā—Hindu sectarianism—Śakti of the Śākta sectary—Great Goddess of the Mediterranean nations—Mother-kin favourable to the growth of Śāktism—Home of Śāktism—Prevalence of mother-kin in the Outer Countries—Śāktism and Magianism—Śāktism and Śākadvīpi Brāhmans 122–161

CHAPTER V.

Race and Caste—The Brāhmans of the Outer Countries.

Outlandic Brahmans claim descent from Vedic Ṛṣis—Their head form—Behāri Brāhmans—Gayāwāl Brāhmans—Bābhans—Genealogical works of the Rāḍhīyas and Vārendra Brāhmans of Bengal—Genealogy of Guravamiśra—Genealogy of Prahāsa—Genealogy of Bhavadeva—Genealogy of Caturbhuja—Brāhmanism in Bengal before Ādiśūra—Marāṭha Brāhmans—Gujarāti Brāhmans—Nāgar Brāhmans of Gujarat—Kulin Kāyasthas of Bengal—Kāyastha surnames—Kāyastha controversy—The legend of Veṇa and the thirty-six castes—Bengali Kāyastha past and present 162–201

CHAPTER VI.

Indo-Aryans and Iranians.

Veda and Avesta—Aryan home and Aryan expansion—Classical writers on the Magi—Rebellion of the Magian Gaumata and Magophonia—Moulton's theory of the surrender of the monopoly of priesthood on the part of

PAGE

the Aryan Medes and Persians to the non-Aryan Magi untenable—Priestly functions of the King—Silence of Herodotus damaging to Moulton's theory—Brāhman and Magi—Dr. Spooner's theory of the Magian invasion of India—His main arguments—Śākadvīpī Brāhmans—Date of their immigration—Popular religion of Magadha in the Maurya period—Gautama Buddha was by birth a Hindu—His repudiation of Hinduism . . 202–244

NOTES.

A. Ārya and Śūdra 245
B. Piśāca affinities of Lahṇḍa, Sindhī and Kāshmīrī . 246
C. Sound changes in Bengali 248
D Un-Vedic Pāñcarātrā 249
APPENDIX Anthropometric Data 253
ADDITIONS AND CORRECTIONS 271

THE INDO-ARYAN RACES.

CHAPTER I.

THE ĀRYAS AND THE ANĀRYAS OF VEDIC INDIA.

THE dawn of history is heralded in India by the hymns sung by the Ṛṣis and enshrined in the Rgveda Saṃhitā. These hymns reveal two hostile peoples in the Land of the Seven Rivers now called the Punjab—the *deva*-worshipping Ārya and the *deva*-less and rite-less Dasyu or Dāsa. The first problem that demands the attention of students of the anthropological history of India is, —who were these Dasyus or non-Āryas of Vedic India ?

It is commonly assumed that in the four-fold division of castes (*varṇa*=colour) the aborigines, who submitted to, or were subdued by, the Āryan invaders, were represented by the Śūdras. "It is reasonable to reckon the Śūdra of the later texts as belonging to the aborigines who had been reduced to subjection by the Aryans."* But this view does not accord well with the data in hand.

* Macdonell and Keith's *Vedic Index of Names and Subjects*, London, 1912, Vol. II, p. 388.

The status of a Śūdra of the later Vedic age resembles that of slaves or serfs of Europe. In the Aitareya Brāhmaṇa (VII. 29) it is said of the Śūdra: "One like a Śūdra shall be born in thy line, the servant of another, who may be expelled or slain at will." According to the Pañcaviṃśa Brāhmaṇa (VI. 1. 11) a Śūdra, even if prosperous (*bahu-paśu*, 'having many cows') could not be other than a servant; his business was the washing of the feet of his superiors (*pādāvanejya*).* This accords well with Manu (VIII. 413-414, 417) who says:—

"The Śūdra, whether bought or unbought, should be made to act as a slave (*dāsyam*), for the Śūdra was created by the Self-existent for the service of the Brāhman.

"Even if freed by his master, the Śūdra is not released from servitude; for this (servitude) is innate in him: who then can take it from him?

"A Brāhman may take possession of the goods of a Śūdra without any hesitation, for nothing that belongs to him is his own, he is one whose property may be taken away by his master."

About the different ways of making slaves or Śūdras, Manu (VIII. 415) writes:—

"A war-captive, one serving as a slave for food, one born (of a female slave) within the house, one bought, one recieved as a gift, one inherited from the father, and one condemned to act as a slave

* *Ibid.* II, p. 389.

as a punishment,—these are the seven kinds of slaves."

Some of these methods of making Śūdras, particularly enslaving a war-captive, must have been in vogue in the Vedic period. In the early Vedic period the Āryas were not only at war with Dāsa foes but also with Ārya foes. About the wars of the Ṛgvedic Āryas Professors Macdonell and Keith write:—

"Āryan foes (*vṛtra*) are referred to beside Dāsa foes, and there are many references to war of Āryan versus Āryan, as well as to war of Āryan against Dāsa. From this it can be fairly deduced that even by the time of the Ṛgveda the Āryan communities had advanced far beyond the stage of simple conquest of the aborigines. In the later Saṃhitās and Brāhmaṇas the wars alluded to seem mainly Āryan wars, no doubt in consequence of the fusion of Ārya and Dāsa into one community."*

It cannot be assumed that the Āryas treated Dāsa war-captives in one way, that is to say, made them slaves, and their Ārya war-captives in a different way, for the hymns breathe as bitter hatred of foes of one class as of the other. Therefore it is unreasonable to hold that the Sūdras of the Vedic period were recruited from among the aborigines alone.

For the true representatives of the Anāryas of the Rgvedic age we should look, not to the

---

* *Ibid.* I, p. 65.

fourth order of the Vedic society, but to the fifth order, the Niṣādas. In the Ṛgveda the term *pañcajanāh* and its synonyms occur very often. According to Yāska (III. 8) the term means, "Gandharvas, manes, gods, demons, and monsters according to some, and the four varṇas with the Nīṣāda as the fifth according to the Upamanyus." But in two other places (X. 3. 5, 7) Yāska himself explains *pañca-kṛṣṭi* of the Ṛgveda as "*pañca manuṣyajātāni*", 'five classes of men', which is explained by the scholiast as the four varṇas with the Niṣādas as the fifth. The author of the Bṛhaddevatā attributes this interpretation to Sākatāyana also (VII. 69). Niṣādas are first named as such in the Rudrādhyāya of the Yajurveda together with the Vrātas (nomads), Takṣans (carpenters), Rathakāras (chariot-makers), Kulālas (potters), Karmāras (blacksmiths), Puñjiṣṭhas (fowlers), Śvanins (dog-keepers), and Mṛgayus (hunters). The Mahābhārata (XII. 59. 94-97) contains the following account of the origin of the Niṣādas:—

"Vena, a slave of wrath and malice, became unrighteous in his conduct towards all creatures. The Ṛṣis, those utterers of Brahma, slew him with kuśa blades (as their weapon) inspired with *mantras*. Uttering *mantras* the while, those Ṛṣis pierced the right thigh of Vena. Thereupon, from that thigh, came out a short-limbed person on earth, resembling a charred brand, with blood-red eyes and black hair. Those utterers of Brahma then said unto him,—Niṣīda, sit here. From him have sprung the Niṣādas, viz. those wicked tribes that have the hills and the forests for their abode, as also those hundreds and thousands of others, called Mlecchas, residing on the Vindhya mountains."*

The same story is repeated in many of the Purāṇas. In the Viṣṇu Purāṇa (I. 13) the Niṣāda is described as "of the complexion of a charred stake, with flattened feature and dwarfish stature." The Bhāgavata Purāṇa (IV. 14. 44) describes the Niṣāda as "black like crow, very low statured, short armed, having high cheek bones, low-topped nose, red eyes and copper-coloured hair."† In the Padma Purāṇa (II. 27. 42—43) it is said, "His (Niṣāda's) descendants are settled in the hills and forests; the Niṣādas, Kirātas, Bhillas, Nāhalakas, Bhramaras, Pulindas, and other Mleccha tribes addicted to vices are all sprung from his body." These epic and Purāṇic legends evidently contain genuine traditions relating to the physical characters of the aborigines whom the Vedic Āryas met in the plains of Northern India. The Niṣādas were too numerous to be annihilated and too powerful to be enslaved or expelled *en masse*. The Āryas were, therefore, compelled to meet them half way. In the Pañcavimṃśa Brāhmaṇa (XVI. 6. 7) the performer of the Viśvajit sacrifice is required "to live for three days among the Niṣādas." In the Śrauta Sūtra

* P. C. Ray's translation.

† काककृष्णोऽतिह्रस्वाङ्गो ह्रस्वबाहुर्महाहनुः ।
ह्रस्वपान्निम्ननासाग्रो रक्ताक्षस्ताम्रमूर्धजः ॥

of Kātyāyana (I. 12) and in the Mimāṃsa Sūtra (VI. 1. 51-52) of Jaimini, Vedic texts are referred to that provided that Brāhman priests should make chiefs who were Niṣādas by descent offer certain sacrifices.

In the mediæval Sanskrit literature, the barbarians of the Vindhya hills, belonging to the Niśāda stock according to the Purāṇas, are called Śabaras, Pulindas, and Kirātas. Bāṇa, who flourished in the first half of the seventh century A.D., thus describes a Savara youth in his Harṣacarita:—"The young mountaineer (*śavara-yuvā*) had his hair tied into a crest above his forehead with a band of Śyāmalatā creeper dark like lamp black, and his dark forehead was like a night that always accompanied him in his wild exploits . . . . . .; his ear had an ear-ring of grass-like crystal fastened in it, and assumed a green hue from a parrot's wing which ornamented it, ... his nose was flat, his lower lip thick, his chin low, his jaws full, his forehead and cheekbones projecting."* This agrees fully with the Purāṇic description of the Niśādas.

Niṣāda characteristics are still conspicuous in the Bhils and Gonds of the Vindhya regions. "The typical Bhil is small, dark, broad-nosed, and ugly, but well-built and active."† "The Gonds are of small stature and dark in colour. Their bodies are well proportioned, but their

* Cowell and Thomas, *Harṣacarita* (Eng translation), p. 230.

† *Rajputana Gazetteer* (Calcutta, 1908), p. 87.

features are ugly, with a round head, distended nostrils, a wide mouth and thick lips, straight and black hair, and scanty beard and moustache."* Dark skin, short stature and broad nose indicate the physical relationship of the Bhils and the Gonds with the old Niśādas on the one hand, and the hill tribes of Chota-Nagpur and Orissa and the Paniyans, the Kadirs, the Kurumbas, the Sholagas, the Irulas, the Mala Vedars and the Kanikars of Southern India, on the other. Sir Herbert Risley classifies these dark, short, and broad-nosed savage tribes of Central and Southern India together with the civilised speakers of Dravidian languages under the head Dravidian type But the first thing that suggests itself at a glance at the summary of measurements of the castes and tribes of the so-called Dravidian type arranged in order of nasal index in Appendix IV p. cxiii of his work, *The People of India* (Calcutta, 1908), is that a line should be drawn between Parayan and Irula in this table. The average nasal indices will be found to vary from 69·1 to 80·0 above the line, whereas they vary from 80·9 to 95·1 below it. Mr. Thurston gives 84·1 as the average nasal index of the Irula of the Nilgiris. So if we exclude the Mukkuvan of Malabar, the Moormen of Ceylon and the Dom and Kurmi of Chota Nagpur and Bengal, we are left face to face with twenty-seven broad-nosed jungle tribes with average nasal indices above 84. We are, there-

Central Provinces Gazetteer (Calcutta, 1908), p. 163.

fore, hardly justified in classifying these broad-nosed tribesmen with the upper group unless it is admitted that the nose-form of the latter has been modified by the influence of environment. Instances may be cited in which physical environment has produced no change in the shape of the nose. Three of the hill tribes of Southern India, the Toda, the Badaga, and the Kota, are medium-nosed like the civilised speakers of the Dravidian languages, the average nasal index of the Toda being 74·9, of the Badaga 75·6 and the Kota 77·2. The climate of the plains of the United Provinces has failed to modify the nose-form of the Pasi toddy-drawer (average nasal index 85·4), Chamar (86·0), Musahar (86·1) and other lower castes.*

In this connection greater weight should be attached to the views of two competent observers who have lived long among the population of Southern India. Mr. Thurston holds that the jungle tribes of Southern India "are the microscopic remnants of a pre-Dravidian people."† Robert Sewell writes, "At some very remote period the aborigines of Southern India were overcome by hordes of Dravidian invaders and driven to the mountains and desert tracts, where their descendants are still to be found."‡ This dark, short and broad-nosed race is termed Pre-Dravidian by the Anthropologists. But since these

* *The People of India*, appendix iv, p. cxiv.

† *Castes and Tribes of Southern India* (Madras, 1904), Vol. I, p. iv.

‡ *The Indian Empire*, Vol. II (Oxford, 1909), p. 32.

physical features characterised the Purāṇic Niṣādas and indicate the affinities of the Purāṇic Niṣādas with the so-called Pre-Dravidian, so I should prefer to classify the dark, short-statured and broad-nosed jungle tribes as the modern Niṣādas representing the old Niṣāda race. The modern Niṣādas speak dialects belonging to three different linguistic families. The Bhils speak an Indo-Aryan language; the Gonds, the Khands, the Oraons and the jungle tribes of Southern India speak Dravidian languages; and the jungle tribes of Chota Nagpur and the Śavaras and Juangs of Orissa speak languages of the Munda family. If our hypothesis relating to the Niṣāda race is correct, we must assume that Mundā was originally spoken by the Niṣāda race as a whole, and Indo-Aryan and Dravidian dialects have been adopted by some of the Niṣāda tribes as a result of their contact with their more civilised neighbours.

The physical characters of the Niṣādas indicate their affinities with the Veddas of Ceylon and the Sakais and Semangs of the Malay Peninsula Thurston writes in his introduction to *Castes and Tribes of Southern India* (p. 33):—

"Speaking of the Sakais, the same authorities [Skeat and Blagden] state that 'in evidence of their striking resemblance to the Veddas, it is worth remarking that one of the brothers, Sarasin, who had lived among the Veddas and knew them very well, when shown a photograph of a typical Sakai, at first supposed it to be a photograph of a Vedda. For myself, when I saw the photographs of Sakais published by Skeat and Blagden, it was difficult to realise that I was not looking at pictures of Kadirs, Paniyans, Kurumbas or other jungle folk of Southern India.''

The linguistic researches of Schmidt and Sten Konow enable us to trace the affinities of the Niṣādas over a still wider range. Pater Schmidt in his *Die Mon-Khmer-Völker* establishes the intimate relationship between the following groups of languages :—the Munda languages of India ; Nikobar spoken in the Nikobar Islands; Khasi spoken in the Khasi hills of Assam; Palong, Wa, and Riang of Salwin basin, Upper Burma; Sakai and Semang languages of the Malay Peninsula; and the Mon-Khmer languages. '' Dr. Konow, working from the point of view of India proper, has been able to show not only that Munda languages are connected with Mon-Khmer, but that the former must once have extended much more widely over India than they do at the present day. There is a line of dialect of the lower Himalaya, stretching from Kunawar in the Punjab to near Darjeeling, —Tibeto-Burman in character, but nevertheless retaining many surviving traces of an old language of undoubted Munda character.'' Schmidt calls these allied groups of languages Austro-Asiatic and further postulates the existence of an Austro-Asiatic race characterised by long or medium head, horizontal non-oblique eyes, broad nostrils, dark skin, more or less wavy hair and short or medium stature. As regards the home of the

Austro-Asiatic race, Schmidt thinks that the point from which the movement of these peoples began is to be found at the extreme western end of the region which they traversed.*

The other division of the Ṛgvedic people—the Ārya folk—did not constitute a homogeneous body. We discern two different social grades within its pale—the Ṛṣi or priest-poet clans such as the Atharvans, Aṅgirases, Bhṛgus (Jamadagnis), Atris, Vasiṣṭhas, Bharadvājas, Gotamas, Kaśyapas, Agastyas, Kaṇvas, and Viśvāmitras (Kuśikas); and the other class included the warrior tribes such as the Yadus, Turvaśas, Pūrus, Anus, Druhyus, Tṛtsus, Bharatas, Sṛñjayas, Ruśamas, Matsyas, Cedis, Krivis and others. These two social grades did not form endogamous castes as yet; nor were the Ṛṣi clans collectively known as Brāhmans and the warrior tribes as Kṣatriyas. But the former constituted a regular social order with a hereditary calling—that of officiating as sacrificial priests and hymn-making, though they did not eschew other occupations. Scholars still differ as to whether the hymns of the Ṛgveda are mere appendages of the soma sacrifice or embody in many cases the sincere outpourings of poets only and not priests. It is not difficult to quote texts supporting either theory. But no reader of the hymns can deny that in many of them sacrifice overshadows everything else. In the evolution of religion rites come first and

* *Journal of the Royal Asiatic Society*, 1907, pp. 187-191.

hymns of praise after. Yajña or sacrificial rite without hymn was not unknown even in the Ṛgvedic age. A Ṛṣi prays in a hymn (X. 105. 8), "With Ṛk verses we shall kill those who are without Ṛk verses. A sacrifice without hymn (*abrahmā yajña*) cannot be pleasing to you." The soma sacrifice had grown so complicated even in what may be termed the early Ṛgvedic age that it required the services of seven Ṛtvijs or sacrificial priests (II. 1. 2). Dakṣiṇā (sacrificial priest's fee) is deified and identified with Uṣas (Dawn) and in one verse (I. 126. 6) the giver of dakṣiṇā is thus extolled: "All kinds (of objects) are intended for the givers of dakṣiṇā; the Sun in heaven shines for the givers of dakṣiṇā; the givers of dakṣiṇā attain long life and immortality." The way in which dakṣiṇā is spoken of in this and in the other hymns indicates that the giving of dakṣinā, that is to say, the employment of sacrificial priests, was an essential part of a sacrificial ceremony in the Ṛgvedic age. And that the office of the priest was in many cases hereditary is amply demonstrated by the hymns of what are called the family books of the Ṛgveda—the eight *mandalas* from the second to the ninth inclusive, attributed respectively to Gṛtsamada of the Bhṛgu clan, Viśvāmitra, Vāmadeva of the Gotama clan, Atri, Bharadvāja, Vaśiṣṭha, Kaṇva, and Aṅgiras and their descendants. Most of the hymns of the first book are attributed to poets of one or other of these clans or of other Ṛṣi clans already mentioned. Of course there were exceptions. There is the case of Devāpi officiating as the *purohita* (domestic priest) in the sacrifice of his brother Saṃtanu (X. 98). In the Ṛgveda itself Devāpi is not stated to be a prince at all. He is called a Kuru prince by Yāska and Śaunaka who flourished long after Śāṃtanu's sacrifice celebrated in the Ṛgveda. The story is thus told by Śaunaka in his Bṛhaddevatā (VII. 155-157; VIII. 1-6):—

"Now Devāpi, son of Ṛṣṭiṣeṇa, and Śaṃtanu of the race of Kuru were two brothers, princes among the Kurus. .

"Now the elder of these two was Devāpi, and the younger Saṃtanu; but the (former) prince, the son of Ṛṣṭiṣeṇa, was afflicted with skin-disease.

"When his father had gone to heaven, his subjects offered him the sovereignty. Reflecting for but a moment, he replied to his subjects:

"'I am not worthy of the sovereignty: let Śaṃtanu be your king.' Assenting to this, his subjects anointed Śaṃtanu king.

"When the scion of the Kuru had been anointed, Davāpi retired to the forest. Thereupon Parjanya did not reign in (that) realm for twelve years.

"Śaṃtanu accordingly came with his subjects to Devāpi and propitiated him with regard to that dereliction of duty.

"Then in company with his subjects, he offered him the sovereignty. To him, as he stood humbly with folded hands, Devāpi replied:—

"'I am not worthy of the sovereignty, my energy being impaired by skin disease; I will myself officiate, O king, as your priest in a sacrifice for rain.'

"Then Śaṃtanu appointed him to be his chaplain (*puro'dhatta*) and to act as priest (*ārtvij-yāya*). So he (Devāpi) duly performed the rites productive of rain."*

This story clearly indicates that the appointment of Devāpi as priest was traditionally considered as something exceptional, and the exception proves the rule.

Not only was the office of the sacrificial priests hereditary in the Ṛgvedic age, but according to traditions preserved in the Taittirīya Saṃhitā, certain functions ot the office were hereditary in particular families. Thus in the Taittirīya Saṃhitā (III. 5. 21) we are told: "The Ṛṣis did not see Indra clearly, but Vasiṣṭha saw him clearly. Indra said, 'I shall tell you a Brāhmaṇa, so that all men that are born will have thee for Purohita; but do not tell of me to the other Ṛṣis.' Thus he told him these parts of the hymns; and ever since, men were born having Vasiṣṭha for their Purohita. Therefore Vasiṣṭha is to be chosen as Brahman priest and the (sacrificer) will have such offspring."† The same *ākhyāyikā*

* Prof. Macdonell's translation.

† "ऋषयो वा इन्द्रं प्रत्यक्षं नापश्यन् वसिष्ठः प्रत्यक्षमपश्यत् सोऽब्रवीद्ब्राह्मणं ते वक्ष्यामि यथा त्वत्पुरोहिताः प्रजाः प्रजनिष्यन्तेऽथ मेतरेभ्य ऋषिभ्यो मा प्रवोच इति तस्मा एतान् स्तोमभागानब्रवीत् ततो वसिष्ठपुरोहिताः प्रजाः प्रजायन्त तस्माद्वासिष्ठो ब्रह्माकार्यः प्रैव जायते ।"

(narrative) is told in the Tāṇḍya Mahābrāhmaṇa (Pañcaviṃśa Brāhmaṇa XV. 5. 24) in a modified form thus :—

"The Ṛṣis did not see Indra with their own eyes. Vasiṣṭha desired how he could see Indra with his own eyes. He saw this Nihavasāman. He (Vasiṣṭha) then saw Indra with his own eyes. He (Indra) said to him (Vasiṣṭha), 'I shall tell you a Brāhmaṇa text by means of which there will be born Bharatas who will have you (only) as their Purohita; but then do not inform other Ṛṣis that I am Indra.' Indra communicated to him this part of the formula. Then were born Bharatas who had Vasiṣṭha for their priest."*

The parts of the formula (*stomabhāgān*) referred to in these texts is "O sun, thou art bright; I pray to thee for propitiating the gods (*raśmir-asi kṣayāya tvā kṣayaṁ jinvati*)." So it was the knowledge of this formula that enabled the Vasiṣṭhas to obtain the monopoly of the office of the Brahman or superintending priest. According to the Śatapatha Brāhmaṇa it was the knowledge of the expiatory formulas that procured the Vasiṣṭhas the same monopoly. Therein we are told in connection with the expiatory oblations of the soma sacrifice (XII. 6. 1. 38-41) :—

---

* "ऋषयो वा इन्द्रं प्रत्यक्षन्नापश्यन् स वसिष्ठोऽकामयत कथमिन्द्रं प्रत्यक्षं पश्येयमिति स एतन्निहवमपश्यत्ततो वै स इन्द्रं प्रत्यक्षमपश्यत् स एनमब्रवीद् ब्राह्मणन्ते वक्ष्यामि यथात्वत्पुरोहिता भरताः प्रजनिष्यन्त ऽथ मान्येभ्यो ऋषिभ्यो मा प्रवोच इति तस्मा एतान् स्तोमभागानब्रवीत्ततो वै वसिष्ठ पुरोहिता भरताः प्रजायन्त ।"

"The Brahman (superintending priest) himself should perform them, and no other than the Brahman; for the Brahman sits on the right (south) side of the sacrifice, and protects the sacrifice on the right side . . . . . . Now as to the meaning of these (formulas) Vasiṣṭha knew the Virāj; Indra coveted it. He spake, 'Ṛṣi, thou knowest the Virāj; teach me it!' He replied, 'What would therefrom accrue to me?' 'I would teach the expiation for the whole sacrifice, I would show thee its form.' . . . . . The Ṛṣi then taught Indra that Virāj . . . . . And Indra then taught the Ṛṣi this expiation from the Agnihotra up to the Great Litany. And formerly, indeed, the Vasiṣṭhas alone knew these utterances, hence formerly one of the Vasiṣṭha family became Brahman; but since nowadays anybody (may) study them, anybody may now become Brahman. And, indeed, he who thus knows these utterances is worthy to become Brahman, or may reply, when addressed as 'Brahman.'"*

Thus efficacious formulas or hymns were originally held as patents by the descendants of the author and thereby hereditability became an essential feature of Vedic sacerdotalism from the earliest times. We may, therefore, hold with Macdonell and Keith "that in the Ṛgveda this Brāhmaṇa, or Brahmin, is already a separate caste, differing from the warrior and agricultural

* Eggeling's translation, *Sacred Books of the East*, Vol. XLIV.

castes,"* and "that the caste system is one that has progressively developed, and that it is not legitimate to see in the Ṛgveda the full caste system even of the Yajurveda; but at the same time it is difficult to doubt that the system was already well on its way to general acceptance."†

Like the regular varṇas (castes) of later days the two sections of the Āryas—the priests and warriors—did not consider themselves as offshoots of the same stock. In the Ṛgveda mankind in general is described as descended from Manu, the son of Vivaśvat (sun-god). Ṛṣis describe Manu as "father Manu" and "our father." But in spite of this clear recognition of Manu as the eponymous ancestor of mankind, a direct divine origin is claimed for most of the Ṛṣi clans. The Aṅgirases are called "sons of heaven" (IV. 2. 15) or "sons of Agni" (X. 62. 5). Vasiṣṭha and Agastya are said to have sprung from Mitra and Varuṇa (VII. 33. 11-13). Regarding the ancestry of Atharvan we are told in the Atharvaveda (V. 11 11): "Since thou, O self-ruling Varuṇa, hast generated father Atharvan, connection of the gods." In the Aitareya Brāhmaṇa (III. 34) Bhṛgu is called Vāruṇi, "son of Varuṇa." According to a legend given in the Bṛhaddevatā (V. 97-101) Atri sprang from Prajāpati along with Bhṛgu and Aṅgiras. In the same work (V. 143) we are told, "The son of Prajāpati was Marīci, Marīci's son was the sage Kaśyapa." The only two Ṛṣi clans

---

* *Vedic Index*, II, p. 81. ‡ *Ibid.* II., p. 250.

for which divine origin is not claimed are the Viśvāmitras and the Kaṇvas, and there is clear traditional evidence to the effect that the founders of these two clans originally belonged to the *yaja-māna* class. The Kuśikas or Viśvāmitras were evidently a branch of the Bharata tribe of the *yajamāna* group. In the Aitareya Brāhmaṇa (VII. 17.6.7) Visvāmitra is addressed as *rājaputra*, 'prince,' and *bharata-ṛṣabha*, 'bull of the Bharatas.' In the Ṛgveda (X. 31. 11) Nṛṣad is given as the name of Kaṇva's father. But according to the Purāṇas Kaṇva was originally a Kṣatriya. Ajamīḍa was a descendant of Pūru, the eponymous ancestor of the Ṛgvedic Pūrus. "From Ajamīḍa was born Kaṇva, from Kaṇva Medhātithi, and from Medhātithi the Brāhmans of the Kaṇva clan (*kāṇvāyanāh*) (Viṣṇu P. IV. 19. 10)." "In one passage of the Atharvaveda (II. 25) they (the Kaṇvas) seem to be definitely regarded with hostility." * Of these two groups ot the Ṛṣi clans—the one claiming divine origin and the other sprung from the *yajamāna* class—the former formed the nucleus of the Ṛṣi class and the latter were Ṛṣi by adoption. According to the Ṛgveda the founders of the Atharvan, Aṅgiras, Bhṛgu, and Vasiṣṭha clans were the founders of the sacrificial cult and are required to be worshipped as *pitṛs*, manes. In one hymn (X. 14) the Aṅgirases, the Atharvans, and the Bhṛgus are called "the soma-loving fathers" and "the makers of the path (*pathakṛdvyah*)." In another hymn

* *Vedic Index*, I, p. 134.

(X. 15. 8) the Vasiṣṭhas are classed in the same category. Atharvan is said to have extracted sacrificial fire by churning Puṣkara (VI. 16. 13). "A Ṛṣi named Atharvan first propitiated the gods by sacrifice; the gods and the Bhṛgus forced their way (to that place) and learnt the sacrifice (X. 92. 10)." "Like a friend Mātariśvan (wind-god) brought this fire to the Bhṛgus (I. 60. 1)." "The Aṅgiras first prepared food for Indra, and worshipped him by offering oblations to the fire (I. 83. 4)." "Atharvan first discovered the path by sacrifice (I. 83. 5)." Similar traditions relating to Aṅgiras, Atharvan and Bhṛgu are also found in the Yajurveda. The only rational interpretation that these hoary traditions admit of is that in the early Vedic age three or four Ṛṣi clans,—the Aṅgirases, Atharvanas, Bhṛgus, and Vasiṣṭhas—were regarded as the original Ṛṣi clans among whom the Vedic sacrificial cult originated, and other clans became members of the sacerdotal class by adoption. This early Vedic sacerdotal class afterwards came to be known as Brāhmans. In the Pariśiṣṭabhāga of the Śrauta Sūtra of Āśvalāyana it is said, "Viśvāmitra, Jamadagni Bharadvāja, Gotama, Atri, Vasiṣṭha and Kaśyapa are the seven Ṛṣis; the descendants of the seven Ṛṣis with Agastya as the eighth are called their gotras (clans)."* Of these eight founders

* "विश्वामित्रो जमदग्निर्भरद्वाजोऽथ गौतमः ।
अत्रि वसिष्ठो काश्यप इत्येते सप्तर्षयः ॥
सप्तानामृषीणामगस्त्याष्टमानां यदपत्यं तद्गोत्रमित्याचक्षते ।"

of the Brāhmanic gotras, Bharadvāja is said to have been the grandson of Aṅgiras (Bṛhaddevatā, V. 102); Gotama also belonged to the Āṅgiras clan; and Jamadagni was the son of Bhṛgu. A tradition to the effect that the Brāhmanic gotras fall into two groups, one representing the original priesthood and the other consisting of priests by adoption, survived down to the time of the Mahābhārata. Thus we are told in the Śāntiparvaṇ (296. 17-18): "Originally only four gotras arose, O King, viz. Aṅgiras, Kaśyapa, Vasiṣṭha, and Bhṛgu. In consequence of good deeds, O ruler of men, many other gotras came into existence in time. These gotras are named on account of the penances of those who have founded them. Good people use them."*

Vedic legends of the conflict between the Vasiṣṭhas and the Viśvāmitras indicate that the Ṛṣis or priest-poets of the original gotras (*mula-gotrāni*) did not recognise the claims of the aspiring members of the warrior tribes to Ṛṣihood without hard struggle. Vasiṣṭha was the priest of Sudās, the king of the Tṛtsus and Bharatas. According to a hymn of the Ṛgveda, Sudās won a great victory over ten allied kings with the assistance of Vasiṣṭha (VII. 18). In the Aitareya-Brāhmaṇa we are told that Vasiṣṭha consecrated Sudās, son

* "मूलगोत्राणि चत्वारि समुत्पन्नानि पार्थिव ।
अङ्गिराकश्यपश्चैव वसिष्ठो भृगुरेव च ॥
कर्मतोऽन्यानि गोत्राणि समुत्पन्नानि पार्थिव ।
नामधेयानि तपसा तानि च ग्रहणं सताम् ॥"

of Pijavana, to sovereignty. The story of the conflict between Sakti, son of Vasiṣṭha, and the Viśvāmitras as referred to in the Ṛgveda (III. 53) is thus narrated in the Bṛhaddevatā (IV. 112-120):—

"At a great sacrifice of Sudās, by Sakti Gāthi's son (Viśvāmitra) was forcibly deprived of consciousness. He sank down unconscious. But to him the Jamadagnis gave speech called Sasarparī, daughter of Brahmā or of the Sun, having brought her from the dwelling of the Sun. Then that speech dispelled the Kuśikas' loss of intelligence (*a-matim*). And in the (stanza) 'Hither, (*upa*: iii. 53. 11) Viśvāmitra restored the Kuśikas to consciousness (*anubodhayat*). And gladdened at heart by receiving speech he paid homage to those seers (the Jamadagnis), himself praising speech with two stanzās 'Sasarparī' (*Sasarparīh*: iii. 53, 15, 16). (With the stanzas) 'strong' (*sthirau*: iii. 53. 17-20) (he praised) the parts of the cart and the oxen as he started for home. And then going home he deposited (them there) in person (*svaśarīreṇa*). But the four stanzas which follow (iii. 53. 21-24) are traditionally held to be hostile to the Vasiṣṭhas. They were pronounced by Viśvāmitra, they are traditionally held to be 'imprecations' (*abhiśāpa*). They are pronounced to be hostile to enemies and magical (*abhicārika*) incantations. The Vasiṣṭhas will not listen to them. This is the unanimous opinion of their authorities (*ācāryaka*): great guilt arises from repeating or listening (to them); by repeating or hearing (them) one's head is broken into a hundred fragments; the children of those (who do so) perish; therefore one should not repeat them.''*

The hymn (III. 53) read with this passage of the Bṛhaddevatā seems to indicate that in a sacrifice, evidently horse-sacrifice, performed by Sudās, Ṛṣis of the Kuśika family including Vismāmitra were invited to take part. Sakti, son of Vasiṣṭha, the family priest of the king, resented this intrusion and made them unconscious by means of a charm. Viśvāmitra and his kinsmen were no match for Vasiṣṭha's son in the use of magical incantations. But the Jamadagnis, who like the Vasiṣṭhas, belonged to the older group of Ṛṣi clans and were as skilful in magic, came to the rescue of the Kuśikas. Visvāmitra thanked the Jamadagnis, started for home in his bullock cart and uttered four imprecatory stanzas against the Vasiṣṭhas. Perhaps this led to a sanguinary conflict between Sudās and Vasiṣṭha which is thus referred to in the Taittirīya Saṃhita (VII. 4. 7, 1), "Vasiṣṭha, when his sons were killed, desired that he might beget children and humble the sons of Sudās. Then he saw this (*sattra* called) *ekonapañcāsadrātra*, adopted it and performed it. Then he (Vasiṣṭha) obtained children and humbled the sons of Sudās.'' †

* Macdonell's translation.

† "वसिष्ठो हतपुत्रो ऽकामयत विन्देय प्रजामभि सौदासान् भवेयमिति। स एतमेकस्मान्नपञ्चाशमपश्यत् तमाहरत् तेनायजत। ततो वै सो ऽविन्दत प्रजामभि सौदासानभवत्।"

Some scholars do not admit that there is any reference to the strife of Viśvāmitra and Vasiṣṭha in the hymn. But in the absence of a more satisfactory explanation we have no other course to follow than to fall back upon the traditional explanation preserved by Śaunaka and referred to by Kātyāyana in his *Sarvānukramaṇi*. Yāska (II. 24) also states that "Viśvāmitra was the Purohita of Sudāsa, son of Paijavana" in connection with Ṛgveda III. 33. The suggestion made by Macdonell and Keith* that Visvāmitra originally held the office of the Purohita of Sudās and was afterwards deposed by Vasiṣṭha does not accord with the statement of the Aitareya Brāhmaṇa that Vasiṣṭha consecrated Sudās to sovereignty and the statement of the Pañcaviṃśa Brāhmaṇa (XV. 5. 24) that the Bharatas adopted Vasiṣṭhas as their domestic priests as soon as they came into being. The fact seems to have been that the Vasiṣṭhas were originally the Purohitas of the Tṛtsus and Bharatas and so of their king Sudās. In the time of Sudās there flourished a number of poets in the Kuśika clan of the Bharata tribe including Viśvāmitra, who claimed the office of the Purohita of their tribal chief. This led to a quarrel with Sakti, the head of the Vasiṣṭha clan. Though Sudās was not loth to recognize their claims, it were the Saudāsas (sons of Sudās) who espoused their cause with zeal and put to death their opponents.

---

* *Vedic Index*, ii. 275-276.

The two sections of the sacerdotal class, Brāhmans by descent and Brāhmans by adoption, were of different physical types. In the Ṛgveda (VII. 33. 1) the Vasiṣṭhas, who represent the first group, are described as *svityam*, 'white', while Kaṇva (X. 31. 11), representing the second group, is *śvāva* or *kṛṣṇa*, 'dark.' In the Gopatha Brāhmaṇa (I. 1. 223) the Brahman's colour is white (*śukla*). The tradition of the existence of a group of Brāhmans with white complexion and yellow hair survived down to the time of the grammarian Patañjali (about 150 B.C.) who writes in his Mahābhāṣya (on Pāṇini V. 1. 115): "Penance, knowledge of the Veda, and birth make a Brāhman. He who is without penance and knowledge of the Veda is a Brāhman by birth only. White complexion, pure conduct, yellow or red hair, etc. are also characteristics that constitute Brāhmanhood."* The Brāhman with white complexion and yellow hair seems so strange a being to Kaiyaṭa, the scholiast of Patañjali, that he assigns him to a previous cycle of existence. He writes, "White complexion, etc., were seen in Brāhmans who flourished in a previous cycle of existence and whose descendants are rarely met with even now.†

* "तपः श्रुतं च योनिश्च एतद् ब्राह्मणकारकम् ।
तपश्श्रुताभ्यां यो हीनो जाति ब्राह्मण एव सः ॥
यथा गौरः शुच्याचारः पिङ्गलः कपिलकेश इति एतानप्यभ्यन्तरान् ब्राह्मण्ये गुणान् कुर्व्वन्ति ।"

† "गौरत्वादयो ब्राह्मणस्य पुराकल्पदर्शनेनाद्यत्वेपि कश्चित्तदन्वयदर्शनेन व्यञ्जका इति तानपि अभ्यन्तरान्भूतत्वेनाश्रयन्तीत्यर्थः ।"

The second division of the Ṛgvedic Āryas, the Yadus (*yādva jana*), Pūrus, Druhyus, Anus, Turvaśas, Bharatas (*bhārata jana*) and other Yajamāna tribes were traditionally akin to the dark section of the Ṛṣis, the Kaṇvas and the Viśvāmitras. The Kāṭhaka Saṃhitā (XI. 6) calls the Vaiśya 'white' (*śukla*), the Rājanya 'swarthy' (*dhūmra*).* To explain the difference of colour of skin and hair between the two groups of Vedic Āryas we have to assume that the ancestors of the "white and yellow-haired" group migrated to India from the temperate region in the far North, and the dark section had their home in the tropics. There is clear traditional evidence in the Ṛgveda to show that two at least of the tribes of the latter group, the Turvaśas and the Yadus, came to India from South-Western Asia. We are told in one stanza (VI. 20. 12): "O hero (Indra)! when you crossed the sea (*samudra*), you brought Turvaśa and Yadu over the sea." Another stanza (VI. 45. 1) tells us, "Indra, who brought Turvaśa and Yadu from afar by his wise policy, is our youthful friend." In X. 62. 10 Yadu and Turva (Turvaśa) are called Dāsas or barbarians. According to some scholars *samudra* in the Ṛgveda does not mean sea, for the Āryas had not yet reached the sea, but only the lower course of the Indus. This interpretation of *samudra* may be traced to the preconceived notion that the Ṛgvedic Aryas were a homogeneous body of men

* *Vedic Index*, Vol. II, p. 247, note 2.

who came from the North-West. But once this notion is dismissed from the mind, there is left nothing to prevent us from accepting *samudra* in its usual sense. The sea that lies nearest to the country of the Ṛgvedic Āryas is the Arabian Sea. So if we are to attach any value to this Vedic tradition, we are forced to assume that the Yadus and the Turvaśas came across the Arabian Sea. The evidences contained in the later Vedic and epic literatures relating to the Indian home of one of these two folks, the Yadus, lend support to this hypothesis.

It is generally assumed that the Yadus and Turvaśas must have been settled somewhere in the Punjab in the Ṛgvedic age. In the list of tribes dwelling in the land of the Five Rivers and in the valleys of the Ganges and the Jumna as given in the later Vedic and early Buddhist literatures neither the Yadus nor the Turvaśas find any mention. Where were they then? According to the Mahābhārata and the Purāṇas the Satvatas or the Bhojas were a branch of the Yadus. Though the Yadus are not mentioned in the Brāmhaṇa texts, the Satvats and the Bhojas are. In the Satapatha Brāhmaṇa (XIII. 5. 4. 21) a verse is quoted wherein it is said that Bharata seized the sacrificial horse of the Satvats. In the Aitareya Brāhmaṇa (VIII. 14) it is said, "Therefore in that southern region all the Kings of the Satvats are consecrated for the enjoyment of pleasures and are called Bhojas." The country of the Satvats and Bhojas is called southern region from the view point of the land in the middle (*asyāṃ dhruvāyāṃ madhyamāyāṃ pratiṣṭhāyāṃ diśi*) or the midland where dwelt the Uśinaras, the Kurus, the Pañcālas and the Vaśas.

The Harivaṃśa and the Purāṇas enable us to define the early Indian home of the Yadus in the south with greater precision. The Harivaṃśa or the supplementary book of the Mahābhārata is the chief repository of legends and traditions relating to the Andhakas and the Vṛṣṇis, the two chief branches of the Yadu stock. The Harivaṃsa in its present form may not be very old, but it must have existed in an embryonic stage even in the time of the grammarian Pāṇini. Suffixes and accents are as a rule prescribed for names of persons according to the actual forms of the words denoting those names and not according to tribes or clans to which the persons named might belong. And yet this is what is done by Paṇini in two of his aphorisms (IV. 1. 115; VI. 2. 34.) In the former aphorism it is prescribed that the affix *aṇ* denoting descendant is added to a word "denoting the name of a Ṛṣi, or the name of a person belonging to the Andhaka, Vṛṣṇi or Kuru clans"; and the latter aphorism provides,—"The first part of a *dvandva* compound formed of names denoting Kṣatriya clans in the plural number retains its original accent when the warrior belongs to the Andhaka or Vṛṣṇi clans." Pāṇini could hardly have made such rules unless he had before him names of descendants of persons of the Andhaka and Vṛṣṇi clans of all possible forms formed by adding *an* and of *dvandva* compounds thus accented. And where could he get materials for such lists except in the narrative literature of his time? The Mahābhārata, of which the Harivaṃsa forms an integral part, is named in the Gṛhya Sūtra of Āśvalāyana and in Pāṇini VI. 2. 38 Pāṇini very probably flourished in the fourth century B.C.,* when genuine traditions of the early Vedic age may be expected to still survive in the Vedic schools. So the legends and traditions relating to the Andhakas and the Vṛṣṇis preserved in the Harivaṃśa may be considered as genuine traditions coming down from the Vedic age.

Two conflicting legends are given in the Harivaṃśa relating to the origin of the Yadus or Yādavas. In chapter 30 Yadu, the eponymous ancestor of the Yādavas, is represented as a son of King Yayāti of the lunar race. But in chapter 94 it is said that Yadu belonged to the solar Ikṣvāku race. As the original Indian home of the Yādavas is very clearly indicated in this version of the legendary history of the Yādava clans and princes, I shall reproduce it in substance. There was a rājā named Haryaśva, the son of Ikṣvāku, in Manu's line. Madhumatī, daughter of the demon Madhu, was Haryaśva's wife. He was driven out of Ayodhyā by his elder brother Mādhava, and, at the instance of his wife, took shelter with his father-in-law at Madhupura, the chief town of

* *Vide* Keith's Introduction to *Aitareya Āraṇyaka* (Oxford, 1909), p. 24.

Madhuvana. "In a short time his (Haryaśva's) kingdom known as Ānarta and Saurāṣṭra enriched by cattle, and also called Anupa adorned by the sea beach and forest, became very prosperous." By his queen Madhumati Haryaśva had a son named Yadu, from whom sprung the Yādava clans, viz. Bhaima, Kakkura, Bhoja, Andhaka, Yādava, Dāsārha and Vṛṣṇi. Yadu's son was Mādhava; Mādhava's son was Satvata; Satvata's son was Bhima. From Satvata one section of the Yādavas came to be known as Sātvatas and from Bhima as Bhaimas. While Bhima was reigning over Surāṣṭra, Satrughna, half-brother of Rāma, the hero of the Rāmāyana, killed Lavaṇa, son of the demon Madhu, destroyed Madhuvana, and there founded a new city called Mathurā. After the death of Satrughna, Andhaka, son of Bhima, succeeded him to the throne of Mathurā.

These legends, by indicating that the Yādavas were originally settled in Saurāṣṭra or the Kathiwar peninsula and then spread to Mathurā, lend indirect support to the Ṛgvedic tradition that the Yadus, together with the Turvaśas, came from beyond the sea. There are strong evidences to show that in the sixteenth and the fifteenth centuries B.C., in Syria and Upper Mesopotamia, there were several colonies of men of Aryan speech, some of whom at least worshipped Vedic gods. In the cuneiform tablets discovered at Tell-el-Amarna in Upper Egypt containing letters from the tributary Kings of Western Asia to Egyptian Pharaohs, we find such Aryan names of chieftains: "Artamanya, chief of Ziribašani, probably about Basan; Bawarzana or Mawarzana (or perhaps Mayarzana), chief of Hazi, probably to the north of Palestine; Šubandu or Šubandi, from Philistæa (cf. S. *Subandhu*); Šuwardata, the adversary of Abdihiba of Jerusalem (cf. S. *Svardatta*); Šutarna or Šuttarna, chief of Mušihuma, probably in Northern Palestine; Yašdata or Wašdata, probably from the neighbourhood of Megidda; Zirdamiašda, probably from Northern Palestine, and so forth. The name of the Kassite sun-god Šuriaš (cf. S. *sūrya*) points to a similar Aryan element to the east of Babylonia . . . . The names of the Mitani Kings are of the same kind. They are Sa-uš-ša-tar, Artatama, Suttarna, Dušratta (or Tušratta); Artaššumara (or Artaššuwara), and Mattiuaza." Regarding the place of the language of these names in the Indo-European family Sten Konow observes: "I think that the explanation of these facts has been given by Professor Bloomfield, who considers it possible that the 'Mitani and other Western Asiatic Iranoid proper names came from a dialect closely allied to Iranian but not yet exactly Iranian, i.e. a dialect which did not change *s* to *h*.' It seems as if the change of *s* to *h* is not so old as the other Iranian characteristics. It only began after Iranian branch had separated itself from the common Aryan stock and did not at once spread over the whole Iranian area."*

* *Journal of the Royal Asiatic Society*, 1911, pp. 44-45.

Another great discovery, cuneiform writings from Boghaz-Kuei, have revealed the religion of the Kings of Mitanni. One of these writings embody a treaty between the Mitanni King Mattiuaza and the Hittite King Subbiluliuma wherein the dieties of the two countries are invoked as protectors of the treaty. Among the gods invoked by the Mitannian king occur the well-known Vedic names Mitra, Varuṇa, Indra, and the Nāsatyas. The Tell-el-amarna and the Boghaz-kuei writings carry us back to the fifteenth century B.C. With peoples of Āryan speech worshipping Indra, Varuṇa, and the Nāsatyas in Upper Mesopotamia in the fifteenth century B.C., it is not inconceivable that some among them should have found their way to Kathiwar through Eridu which had an immemorial coasting trade with India.* One probable link of the chain connecting ancient India with Mesopotamia seems to have been discovered. It is the Babylonian seal in the Central Museum of Nagpore. Unfortunately, as the seal has so long been mistaken for an ornament, no record has been kept to show where, when, and how it was found. Mr. L. W. King of the British Museum, who has deciphered the inscription writes: "The scene engraved on the seal represents a goddess standing with hands raised in adoration before the weather god Adad, or his West-Semitic equivalent Amurru . . . The inscription gives the owner's name and reads 'Liburbeli,

* J. L. Myres, *The Dawn of History*, p. 109.

the servant of (. . . .).' The seal dates from about 2000 B.C., the period of the first dynasty of Babylon." * As the find-place of the seal is unknown, it is difficult to base any conclusion upon it. But had not the seal with a golden handle been found in India, and presumably in Central India, it could hardly have found its way to the Nagpore Museum. The Āryas of the Ṛgvedic age were not unfamiliar with sea voyage. "There are references," observe Macdonell and Keith, "to the treasures of the ocean, perhaps pearls or the gains of trade, and the story of Bhujyu seems to allude to marine navigation." † There are references to sea voyage in the Brāhmaṇas also indicating the maritime activity of the Aryas in the later Vedic age. In the Pañcaviṃśa-Brāhmaṇa (XIV. 5. 17) it is said, "Those who go to the sea without boat (*aplavah*) do not come out of that." ‡ Again in the Aitareya Brāhmaṇa (VI. 21) we are told, "Know that this *tristup* formula is the first among the hymns that I am to recite. Those who perform the annual *satra* or Dvādaśāha are like men who wish to cross the sea As men who desire to cross the sea get into boat full of provisions, so these performers of *satra* use *tristup* formula."§

* *Journal of the Asiatic Society of Bengal*, Vol. X (1914), p. 462.

† *Vedic Index*, Vol. II, p. 432.

‡ "यो वा अप्लवः समुद्रं, प्रस्नाति न स ततः उदेति ।"

§ "त्रिष्टुभो वा इमाः सत्त्रप्रतिपद इत्येव विद्यात् तद्यथा समुद्रं, प्रप्लवेरन्नेवं हैव ते प्रप्लवन्ते ये संवत्सरं द्वादशाहं वासते तद्यथा सैरावतीं नावं पारकामाः समारोहेयुः एवमेवैता त्रिष्टुभः समारोहन्ति ।"

So we may assume a continuous maritime connection of Āryāvarta with Western Asia from the Ṛgvedic period till the time of the Bāveru Jātaka of the Pāli canon.

The Ārya immigrants from Mesopotamia must have absorbed a good deal of Semitic blood in their Syrian home and were probably dark like the Semites. The Pūrus, Druhyus and Anus, mentioned in the Ṛgveda along with the Yadus and Turvaśas, may have come from the same quarters and were probably of the same physical type. The fair and fair-haired invaders who formed the nucleus of the Brāhman caste came earlier direct from the cradle of the Aryan folk in the far north and elaborated the vedic sacrificial cult in their Indian home from the primitive worship of Indra, Varuṇa and the other gods of nature. They were probably akin to the Āthravans and Magi of Ancient Iran, for the Iranians, like the Indo-Āryans, but unlike all other Indo-Germanic peoples, had, and the Parsis still have in their Dasturs, a hereditary priesthood. The ancestors of the Ṛṣi clans probably came earlier. When later on the ancestors of the Ṛgvedic warrior tribes entered India and came in contact with the Ṛṣi clans, the former recognized the cultural superiority of the latter and accepted them as their religious guides.

Fair and fair-haired Ṛṣi clans from the north, dark or brown *yajamāna* tribes from South-Western Asia, and the very dark aboriginal Niśādas were the ethnic elements out of which grew up the five primary *varṇas* or castes, viz. the Brāhmans, Rājanyas (Kṣatriyas), Vaiśyas, Śūdras, and Niśādas. Now the question is, how did this transformation take place. The earliest account of the origin of *varṇas* is found in the following stanzas of the Puruṣa hymn of the Ṛgveda (X. 90. 11-12):—

"When they divided the Puruṣa, into how many parts did they divide him? What was his mouth? What were his arms? What were his thighs and feet called?

"The Brāhman was his mouth; of his arms, the Rājanya was made; the Vaiśyas were his thighs; the Śūdra sprang from his feet."

The Vedic theory of the origin of castes finds a clearer expression in a Yajus text (*Taittirīya Saṃhitā*, VII. 1. 1. 4-6) wherein we read:—

"Prajāpati, desirous of offspring [performed the Agniṣṭoma sacrifice] and created trivṛt hymn, god Agni, Gāyatri metre, Rathantara sāman, Brāhman among men and goats among brutes from his mouth. As they were created from the mouth, therefore they are superior to all others.

"[He] created Pañcadaśa hymn, god Indra, Triṣṭup metre, Vṛhat sāman, Rājanya among men and sheep among brutes from his chest and arms. Therefore they are strong because they have been created from strength (strong arms). [He] created Saptadaśa hymn, Viśvadevas among the gods, Jagati metre, Vairupa Sāman, Vaiśya among men and the cows among brutes from the belly. As they have been created from the storehouse of food (belly), so they are the food (or intended to bc enjoyed by others). Thereforc thcy (Vaiśyas) are more numerous than others (among men) because many gods were created.

"[He] created ekaviṃśa hymn, anuṣṭup metre, Vairāja Sāman, Śūdra among men and horse among brutes from his feet. Therefore the Śūdra and the horse are dependent on other (castes). As no god was created from the feet, so the Sūdra is not competent to perform sacrifice. As the Śūdra and the horse were created from the feet, so they live by exerting their feet."*

Here the four varṇas are recognized as separate creations of the creator, differing as widely as do goat, sheep, cow and horse; or in the language of natural history, the four varṇas were considered as four different species of animals and not merely four different groups of the same species. The conception that the difference between the different groups of men is congenital and not artificial was founded on the fact that the earliest social groups known to the Āryas,—the priests, the *yajamānas*, and the godless aborigines actually

---

* प्रजापतिरकामयत प्रजायेयेति स मुखतस्त्रिवृतं निरमिमीत तमग्निर्देवतान्वसृज्यत गायत्रीछन्दो रथन्तरं साम ब्राह्मणो मनुष्याणामजः पशूनां तस्मात्ते मुख्या मुखतो ह्यसृज्यन्त। उरसो बाहुभ्यां पञ्चदशं निरमिमीत तमिन्द्रो देवतान्वसृज्यत त्रिष्टुप् छन्दो बृहत्साम राजन्यो मनुष्याणामविः पशूनां तस्मात्ते वीर्यावन्तो वीर्याद्ध्यसृज्यन्त। मध्यतः सप्तदशं निरमिमीत तं विश्वेदेवा देवता अन्वसृज्यन्त जगतीछन्दो वैरूपं साम वैश्यो मनुष्याणां गावः पशूनां तस्मात्त आद्या अन्नधानाद्ध्यसृज्यन्त तस्माद्भूयांसोऽन्येभ्यो भूयिष्ठा हि देवता अन्वसृज्यन्त। पत्त एकविंशं निरमिमीत तमनुष्टुप् छन्दोऽन्वसृज्यत वैराजं साम शूद्रो मनुष्याणामश्वः पशूनां तस्मात्तौ भूतसंक्रामिणावश्वश्च शूद्रश्च तस्माच्छूद्रो-यज्ञेऽनवक्लृप्तो न हि देवता अन्वसृज्यत तस्मात्पादावुपजीवतः पत्तो ह्यसृज्येताम्।

differed from one another in colour (*varṇa*) and other prominent physical characters. This, "the sense of distinctions of race indicated by differences of colour," to use the language of Risley, is "the basis of fact" in the development of caste system. When the slaves came to be recognized as a separate group termed Śūdra, and the tax-paying subject section of the *yajamāna* tribes as a separate social group termed Vaiśya, as distinguished from the ruling or Rājanya section, the conception of the identity of racial or colour difference and social difference was extended to them by fiction, and the Vaiśyas and Śūdras were recognized as separate *varṇas* or colours. With these two elements, fact and fiction, was combined a third element, heredity of function, copied from the Ṛṣi clans. Colour or race differences, real and fancied, together with hereditary function, gave birth to the caste system. But as newer groups formed or attached themselves to the Ārya nations, the absurdity of regarding them all as distinct colours or varṇas was recognized, and the theory of *varna-śaṅkara* or mixed caste was started to explain their origins.

CHAPTER II.

INDO-ARYANS OF THE OUTER COUNTRIES.

Vedic Aryandom or the country inhabited by the people who called themselves Āryas and among whom the Vedic civilization originated and developed, comprised only a limited portion of Northern India. The boundaries of this land in the later Vedic period may be ascertained from a list of nations given in the Kauṣītaki Upaniṣad (VI. 1). This list contains the following names—the Uśīnaras, the Vaśas, the Matsyas, the Kurus, the Pañcālas, the Kāśis and the Videhas. One important name, that of the Kośalas, is omitted from this list. The land of the Uśīnaras marked the western boundary of Vedic India and the land of the Videhas marked the eastern boundary. From Pāṇini (IV. 2. 117-118) we learn that Vāhika villages were situated within Uśīnara. So Uśīnara formed a part of, if not identical with, the Vāhika country. According to the Mahābhārata (Karṇaparvaṇ XLV. 40) the land of the five rivers was known as the country of the Vāhikas. Videha is now represented by Tirhut or North Bihar and the Kośi river formed its eastern boundary in ancient times. The Āryas who lived within these limits were very hostile to the peoples that lived around them. In a well-known hymn of the Atharvaveda *takman* or fever is thus addressed (V. 22. 5-14):—

"His home is with the Mujavants, his home is with the Mahāvṛṣas. From the moment of thy birth thou art indigenous with the Bāhlikas.

"To the Gandhāris, the Mujavants, the Aṅgas and the Magadhas we deliver over *takman* like a servant, like a treasure."

Gandhāri is the modern Peshawar district of the North-West Frontier Province, and Magadha and Aṅga make up South Bihar. In the Vrātya-book of the Atharvaveda (XV) the Māgadha or the native of Magadha is represented as closely related to the Vrātya who is there deified. The account of the Vrātya as given in the Pañcaviṃśa Brāhmaṇa (XVII. 4) is thus summed up by Keith: "We are there told that they do not practise Kṛṣi [agriculture] or trade, i.e. that they are distinct in culture from the Brāhmanical Indians who practise in the time of the Brāhmaṇas both. Moreover they have a different code of law, for that is the real meaning of *adaṇḍyam daṇḍena ghanntas caranti*, and they have different speech, for they call what is easy to say difficult, a point indicating at the least a Prākṛta speech in which conjunct consonants had been softened. They are described as speaking '*dīkṣitavācam* [the language of the initiated] though *adīkṣita* [uninitiated], but this characteristic is really unintelligible."* This last characteristic probably indicates that the Vrātyas had adopted the vocabulary of the Vedic religion while retaining their

* *Journal of the Royal Asiatic Society*, 1913, p. 159.

own faith. They had evidently adopted the names of the Vedic gods while attributing to them the characteristics of their own gods. That Magadha was recognized as the chief centre of Vrātya culture is evident from the fact that in the Śrauta Sūtras of Kātyāyana (VIII. 6. 28) and Lāṭyāyana (XXII. 4. 22) it is enjoined that after the *Vrātya-stoma*, a rite that procured the admission of the Vrātya to the Brāhmanic fold, his belongings or outfit had to be bestowed either upon an inferior Brāhman or Brāhman in name only (*brahma-bandhu*) of Magadha, or one who had not given up the Vrātya practices. This shows that the Brāhmans of Magadha were looked down upon as priests of the Vrātya and consequently the mass of the population of Magadha were regarded as Vrātyas.

In connection with the shape of the burial mound (*śmaśāna*) built on charred bones the Easterners are called Asuras in the Śatapatha Brāhmaṇa (XIII. 8. 1. 5):—"Four-cornered (is the sepulchral mound). Now the gods and the Asuras, both of them sprung from Prajāpati were contending in the (four) regions (quarters). The gods drove out Asuras, their rivals and enemies, from the regions, and being regionless, they were overcome. Wherefore the people who are godly make their burial-places four-cornered, whilst those who are of the Asura nature, the Easterners and others, (make them) round, for they (the gods) drove them out from the regions." Here the 'Easterners and others' are evidently the

Magadhas, Aṅgas and their eastern neighbours; and differences in the size of the sepulchral mound is recognised as a mark of ethnic difference.*

In the Smṛti literature Magadha and Aṅga are included among countries migration to which is strictly forbidden. Thus Baudhāyana ordains in his Dharmasūtra (I. 1. 32-33):—

"The inhabitants of Ānarṭṭa, of Aṅga, of Magadha, of Saurāṣṭra, of the Deccan, of Upavrit, of Sind, and the Sauvīras are of mixed origin. He who has visited the (countries of the) Āraṭṭas, Kāraskaras, Puṇḍras, Sauvīras, Vaṅgas, Kaliṅgas, (or) Pranunas shall offer a Punastoma or Sarvapṛṣthi."

Another law-giver, Devala (as quoted by Vijñāneśvara on Yājñavalkya III. 292), says:—

"He who has visited the (countries of the) Sindhus, Sauvīras, Saurāṣṭras, inhabitants of the frontier regions, of the Aṅgas, Vaṅgas, Kaliṅgas, and Andhras, should go through the ceremony of intiation anew."

How this injunction will be violated in the Kaliyuga or the iron-age is thus predicted in the Harivaṃśa (CXCIV. 11199-11203)·—

"At that time, owing to the lapse of time, all men, having been reduced to poverty, will leave their native land with their relatives. Pressed by hunger and fear, taking their children on their shoulders, men will cross the Kauśikī (Kośi) river in haste out of fear. Men will take shelter in the

Rhys Davids, *Buddhist India*, p. 80.

(countries of the) Aṅgas, Vaṅgas, Kaliṅgas, Kāśmīras, Mekalas, the caves of the mount Ṛṣika, the borderland of the Himalaya and the shore of the sea. Men will live in the forest with the Mlecchas."*

These outer countries to which migration from Vedic Aryandom was so strictly forbidden formed a ring round it. To begin with the east, the Kośi (Kauśikī) formed the boundary between the countries of the Videhas and the Puṇḍras (Varendra). To the south-east of the Puṇḍras lived the Vaṅgas (Eastern Bengal) and to the west of the Vaṅgas lay the country of the Suhmas or Rāḍhās which is omitted from the lists. The country of the Kaliṅgas lay to the south of the Rāḍhās and that of the Andhras south of the Kaliṅgas. Dākṣiṇātya or the Deccan extended to the west of the Kaliṅgas, and Saurāṣṭra (Kathiwar), Ānartta (Gujarat), Sind and probably the country of the Sauvīras lay to the north-west of the Deccan. The Ārattas and the Kāraskaras lived in the Western Punjab. The following extract from the Mahābhārata (Karṇaparvaṇ XLV) adds the Khasas, who

---

* स्वदेशेभ्यः परिभ्रष्टा निःसाराः सह बन्धुभिः ॥
नराः सर्व्वे भविष्यन्ति तदा कालपरिक्षयात् ।
ततः स्कन्धैः समादाय कुमारान् विद्रुता भयात् ॥
कौशिकीं प्रतरिष्यन्ति नराः क्षुद्भयपीड़िताः ।
अङ्गान् वङ्गान् कलिङ्गांश्च काश्मीरांश्च मेकलान् ॥
ऋषिकान्तगिरिद्रोणीः संश्रयिष्यन्ति मानवाः ।
कृत्स्नञ्च हिमवत् पार्श्वं कूलञ्च लवणाम्भसः ॥
अरण्येषु निवत्स्यन्ति नराः म्लेच्छगणैः सह ।

Harivaṃśa, Calcutta, 1839.

still live on the southern slope of the Himālayās, to the list of the Outer nationalities and indicates the reason why immigration to their countries was forbidden :—

"The lands through which the five rivers flow after issuing from the mountains are called Āraṭṭa; virtuous men should not spend there more than two days. There are two Piśācas called Vāha and Hika in the Vipāsā (Beas). The Vāhikas are their offspring. They have not been created by Prajāpati, therefore, being low-born, how can they know the rules of piety prescribed in the sacred books? One should avoid the Kāraskaras, Māhisakas, Kaliṅgas, Keralas, Karkotas and Virakas who follow the path of vice . . . . The Vāhikas dwell in the Āraṭṭa country; and the low Brāhmans of that country, who have been living there from the time of Prajāpati, do not either study Veda or perform sacrifice. The gods do not eat food offered by these wicked Vrātyas. The Prasthalas, Madras, Gandhāras, Āraṭṭas, Khaśas, Vasātis, Sindhus, and Sauvīras are mostly very wicked."

Baudhāyana's statement that the inhabitants of Ānarta, Aṅga, Magadha and other Outer countries are of mixed origin, and the statement in the above extract that the Vāhikas were not created by Prajāpati, clearly indicate the belief of the dwellers of Vedic Aryandom that the Outer nationalities originated from ethnic stock or stocks that were quite different from the stock or stocks from which they themselves originated and culturally the latter were Vrātyas or heathens who had not yet adopted the Vedic cult.

The fundamental cultural difference that separated the two groups of Indo-Aryan nationalities—the Inner or the Vedic group and the Outer group—in the olden days is still manifest in the different types of social organisations existing among the modern representations of the two groups. In the Punjab, Rajputana, and the United Provinces, and among the countries of the Outer ring, in Gujarat and Bihar, the fourfold division of society still survives. Besides the Brāhmans and the Śūdras, there are the Rajputs or the Chatris who represent the ancient Kṣatriya order and the Vanias who follow the usages of the Vaiśyas. But the social organisation of the Maraṭhā country, of Orissa, of Bengal and of other countries lying beyond, is of a different type. In these countries there are only two orders from the Brāhmanic standpoint,—the Brāhman and the Śūdra. Mādhava, who flourished in the fourteenth century in Vijaynagar, writes in his commentary on Parāśara Smṛti, "The Kṣatriyas and the Vaiśyas have totally disappeared." Raghunandana, a Bengali writer who flourished in the sixteenth century, writes in his Śuddhitattva: "The Kṣatriyas of modern times have been degraded to the status of Śūdras. On account of the abandonment of rites the Vaiśyas and the Ambaṣṭhas also have degenerated [into Śūdras]." To explain away the absence of regular Kṣatriya and Vaiśya orders in the Outer countries the orthodox students of the Brāhmanic codes were compelled to assume the existence of these orders in the remote past and their subsequent disappearance or degeneration. But if it were really so, the Kṣatriya and Vaiśya orders would have been non-existent in Hindusthan proper, which roughly corresponds to ancient Vedic Āryāvarta, as well. It is, therefore, more reasonable to suppose that the fourfold division of society was not indigenous in the Outer countries, but was imported from Vedic Aryandom in an imperfect form and the Kṣatriya and Vaiśya usages failed to make their way therein. This could hardly have been so if the two groups of Indo-Aryans—the Inner or the Hindusthani group and the Outer group—had come of the same stock—if the Outer group had been mainly descended from immigrants from the Vedic country.

The linguistic difference between the two groups of the Indo-Aryan folk is still more significant. Sir George Grierson writes :—

"The Midland extended from the Himālayas on the north to the Vindhya Hills on the south, and from Sarhind (*vulgo* Sirhind) in the Eastern Punjab on the west to the confluence of the Ganges and the Jumna on the east. It thus consisted of the Gangetic Doāb, and of the country immediately to its north and south. The population of this tract had extended from its original seat near the Upper Doāb and the sacred river, the Sarasvatī. The particular Indo-Aryan dialect of these people developed into the modern language of the Midland.

* * * *

"Round it, on three sides—west, south, and east—lay a country inhabited, even in Vedic times, by other Indo-Aryan tribes. This tract included the modern Punjab, Sind, Gujarāt, Rājputāna, and the country to the east—Oudh and Bihar. Rajputāna belongs geographically to the Midland, but it was a late conquest, and for our present purposes may be considered as belonging to the Outer Band. Over this band were scattered different tribes, each with its own dialect; but it is important to note that a comparison of the modern vernaculars shows that these outer dialects were all more closely related to each other than any of them were to the language of the Midland. In fact, at an early period of the linguistic history of India there must have been two sets of Indo-Aryan dialects—one the language of the Midland, and the other the group of dialects forming the Outer Band. From this it has been argued, and the contention is entirely borne out by the results of the ethnological enquiries, that the inhabitants of the Midland represent the latest stage of Indo-Aryan immigration. The earliest arrivals spoke one dialect, and the new-comers another. According to Dr. Hœrnle, who first suggested the theory, the latest invaders probably entered the Punjab like a wedge, into the heart of the country already occupied by the first immigrants, forcing the latter outwards in three directions, to the east, to the south and to the west.

"The next process which we observe in the geographical distribution of the Indo-Aryan languages is one of expansion. The population of the Midland increased, and history shows that it exercised an important influence over the rest of India. The imperial cities of Delhi and Kanauj, and the holy city of Mathurā . . . . lay within its territory. With increased population and increased power it expanded and conquered the Eastern Punjab, Rājputāna and Gujarāt (where it reached the sea, and gained access to maritime commerce), and Oudh. With its armies and with its settlers it carried its language, and hence in these territories we find mixed form of speech. The basis of each is that of the Outer Band, but its body is that of the Midland. Almost everywhere the nature of the phenomena is the same. In the country near the borders of the Midland, the Midland language has overwhelmed the ancient language and few traces of the latter can be recognized. As we go farther from the centre, the influence of the Midland weakens and that of the Outer Band becomes stronger and stronger, till the traces of the Midland speech disappear altogether. The present language of the Eastern Punjab is closely allied to that of the Upper Doāb, but it gradually becomes the Lahndā of the Western Punjab, which has nothing to do with the Midland. So the language of North-eastern Rājputāna is very similar to that of Agra, but as we go south and west we see more and more of the original language of the Outer Band, until it is quite prominent in Gujarāt. Again in Oudh, which was a country with a literature and history of its own, there is a mixture of the same nature, although here the Midland language has not established itself so firmly as it has in the west and south.

"Finally, where possible, the inhabitants of the Outer Band also expanded to the south and east. In this way we find Marāṭhī in the Central Provinces, Berār, and Bombay; and, to the east, Oṛiyā, Bengali, and Assamese, all of them true Outer languages unaffected in their essence by the speech of the Midland.

"The state of affairs at the present day is therefore as follows:—There is a Midland Indo-Aryan language, occupying the Gangetic Doāb and the country immediately to its north and south. Round it on three sides is a band of Mixed languages, occupying the Eastern Punjab, Gujarāt, Rājputāna and Oudh, with extensions to the South in Bāghelkhand and Chattīsgarh. Again, beyond these, there is a band of Outer languages, occupying Kashmīr, the Western Punjab, Sind (here it is broken by Gujarāt), the Marāṭhā country, Orissa, Bihār, Bengal and Assam."*

This long extract perhaps embodies the final classification of the Indo-Aryan languages and therefore deserves careful attention from all students of Indian ethnology and history. But Grierson's reconstruction of the history of the Indo-Aryan movements mainly based on this classification can not be reconciled to what we

* *The Indian Empire*, Vol. I, pp. 357-359.

learn from other sources. Grierson's statement that in Vedic times there lived in the Punjab and Oudh other Indian tribes speaking dialects that differed widely from the language of Midland is baseless. Uśīnara, as we have already seen, evidently corresponding to the Eastern Punjab, formed an integral part of the Vedic Aryandom. In the ethnographical list of the Aitrareya Brāhmaṇa (VIII. 14) we are told:—"In this firmly fixed middle country (*asyāṃ dhruvāyāṃ madhyamāyāṃ diśi*) all the rulers of the Kurus and the Pañcālas, together with those of the Vaśas and the Uśīnaras, are consecrated to kingdom and called Rājās." "In treating of other territories" as Oldenberg observes, "instead of *asyām*, the word *etasyām* is used: *asyām* contains a significant hint that the compiler of the text belongs to this territory." The Vaśas of the Vedic literature corresponds to the Vaṃsas of the Pali Buddhist texts and Vatsya of the later Sanskrit literature with Kanśāmbī as their capital, and their country extended as far as the junction of the Ganges and the Jumna. So that Vedic Midland as defined in the Aitareya Brāhmaṇa included the whole area where Grierson's Midland Indo-Aryan language is spoken as well as Eastern Punjab or the country of the Uśīnaras.

. Though geographically outside Vedic Midland, Vedic culture flourished in full vigour in Kośala, Kāśī and Videha and the Brāhmans of the Kurupañcālas were held in great esteem by the rulers of these countries. The *satra* or the twelve years sacrificial session of Prajāpati performed by the Ṛṣis of Naimiṣa is referred to in the Pañcaviṃśa (XXV. 6. 4) and the Jaiminīya Brāhmaṇa.* Kośala was the home of the Ikṣvākus. According to the Jaiminīya Upaniṣad Brāhmaṇa (IV. 6. 1) King Bhageratha Aikṣvāka wishing to perform a wish-fulfilling sacrifice sought the advice of the Brāhmans of the Kuru-Pañcālas.† According to the Śatapatha Brāhmaṇa (XIII. 5. 4. 4) the Kośala king Para Ātṇāra Hairaṇyanābha is described as having performed the Aśvamedha or horse sacrifice. According to the Bṛhadāraṇyaka and Kauṣītaki Upaniṣads, Ajātasatru, King of Kāsi, instructs a proud Brāhman on the real nature of self (*ātman*). According to the Pañcaviṃsa Brāhmaṇa (XXV. 10. 17) Namī Sāpya, King of Videha, attained to heaven quickly by performing a sessional sacrifice at the place where the Sarasvatī disappears in the sands of the desert. The story of the great sacrifice performed by Janaka, King of Videha, and attended by Brāhmans of the Kuru-Pāñcālas where thousand cows were set apart for the most learned Brāhman and seized by Yājñavalkya, is told in the Jaiminīya (II. 76-77) and the Śatapatha Brāhmaṇa (XI. 6. 3; XIV. 6. 1. 9). It is highly probable that Yājñavalkya, the founder of the Vājasaneya school of the Yajurveda, was a native of Videha. But he was a pupil of Uddālaka Āruni, a Pāñcāla Brahman.

* *Journal of the American Oriental Society*, Vol. 26, p. 193.
† *Ibid.*, Vol. 16.

But the reason why Kośala and Kāśi were not considered as holy as Kuru and Pañcāla probably was, that there was a tendency to heterodoxy among the inhabitants of these countries. In the Jaiminīya Brāhmaṇa (III. 94-95) we are told the story of a dispute between an Aikṣvāka King and his priest, Vṛśa Jāna. King Tryaruna Traivṛṣṇa Aikṣvāka was being driven by the latter in a chariot. A Brāhman boy who was playing on the road was run down by the wheel of the chariot. Then there was a dispute between the King and the priest as regards the responsibility of the crime. The two said, "Let us submit the question." To the Ikṣvākus they submitted the question. The Ikṣvākus said, "None other than he who drives the chariot is controller of the chariot." It was to Vṛśa that they declared: "It is thou that hast killed him!" Vṛśa revived the child with a *sāman*, but went away in anger. Thereupon strength departed from the fire of the Iksvākus and consequently they had to recall Vṛśa.* As regards the heterodoxy of the Kāśis we learn from the Śatapatha Brāhmaṇa (XIII. 5. 4. 19): "Śatānīka Sātrājita performed the Govinata (form of Aśvamedha) after taking away the horse of the Kāśya (King); and since that time the Kāśis do not keep up the (sacrificial) fire, saying 'The Soma-drink has been taken from us.'"† According to Jaina and Bauddha traditions Pārśva, the predecessor of Mahāvīra, and Kassapa Buddha, the

* *Ibid.*, Vol. 18. † Eggeling's translation.

predecessor of Gautama Buddha, were both born in Benares. At one time Kośala and Kāśi had closer social intercourse with Magadha, Aṅga and other outer countries than with Kuru-Pañcāla. In the Rāmāyaṇa (I. 13, 21-28) Vasiṣṭha advises Daśaratha, King of Ayodhyā, to invite the Kings of Mithilā, Kāśi, Kekaya, Aṅga, Kośala, Magadha, the Eastern countries (*prācinān*), Sindhu, Sauvīra, Saurāṣṭra and Dākṣinātya to his horse sacrifice. It will be observed that the rulers of Kuru-Pañcāla, Matsya and other countries of Madhydeśa are omitted from the list. But heterodoxy and absence of social intercourse between the Kṣatriyas of Kuru-Pañcāla on the one hand and of Kāśi-Kośala on the other do not warrant us to assume any great linguistic difference in the Vedic period. It is to be noted that Daśaratha's domestic priest was a Vasiṣṭha, a clan that originally lived among the Bharatas on the Sarasvatī.

The case of Videha or Mithilā, where Maithili, a language belonging to the Outer Band, is now spoken, is somewhat different. The following well-known legend of the Śatapatha Brāhmaṇa (I, 4, 1, 14-17) throws light on the colonisation of Videha by the Vedic Āryas:—

"Māthava, the Videgha, was at that time on the (river) Sarasvatī. He (Agni) thence went burning along this earth towards the east; and Gotama Rāhūgana and the Videgha Māthava followed after him as he was burning along. He burnt over (dried up) all these rivers. Now that (river), which is called 'Sadānirā', flows from the northern (Himālaya) mountain: that one he did not burn over. That one the Brāhmans did not cross in former times, thinking, 'it has not been burnt over by Agni Vaiśvānara.'

"Nowadays, however, there are many Brāhmans to the east of it. At that time it (the land east of the Sadānirā) was very uncultivated, very marshy, because it had not been tasted by Agni Vaiśvānara.

"Nowadays, however, it is very cultivated, for the Brāhmans have caused (Agni) to taste it through sacrifices. Even in late summer that (river), as it were, rages along: so cold is it, not having been burnt over by Agni Vaiśvānara.

"Māthava, the Videgha, then said (to Agni), 'where am I to abide?' 'To the east of this (river) is to be thy abode!' said he. Even now this (river) forms the boundary of the Kośalas and Videhas; for these are the Māthavas (or descendants of Māthava)." *

This legend clearly indicates that at the time of the composition of the Śatapatha Brāhmaṇa it was distinctly remembered that at one time Videha lay outside Vedic Aryandom, and that the Brāhmans and Kṣatriyas who introduced Vedic culture came from the land watered by the Sarasvatī. The Brāhmanic codes name an inferior caste (mixed caste) called Vaideha who are evidently named after Videha and probably represented the pre-Vedic folk of the country. In the

* Eggeling's translation.

Vedic literature and the epic Rāmāyaṇa we find Videha ruled over by a line of hereditary sovereigns. But a different order of things prevailed in the sixth century B.C., at the time when Gotama Buddha flourished. Videha was no longer a monarchy, but there had sprung up a number of oligarchies headed by ruling tribes and clans within and in the neighbourhood of Janaka's realm. Chief among these were the Vajjians and the Licchavis of Vesāli, the Mallas of Pāvā and Kusināra, the Bulis of Allakappa, the Koliyas of Rāmagrāma and the Moriyas of Pipphalivana. The Licchavis (Licchivis) and the Mallas are named by Manu (X. 22) among the Vrātyas along with the Khasas and the Draviḍas. These and the other independent tribes of Videha were probably akin to the people of the Outer countries and were only partially Brāhmanised.

Though Videha, therefore, in spite of a veneer of Vedic culture, was only partially Aryanised, the Eastern Punjab on the one hand and Kośala and Kāśi on the other can not be excluded from the same ethnic sphere, and it can not be held with Grierson that Indo-Aryan tribes who originally occupied these areas spoke languages differing from the language of the Midland, and that owing to their nearness to "the borders of Midland, the Midland language has overwhelmed the ancient language." To explain the peculiar position of the mixed or intermediate Indo-Aryan languages, Grierson assumes that the population and power of the Midland increased and its armies and its settlers carried its language to the Eastern Punjab, Gujarāt and Oudh. But the Vedic, the Pali-Buddhist, and Purāṇic literatures preserve no tradition relating to the conquest and annexation of Uśīnara on the one hand, Kośala and Kāśi on the other, by the Kurus, Pañcālas, Matsyas or Vaśas. According to the Aitareya Brāhmaṇa (VIII. 14) while the kings (rājās) of the Middle country,— of Uśīnara, Kuru, Pañcāla, and Vaśa,—were consecrated to "kingdoms" (*rājyāya*), in the eastern country (*prācyām diśi*), the rulers (rājās) of the eastern peoples,—of the Kośalas, and Videhas,—were consecrated to "empire" (*sāmrājyāya*). This seems to indicate that at the time of the composition of this Brāhmaṇa, the rulers of the East were much more powerful than the rulers of the Middle country.

The dynasties and clans that held sway contemporaneously in the Middle and Outer countries of Northern India according to the Brāhmaṇas and the Upaniṣads survived down to about a century after Buddha. Pali texts give a list of sixteen powers of Northern India in Buddah's time, viz. Aṅgā, Magadhā, Kāśī, Kośalā, Vajji, Mallā, Cetī, Vaṃsā, Kuru, Pañcālā, Macchā, Sūrasenā, Assakā, Avanti, Gandhārā and Kambojā. The Purāṇas also bear witness to the same state of affairs. After giving the genealogies of the different dynasties that reigned in Magadha in succession down to the last of the Siśunāgas the Purāṇas tell us:—

"Contemporaneous with these aforesaid kings

there will be other kings; all these following kings will endure an equal time: namely, 24 Aikṣvākus, 27 Pañcālas, 24 kings of Kāśi, 28 Haihayas, 32 Kaliṅgas, 25 Aśmakas, 36 Kurus, 28 Maithilas, 23 Śūrasenas and 20 Vītihotras. All these kings will endure the same time."*

The tide of conquest, when it started, started not from the west but from the east—from Magadha, for we are told of Mahānandin, the last Śiśunāga King of Magadha:—

"A son of Mahānandin by a śūdra woman will be born a king, Mahāpadma (Nanda), who will exterminate all kṣatriyas. Thereafter kings will be of śūdra origin. Mahāpadma will be sole monarch, bringing all under his sole sway. He will be 88 years on the earth. He will uproot all kṣatriyas, being urged on by prospective fortune." †

The Purāṇic story of Nanda Mahāpadma is not a mere fable, but a historical event of very great moment. The historians of Alexander the Great, who invaded the Panjab only a generation after Nanda, corroborate the story in substance. Alexander reached the Hyphasis (Beas) towards the end of 326 B.C. Beyond the Sutlej lay the territories once ruled over by the Kuru, Pañcāla, Matsya, Vaṃśa and Ikṣvāku dynasties. But Alexander heard not a word about the princes of these dynasties. On the contrary, he was informed

* Pargiter, *The Purāna Text of the Dynasties of the Kali Age*, Oxford, 1913, p. 69.

† *Ibid.*, p. 69.

that the king of the Prasii (Magadha) was waiting to offer him resistance with an army of 80,000 horse, 200,000 foot, 8000 war chariots and 6000 fighting elephants. Where were the representatives of the old dynasties then? We have no other alternative but to accept the Purāṇic story of their overthrow by Nanda of Magadha as genuine history. It is corroborated from the south-eastern side by the Hāthigumphā inscription of Khāravela, King of Kaliṅga. According to the Purāṇas an old dynasty ruled over Kaliṅga contemporaneously with the Śiśunāgas, and, according to the Pāli Buddhist texts, Dantapura was the capital of the kingdom. In the Hāthigumphā inscription we are told of King Khāravela that, "In the fifth year he had an aqueduct that had not been used for 103 years since King Nanda (*or* since the Nanda kings?) conducted into the city." * This shows that Nanda was in possession of Kaliṅganagarī 103 years before the fifth year of Khāravela's reign.

The subjugation of Vedic Aryandom by a low-born conqueror from semi-barbarous Magadha probably contributed much more towards the overthrow of the Vedic culture than the teachings of Buddha and Mahāvīra. It inaugurated the real kaliyuga or iron age. We are told in the Viṣṇu Purāṇa (IV. 24) "When the seven Ṛṣis are in Pūrvāṣāḍhā, then Nanda will begin to reign; and thenceforward the influence of the Kali will augment."

* Luders, *List of Brahmi Inscriptions*, No. 1345.

The Nandas were succeeded by the mightier Mauryas of Magadha who exercised imperial sway over the whole of Northern India for nearly a century. Then the empire fell a prey to invaders from beyond the North-west frontiers such as the Yavanas (Bactrians), Pahlavas (Parthians), Tuṣāras (Yeutis) and Śakas.

Then there arose in Magadha a second Mahāpadma Nanda. We are told in the Purāṇa:—

"Of the Māgadhas the king will be very valiant Viśvasphāṇi. Overthrowing all kings he will make other castes *kings*, *namely*, Kaivartas, Pañcakas, Pulindas, and Brāhmans. He will establish those persons as kings in various countries. Viśvasphāṇi is called eunuch-like in appearance. Overthrowing the Kṣatriya caste he will create another Kṣatriya caste. After gratifying the gods, the pitṛs and Brāhmans once *and* again, he will resort to the bank of the Ganges and subdue his body; after resigning his body he will go to Indra's world." *

Though no contemporaneous record bearing witness to the existence of this king has hitherto come to light, yet his account given after the accounts of the historical Andhras, Ābhīras, and the foreign dynasties and immediately before those of the historical Nāga and Gupta dynasties, can not be treated lightly. The founders of the Gupta empire were also natives of Magadha, and owed their elevation to an alliance with the Licchavis of Vaiśāli. The only native of the holy Madhya-

* *The Purāna Text of the Dynasties of the Kali Age*, p. 73.

deśa who ever succeeded in subduing the whole of Northern India was Harśavardhana of Thaneśvara and Kanauj. After his death his empire broke up into small kingdoms which lasted till the Mussalmān conquest. It was not, therefore, the conquering armies of the Midland, but the armies and settlers from Magadha and other Outer countries that carried their languages to Oudh and other places where mixed languages are now spoken.

To the north-west and the north of the Midland lived the Khaśas whose early history is thus summed up by Sir George Grierson:—

"We gather that according to the most ancient Indian authorities in the extreme north-west of India, on the Hindu Kush and the mountainous tracts to the south, and in the Western Punjab there was a group of tribes, one of which was called Khaśa, which were looked upon as Kṣatriyas of Aryan origin. These spoke a language closely allied to Sanskrit, but with a vocabulary partly allied to that of the Iranian Avesta.

"It is probable that they occupied an important position in Central Asia, and that countries, places and rivers, such as Kashmir, Kashgar in Central Asia, and the Kashgar of Chitral were named after them. They were closely connected with the group of tribes nicknamed 'Piśāchaś' or 'cannibals' by Indian writers, and before the sixth century they were stated to speak the same language as the people of Balkh. At the same period they had apparently penetrated along the southern slope of the Himālayas as far east as Nepāl, and in the twelfth century they certainly occupied in considerable force the hills to the south, south-west and south-east of Kashmir.'' *

'Not only social institutions, and language, but an important physical feature also—the shape of the skull—lends support to the testimony of the Śruti, Smṛti, and Purāṇa, that the Indo-Aryans of the Outer countries originally came of an ethnic stock that was different from the stock from which the Vedic Āryas originated. Long heads preponderate in all ranks of society in the provinces that now represent the ancient Vedic Aryandom and among the Maithil Brāhmans of Bihar with only 25 per cent of medium heads and 1·5 per cent round heads.† But among the typical

---

* *Indian Antiquary*, vol. XLIII, p. 150.

† *Summary of measurements of headforms of typical Hindustani Castes.*

No. of subjects measured.	Name of caste.	Province of birth.	Percentage of long or dolichocephalic heads (index under 75).	Percentage of medium or mesaticephalic heads (index 75 to under 80).	Percentage of broader brachycephalic heads (index 80 and above).
100	Brahman ..	United Provinces.	74	24	2
26	Bhuinhār ..	,,	73	27	0
100	Chāmār ..	,,	78	20	2
100	Kāyastha ..	,,	79	21	1
100	Kurmi ..	,,	68	31	1
100	Goala (Ahir) ..	,,	80	19	1
60	Khatri ..	Punjab ..	64	33	3
80	Chuhrā ..	,,	71	28	1
420	Rajput ..	Rājputāna	79	20	1
50	Maithil Brāhman ..	Bihar ..	70	26	4

castes of the Outer countries there is a preponderance of medium and round heads indicating, roughly speaking, an admixture of 50 per cent round heads, with the exception of Bihar where a larger percentage of long heads as well as the survival of the four-fold division of caste, are due to the absorption of larger Midlandic elements.* Other Indian peoples among whom broad or medium heads are present in as large numbers as

With the exception of the Maithil Brahmans of the previous table and the Pāścātya Vaidik Brahmans and the Uttararādhīya Kayasthas of the following table all other figures are taken from Sir Herbert Risley's *Tribes and Castes of Bengal* and *People of India*.

No. of subjects measured.	Name of caste.	Province of birth.	Percentage of long or dolichocephalic heads.	Percentage of medium or mesaticephalic heads.	Percentage of broader brachycephalic heads.
100	Nagar Brahman ..	Bombay Presy.	15	39	46
127	Bania	,,	12	49	39
100	Marāṭha ..	,,	37	42	21
100	Prabhu	,,	11	37	52
100	Chitpavan Brahman	,,	31	40	29
100	Kunbi	,,	29	47	24
68	Brahman ..	Bengal ..	13	52	35
50	Pāścātya Vaidik Brahman	,,	6	48	46
50	Uttararāḍhi Kayastha	,,	32	54	14
100	Kayastha .	,,	11	50	39
67	Namasūdra ..	,,	21	51	28
59	Bhuinhar .	Behar ..	30	53	17
62	Chamar .	,,	44	35	21
71	Kurmi.. ..	,,	37	48	15

among the Indo-Aryans of the Outer countries are the Telugu, the Kodagu and the Canarese-speaking population of the Deccan. After analysing the head-measurements of the population of the different linguistic areas of the Madras Presidency, Thurston writes :—

"I am not prepared to hazard any new theory to account for the marked difference in the type of cranium in the various areas under consideration, and must content myself with the observation that whatever may have been the influence which has brought about the existing sub-brachycephalic or mesaticephalic types in the Northern areas, this influence has not extended into the Tamil and Malayalam countries, where Dravidian man remains dolicho or sub-dolichocephalic."*

The speakers of Tamil and Malayālam languages of Southern India who represent the ancient Cholas, Pāndyas, and Keralas, are long-headed, and so are the tribesmen of the Niṣāda stock. So to account for the presence of round and medium-headed elements in such large numbers in the population of the Indo-Aryan Outland we are constrained to assume the immigration of round-headed and medium-headed tribes who have commingled with the long-headed men of Niṣāda, Vedic Ārya, and Tamil stocks in different proportions in different parts of the wide area inhabited by them.

Physical characteristics, and, particularly the head index, do not find recognition in certain

---

* *Castes and Tribes of Southern India*, Vol. I.

quarters as tests of physical relationship. Mr. O'Malley writes:—

"Of late years anthropometry as a test of race has begun to fall out of favour. Professor Ridgeway considers that physical type depends far more on environment than on race. 'From the evidence already to hand there is high probability that intermarriage can do little to form a new race, unless the parents on both sides are of races evolved in similar environments.' Elsewhere he points out that 'as the physical anthropologists cannot agree upon any principles of skull measurement, the historical inquirer must not at present base any argument in this class of evidence.' Another writer (Professor Homersham Cox) remarks:—'Neither cephalic nor nasal index is of much use in determining race. The truth is, the method on indices has been thoroughly discredited among anthropologists, and were it not employed in the 'People of India,' a book published in 1908, we should have supposed it had no longer any followers.' . . . . . . His (Prof. Ridgeway's) views appear to be confirmed by the recent discoveries of Walcher, who has drawn attention to the changes which can be made in the shape of the skull of newly-born infants by inducing them to lie constantly on the side or on the back, according as it is desired to make the head long or short." *

---

* *Census of India*, 1911, *Vol. V*, *Bengal, Bihar and Orissa and Sikkim. Part I. Report* by L. S. S. O'Malley, Calcutta, 1913, p. 517.

Regarding the recent discoveries of Walcher it may be observed that though it is possible to make changes in the shape of the skull of newly-born infants, there is no evidence to show that in countries where long-heads predominate the infants are deliberately and invariably made to lie on the side, and in countries where short heads predominate the infants are similarly made to lie on the back. Students of physical anthropology do not seem to have taken serious notice of the views of the two other authorities cited by Mr. O'Malley, but have gone on with their researches as before. We are here mainly concerned with one physical character, the shape of the skull as indicated by the cephalic index, as a test of race. The influence of environment on the head-form has been a subject of keen controversy in America. I reproduce Dr. W. L. H. Duckworth's summary of the discussion:—

"The contribution to the study of environment provided by Dr. Boas in his report on the immigrants into the United States deserves special attention here. Two striking announcements are made in that report. In the first place, it is claimed that in regard to head-form, the offspring of immigrants stand in distinct and even marked contrast to their parents. Again the data are said to show that a change in every case takes place in the direction of convergence towards a common form or type. So that whether the parents themselves be of long-headed or of the bullet-headed type, these characteristics are not transmitted.

The offspring tends towards an intermediate form. Environment is made prominent in the speculations as to the influence determining these results. The latter are extraordinary for two reasons. First on account of the acting force, and again for the rapidity with which it acts. Acceptance of the conclusions in such a matter must depend on the nature of the evidence, including *inter alia* the method of collection and the actual numerical differences shown by the figures. Having regard to such points, the severe criticism which has been passed on these statements is not without justification, and it is clear that further support is needed before anything like complete recognition can be accorded to the conclusions." *

The anthropological history of Europe, of which Prof. Arthur Keith has given a luminous summary in his Presidential Address delivered to the Royal Anthropological Institute of Great Britain and Ireland (on January 26th, 1915) furnishes unerring testimony of the value of head-form as a test of race. This history covers a period of 4000 to 5000 years and is thus put in a nutshell:—

"In the first place we have clear proof that at one time — some 4000 or 5000 years ago — the round-headed stock did break through and reached the western shores of Europe. It leavened England, but became submerged; it met a similar fate in Western Germany and in Holland. In the earlier centuries of the present era the long-heads

* *The Britannica Year Book*, 1913, p. 155.

in North-Western Europe must have undergone a recrudescence in numbers and in power. They broke eastwards in the plains of the Vistula and the Danube; they imposed their speech on the conquered peoples, but the vanquished imposed on them their features of face, head, and body. They broke westwards in France and lost both their tongue and their head-form; they crossed the North Sea and kept both their tongue and their shape of head." *

Sir Herbert Risley traces the round-headed elements among the Gujarātis, Marāṭhis, and Coorgs to Scythian admixture; and those among the Bengalis and Oriyas to Mongoloid admixture. The Central Asian nomads who followed the Bactrians and Parthians to India in the centuries immediately preceding and succeeding the Christian era and are generally known as Indo-Scythians consisted of Śaka and Yeuti or Tokhāra (Skt. Tuṣāra) hordes. The history of their dominion in India is involved in obscurity. But it is possible to distinguish two different phases of Indo-Scythian rule. First, the dominions of the Kṣatrapas or Satráps of North-Western and Western India who were the representatives of Parthian suzerains; second, the empire of the Kushan branch of the Yeutis. The inscriptions of the Kṣatrapas and Mahākṣatrapas of North-Western India have been discovered at Taxila and Mathura, and their coins have been found in the Punjab and in the western

* The Bronze-Age Invaders of Britain—*Nature*, February 11, 1915, pp. 660-561.

districts of the Agra province. Śaka-Parthian dominion in the North-West was probably overthrown by the Kushan branch of the Yeutis. We know the names of no less than seven Kushan kings from their coins and inscriptions. Inscriptions dated in the reign of Kanishka have been found as far east as Sārnath, and, according to tradition, his kingdom extended as far as Pațaliputra in Magadha. An inscription dated in the reign of the Kushan King Vāsashka has been found on a Buddhist statue at Sanchi.* Coins of the Kushan Kings have been found all over Northern India. These Indo-Scythians were evidently round-headed. But the Indo-Scythian strain has failed to modify the physical type of Hindusthān which is predominantly long-headed. This is no doubt due to the fact that Indo-Scythian invaders were too small in number to produce any impression on the physical features of the general population that absorbed them. If this was the case in Northern India, it cannot be assumed that the Indo-Scythians who invaded Western India and the Deccan modified the physical character of the long-headed Dravidian or Niṣāda aborigines. Indo-Scythian Kṣatrapas ruled over Gujarat and part of Mālava for above three centuries beginning from A.D. 78, but their dominion farther south was short-lived and intermittent. Both Northern Konkan and Northern Mahārāṣṭra were in possession of the Kṣaharātas under Nahapāna (A.D.

* *Journal of the Royal Asiatic Society*, 1903, p. 325.

119-124) and were then re-conquered by the Andhra King Gautamiputra. Northern Mahārāṣṭra continued under the Andhras till it passed into the possession of the Ābhīras early in the third century A.D. Mahākṣatrapa Rudradāman conquered Northern Konkan about A.D 150; but it was recovered by the Andhra King Yajña-Śrī (A.D. 169-198). The Indo-Scythians who held only the outskirts of the Deccan for such short intervals can hardly be regarded as the ancestors of the vast broad or medium-headed population of the entire table-land. We must therefore reject Risley's Indo-Scythian theory and trace their origin to brachycephalic hordes who migrated in large numbers in the prehistoric period and by intermingling with the Niṣāda, Dravidian, and Vedic Aryan, elements produced the hybrid population of Gujarāt, Mahāraṣṭrā, Coorg, Karṇāta and Andhra (Telugu Country).

From the same group of prehistoric immigrants are derived the round-headed and medium-headed elements in the population of Bihar, Orissa, and Bengal. Mongoloids are not recognised as autochthones in India but are immigrants,* and Risley's theory of Mongolo-Dravidian origin of the Bengalis and Oriyas involves the assumption that Mongoloid invaders preceded in large numbers the carriers of Aryan speech and culture in Bengal and Orissa. But neither the physiognomy of the bulk of the Bengali and Oriya folk,

---

* *The Indian Empire*, Vol. I, p. 384.

nor the legends and traditions relating to their origin, support this hypothesis, while legends and traditions bearing testimony to Mongoloid affinities are well-known relating to the Nepalese and Assamese among whom men with Mongoloid physiognomy still predominate. According to the *Svayambhu Purāna* and the local annals the valley of Nepal was originally a lake called *Kālihrada* or 'dark lake'. Mañjudeva (Bodhisatva Mañjuśrī or Mañjughoṣa) came from China with a body of Chinese (*cinadeśajamānuṣāh*), drained the lake by cutting out a passage, and colonized the valley with his followers. He also imported from China a prince named Dharmākara and made him the ruler of the Chinese colony. These legends bear strong resemblance to the legends contained in the *Nilamata* relating to the origin of the population of Kashmir which will be referred to presently. According to the *Kālikā-Purāṇa* (XXXIX.104)*, Kāmarūpa or Assam, bounded on the west by the Karatoyā, was inhabited "by powerful, cruel, and ignorant Kirātas." Naraka, a demon, with the help of Viṣṇu, drove out the Kirātas and established Brāhmans well versed in the Vedas and other castes in Kāmarūpa. But Purāṇic legends relating to the origin of the people of Aṅga (south-eastern Bihar), Kaliṅga (Orissa), and the three main divisions of Bengal—Puṇḍra (Varendra), Suhma (Rāḍha) and Vaṅga (Eastern Bengal)—know nothing of Chinese and Kirāta immigrants or

Published by Kṣemaraja, Bombay, 1814 Sáka.

aborigines. According to these legends as told in the Harivaṃśa (chapter 31), in the line of Pūru, son of Yayātī, there was a king named Bali who had five sons,—Aṅga, Vaṅga, Kaliṅga, Suhma and Puṇḍra. The five kingdoms ruled over by them came to be known after them. "Anga was first born, then Vaṅga, Suhma, Puṇḍra and Kaliṅga. These are called Bāleya Kṣatriyas. Bāleya Brāhmans on earth are also his descendants. O Bhārata, Brahmā, being pleased with him, granted him this boon . . . Here you will establish the four permanent castes."* These verses also occur in the Matsya Purāṇa (48. 24·28). Vāyu Purāṇa (99, 27) says of Bali, "He gave birth to sons that created the four castes on earth." † These legends also throw light on the question of the origin of caste in the Outer countries.

Head-form alone, unless accompanied by other Mongoloid characteristics, can not be accepted

* महायोगी स तु बलिर्बभूव नृपतिः पुरा ॥
पुत्रानुत्पादयामास पञ्चवंशकरान् भुवि ।
अङ्गः प्रथमतो जज्ञे वङ्गः सुह्मस्तथैव च ॥
पुण्ड्रः कलिङ्गश्च तथा बालेयं क्षत्रमुच्यते ।
बालेया ब्राह्मणाश्चैव तस्य वंशकरा भुवि ॥
बलेस्तु ब्रह्मणा दत्तो वरः प्रीतेन भारत ।
* * * *
चतुरो नियतान् वर्णांस्त्वं च स्थापयितेति च ॥
* * * *
तेषां जनपदाः पञ्चः अङ्गवङ्गाः ससुह्मकाः ।
कलिङ्गाः पुण्ड्रकाश्चैव ॥

† "पुत्रानुत्पादयामास चातुर्वर्ण्यकरान भुवि ।"

as a sign of considerable Mongolian strain, for all the Mongoloid tribes within the Indian border are not round-headed. Among 84 male members of the Abor tribe measured by Messrs. J. Coggin Brown and S. W. Kemp, 32 per cent are long-headed and only 6 per cent are round-head.* The Koch, Paliya, and the Rajvaṃśis of Northern Bengal, whose physiognomy displays Mongoloid traits, are evidently the descendants of Mongoloid invaders from the Himālayas or the Brahmaputra Valley who settled in the historic period. To account for the linguistic, social, and physical differences between the Hindusthānis on the one hand and the Indo-Aryans of the Outer countries on the other, we have to assume the immigration of round and medium-headed invaders of Aryan speech in the pre-historic period. Now the question is, wherefrom did these pre-historic round-headed Aryan invaders come?

The home of the round-headed Aryans is not far to seek. Beyond the Indus, in Baluchistan and Afghanistan, live the Baluch and the Pathans who are Aryan in speech (Iranian) and medium-headed. Sir Herbert Risley classified these Baluch and Pathans as Turko-Iranian type on the assumption that the dolichocephalic elements among them are of Iranian stock and the brachycephalic elements are of Turanian stock. But the physical anthropology of the Pāmirs and Chinese Turkistan

* *Memoirs of the Asiatic Society of Bengal*, Vol. V, Extra No., p. 91.

as gathered from data collected by Ujfalvy and Sir Aurel Stein indicates that we need not lay the Turks, the Scythians, and the Mongolians under contribution to explain the presence of broad or medium heads among Outlandic Indo-Aryans or Indo-Afghans. The final conclusions from these data are thus stated by Mr. T. A. Joyce*:—

"To sum up, the measurements show that the majority of people surrounding the Taklamakan desert have a very large common element. Further, this element is seen in its purest form in the Wakhi. The fact that the Wakhi display so close a relationship with the Galcha proves that the basis of the Takla makan population is Iranian (?). At the North-Western edge of the desert an intrusive element, which can be sharply differentiated from the Iranian (?), makes its appearance, the Turki element. Besides this there seems to be some common bond between the peoples of the desert and of Tibet. This probably means that the Iranian (?) element has penetrated to Northern Tibet, though it is not unlikely that Tibetan (modified Mongolian) influence has been exercised, *to slight degree*, upon the desert peoples. In any case the relationship with Tibet required confirmation by more measurements taken in the latter country. In the Pamirs is a series of tribes, who, though chiefly of Iranian (?) stock, begin to exhibit slight traces of Indo-Afghan blood. In at least one tribe,

* *Journal of the Royal Anthropological Institute*, 1912, pp. 467-468.

the Kāfir, these traces are considerably more than slight. The Chitrali also seem to stand in closer relationship to an Indo-Afghan people (but a rather specialized Indo-Afghan people) than the other Pamir tribes. Some admixture has taken place between the Turki and Desert folk. In the case of Aksu, the Turki element predominates. In the case of Niya and Keriya, who should be classed as rather aberrant members of the Desert group, it seems probable that their departure from the North is due to Turki admixture. Faizabad appears to be a mixture of all three groups, Pamir, Turki, and Desert; and this is what might be expected, the root stock of the population would thus be Iranian (?), though it has been exposed to Turki influences since Indo-Scythian times and has thus become somewhat modified. In the East, Chinese influence begins to make itself felt, but only over a very restricted area. Hami, Turfan, and Korla have been thus affected, and it is not unlikely that the desert people have had some corresponding, though perhaps slight, effect upon the population of Nan-huo and Tun-huang. . . . . The great differentiation of the Chinese and Turki groups is interesting, since both are regarded as 'Mongolian.' It is evident that they belong to widely different branches of the Mongolian race, and it must be concluded that the Turki are allied to the Southern Mongolian. . . . . If this is so, and the Turki peoples do, in fact, contain a large Southern Mongolian element, their stature has been greatly increased in the course of their wanderings, by contact, probably, with Iranian (?) peoples. This leads us to the question to what extent we may regard the Turki as a distinct branch of Mongolians, and whether it would not be more correct to look upon the various tribes which fall under this heading as being originally mixtures, in varying proportions, of Mongolian and Iranian (?) elements, which time has reduced to comparative homogeneity. Finally, the point which emerges most clearly from the welter of measurements and descriptive data contained in this paper is this : that the original inhabitant of the Pamirs and Takla-Makan Desert, including the cities now buried beneath the sand, is that type of man described by Lapouge as *Homo Alpinus*, with, in the west, traces of the Indo-Afghan; and that the Mongolian has had very little influence upon the population. In using the Homo Alpinus term, I wish it to be understood that I employ it merely as the name of certain type already described, and not necessarily imply that the actual population of the Alps is closely allied to the population of Chinese Turkistan.

"In conclusion, I will quote from my previous paper (already cited) the description of these types:—

"1. A white-rosy race, very brachycephalic, stature about the average, with thin prominent nose, varying from aquiline to straight, long, oval face, hair brown, usually dark, always abundant and wavy (I think this should now be altered to curly), eyes medium in the main. This is Lapouge's *Homo Alpinus*.

"2. A race, also white, but with a slight tendency to brownish, also very brachycephalic and with stature above the average, nose broader and usually straight, cheekbones broad, hairs straighter, darker and less abundant, eyes dark. The 'Turkish' race.

"3. A brown mesaticephalic, tall type, thin, prominent and aquiline nose, long, oval face, black, wavy hair, dark eyes. This race may be termed the Indo-Afghan."

From this classification of the physical types of Chinese Turkistan and the Pāmirs, it is evident that in the pre-historic period the Takla-Makan desert and the Pamirs were inhabited by a very brachycephalic population of Aryan or Indo-European speech. Mr. Joyce calls this root stock Iranian. But several documents written in the language spoken in Chinese Turkestan that have been unearthed indicate that the language spoken in the ancient kingdoms of Khotan and Kucha was neither Indo-Aryan nor Iranian. Some savants designate this language "Tokharian" (A and B). The 'B' dialect of the Tokharian language was spoken in the small kingdom of Kucha in the seventh century A.D. Professor Sylvain Levi names this dialect Kuchean, and about its place in the Indo-European family he writes, "One would expect the Kuchean to be intimately connected with the Aryan languages of Iran and India. Not at all. Special features show its near relationship to the

Western languages of Europe, particularly Italo-Celtic.'' * In the North-Western Frontier Province and Baluchistan this *Homo Alpinus* type has been modified into medium-headed Indo-Afghan by contact with the long-headed Vedic Ārya and the Avestic Ārya on the one hand, and the Dravidian, whose language, the Brahui, still survives in Baluchistan, on the other. In India the same type has been turned into the mesaticephalic Indo-Aryan of the Outland by Nisāda, Vedic Ārya, and Draviḍa, admixture.

According to Hoernle's theory adopted by Grierson, the Indo-Aryans of the Outer countries came earlier and the inhabitants of the Midland represent the latest wave of immigration. There is no clear evidence to show that the Magadhas, the Aṅgas, and the Puṇḍras preceded the Vedic Āryas. It is more reasonable to suppose that when immigrants of the *Homo Alpinus* type entered India they found the middle portion of the Gangetic plain in possession of the Vedic Āryas, and therefore the first batch found their way to the lower Gangetic plain (Bihar) across the tableland of Central India. Other bands, the Rāṣṭikas or Raṭṭas after whom Mahārāṣṭra and Saurāṣṭra are named, wandered into the Kathiwar Peninsula and the Deccan.

A later wave consisted of the Vāhikas of the Land of the Five Rivers who are referred to in the Satapatha Brāhmana (I. 7. 3. 8) as worshippers

* *Journal of the Royal Asiatic Society*, 1914, p. 959.

of Rudra under the name of *Bhava*. The latest wave is represented by the speakers of what Grierson calls the modern Piśāca languages,—the Kashmīris, the Darads, and the Kāfirs of the Hindukush. The legends of *Nilamata* enshrine the traditions of the movements of the different strata of the population of Kashmir. Like Nepal, Kashmir was originally a lake called Satīsara. The Nāgas with Nila their king lived in this lake. Śiva drained off the water of the lake and produced Kashmir. Kaśyapa, Nila's father, peopled Kashmir with gods and goddesses as well as Nāgas. He wished to introduce men, but the Nāgas objected to their company. Kaśyapa cursed and condemned the Nāgas henceforth to dwell with Piśācas. Nila interceded on behalf of the Nāgas. Kaśyapa said there was an island, six yojanas in area, in the sand ocean. Fierce Piśācas, Yakṣas, and Daityas lived in that island. Every year Nikumbha, the King of the Piśācas, would lead five crores of Piśācas to Kashmir and live there six months. The Nāgas would live with men for the remaining six months. Regarding the ethnographical significance of these legends Grierson writes:—

"By the expression 'an island in the sand ocean' to the north of Kāśmir, the Nilamata can only mean an oasis in the Central Asian desert lately explored by Dr. Stein. . . . . That these mythological Nāgas represented an actual people has never, I believe, been doubted; and here, in the Nilamata, we see them described as the original inhabitants of Kāśmir, and as half conquered by

Piśāca invaders from an oasis in the Central Asian desert. If we now turn to the Sūryagarbha Sūtra of the Mahasaṃnipāta, the Māhātmya of Khotan, we find the same story repeated. The Yakṣas (i.e, Piśācas) are again brought into prominence as superseding the Nāgas. The latter refuse to accept the charge of the twenty holy places of Buddhism. The Yakṣas then accept the responsibility of nineteen, the twentieth, Gośringa in Khotan, being left to the Nāgas.''*

Regarding the Nāgas, Grierson adds in a note, "I am inclined to believe that they may have been the ancestors of the Non-Aryan inhabitants of Hunza-Nagar, whose language, Burusaskī, has not yet been identified as belonging to any known family of speech." The Piśāca characteristics are not confined to the dialects of Kāshmir and Hindukush but are found in most of the Outer Indo-Aryan languages. Grierson writes :—

"But there are traces of the former prevalence of these languages over an area much wider than North-Western India. The Khasa languages of the Western Himalaya as far as Kumaon present many peculiarities which are also found in 'Modern Piśāca' forms of speech; and only in these. So also the Lahndā of the Western Punjab, Sindhī, and Punjābī itself. . . . .

"But these 'Modern Piśāca' features have spread much further than the Punjab. They have

---

* *Zeitschrift der Deutschen Morgenlandischen Gessellschaft*, 1912, p. 72.

gone from Sindhī into Northern Gujaraṭhi, and thence, as already stated, into the Vindhya country of the Bhils. They are traceable so far south as the Konkaṇi dialect of Maraṭhī." *

These Piśāca peculiarities are probably derived not from invaders of Piśāca speech, but from the stock language spoken by the invaders akin to the *Homo Alpinus* of Eastern Turkestan, and the dialects of the Hindukush and Kaśmir retain a greater number of these peculiarities because they have been much less influenced by the Midlandic Indo-Aryan language than the other Outer Indo-Aryan languages.

---

* *Ibid.*, p. 77.

CHAPTER III.

RACE AND CULT—VAIṢṆAVISM.

The Vedic literature—Mantra, Brāhmaṇa and Sūtra—yields materials for reconstructing the history of the culture of the Vedic Aryans as Avesta does of the Iranians. But no ancient literary monument of the Outlandic Indo-Aryans revealing any aspect of their primitive culture has come down to us. The little that we as yet know of their distant kinsmen of Central Asia (Chinese Turkestan) does not throw any light on this question. The earliest documents hitherto discovered in the sands of Turkestan do not carry us further than the early centuries of the Christian era when the whole local civilization was Buddhistic, and nothing has as yet come to light that enables us to obtain a glimpse of the pre-Buddhistic culture of the Aryan round-heads of Central Asia. But by analysing the post-Vedic Indo-Aryan cults ethnographically, it may be possible to trace some elements of the primitive culture of the Outlandic Indo-Aryans and to ascertain their share in building up the latter-day Hindu culture as distinguished from the early Vedic culture. I shall here deal with the history of Vaiṣṇavism from the ethnographical standpoint.

The origin of the different phases of Vaiṣṇavism has long been a subject of keen controversy. In 1868 Weber first called attention to the strange coincidences between the legends of child Kṛṣṇa and Christ. He writes, "Now, when Christianity, by whatever way it arrived, became known to the Indians, the similarity of the names of Kṛṣṇa (which in Southern India is pronounced Krishtna, with a 't') and of Christ seems to have given rise to the identification of the two personalities, and to have caused the transfer of the stories regarding our Lord, the birth of the Babe in the manger, and so forth, to Kṛṣṇa, whose mother's name, Devakī, it may be remarked, can also be interpreted as meaning 'the divine one'."* About the way in which Christianity arrived in India and influenced Kṛṣṇa worship Weber writes:—

"The observance of the feast of the birth of Christ in connection with that of His baptism is traceable in Egypt from the second half of the fourth century up to the year 431 A.D.; and it is natural to assume that it was about this time that the transfer of this kind of festival to India took place, and, with it, the other connected materials which point to Christian legends and conceptions in the story of Kṛṣṇa. Two ways lay open for their communication. In the first place, Indian travellers, merchants, and the like may have come to Alexandria. There they may have learnt about Christianity, and on their return home may have transferred its legends to their own Kṛṣṇa, whom they already worshipped in

* *Indian Antiquary*, Vol. XXX (1901), p. 286.

India as a demigod. In the second place Christian missionaries may have gone to India, and have found there among the Kṛṣna worshippers a good soil for the propagation of their doctrines.''*

Weber's theory of the Christian origin of the cult of Gopāla or child Kṛṣṇa has been adopted by almost all scholars with the exception of Barth, but Weber's view relating to the time and way of the arrival of Christianity in India has not met with general approval. Hopkins, considering how late are these legends about the child Kṛṣṇa, dated them tentatively as arising after A.D. 600.† Kennedy holds that in the fifth or sixth century A.D. Scythian nomads from Central Asia, called Gurjaras or Gujars, ''who roamed through the woods of Braj, brought with them a child-god, a Christian legend, and Christmas festival; and in a city of lax Buddhists and eager Hindus this germ sufficed for the birth of a new if hybrid divinity ..... The name of the new god sounded in the ears of the Hindus like that of elder Kṛṣṇa, whom the popular epic had exalted to the highest rank: the new god, like the elder Kṛṣṇa, was an incarnation of the Most High; and so the youthful Kṛṣṇa was born.''‡ Grierson, following Weber, Hopkins and Kennedy, writes: ''It is possible, and perhaps probable, that the worship of the infant Kṛṣṇa was a local adaptation of the worship of the infant Christ introduced to India from

* *Ibid.*, p. 287.

† *The Religions of India*, 1894, p. 431.

‡ *Journal of the Royal Asiatic Society*, 1907, pp. 989—990.

the North-West, and the ritual of Kṛṣṇa's birth-festival was certainly borrowed from Christian authorities."*

The distinguished Indian scholar, Sir Ramskṛṣna G. Bhandarkar, pushes back the importation of the Christian influence to an earlier epoch. He says that inscriptions, the work of Patañjali, and the Nārāyaṇīya section of the Mahābhārata indicate no knowledge of the cowherd (Gopāla) Kṛṣṇa. The only passage of the Mahābhārata (II. 41), northern recension, which refers to the deeds of cowherd Kṛṣṇa, is an evident interpolation. "The Harivaṃśa, which is the chief authority, contains the word *dināra*, corresponding to the Latin word *denarius*, and consequently must have been written about the third century of the Christian era." "The cowherds among whom the boy-god Kṛṣṇa lived were the nomadic Ābhīras "who must have migrated into the country in the first century A.D." "They probably brought with them the worship of the boy-god and the story of his humble birth, his reputed father's knowledge that he was not his son, and the massacre of the innocents. The two last correspond to Nanda's knowing that he was not the father of Kṛṣṇa and Kaṃśa's killing all children .... It is possible that they brought with them the name of Christ also, and this name probably led to the identification of the boy-god with Vāsu-

---

* *Encyclopædia of Religion and Ethics*, Vol. II, art. 'Bhakti-Mārga', p. 550*b*.

deva-Kṛṣṇa. The Goanese and the Bengalis often pronounce the name Kṛṣṇa as Kusto or Kṛsto, and so the Christ of the Ābhīras was recognised as the Sanskrit Kṛṣṇa.''*

The main reason that has led these eminent authorities to assume a Christian origin of the cult of child Kṛṣṇa is the presence of certain common elements in the legends of child Kṛṣṇa and those of Christ. If these elements remind one of the story of Christ as told in the gospel, there are other elements in the legend of Gopāla, such as Nārada's prediction to Kaṃśa (according to *Harivaṃṣa*) that he would be killed by the eighth child of Devaki, precautions taken by Kaṃśa, and Kṛṣna's ultimately killing Kaṃśa, bear striking analogy to the legends of the Greek hero Perseus whose maternal grandfather Acrisius was forewarned by a prophet that he would be killed by the hand of his daughter Danae's son and was ultimately killed by Danae's son Perseus. If we admit the possibility of the independent origin of these legends, it is not necessary to postulate borrowing from Christianity of such elements in the Kṛṣṇa legend as Nanda's knowledge that Kṛṣṇa was not really his son and Kaṃśa's massacre of Devaki's children. There is a great deal of resemblance between the career of boy Kṛṣṇa and of young Perseus, whereas Christ is a character of different type. Two of Perseus's greatest

---

* Encyclopedia of Indo-Aryan Research, III, 6. *Vaisṇavism, Śaivism and Minor Religious Systems*, Strassburg, 1913, pp. 37-38.

feats, slaughter of Medusa the Gorgon, and of the sea-monster bred of slime to save Andromeda, have their counterparts in Kṛṣṇa's slaughter of Putanā and the subjugation of Kāliya, the snake-demon.

Another argument advanced by Bhandarkar is, that Ghoṣa, where, according to the Harivaṃśa, child Kṛṣna's foster-father lived, "is defined as Ābhīrapallī, which is generally understood as the enclosure of cowherds. But the original signification of the word Ābhīra is not a cowherd. It is the name of a race." Amara and later lexicographers define *ghoṣa* as *ābhīrapallī* or Ābhīra settlement. But the term also occurs in Patañjali's Mahābhāṣya (on Pāṇini II. 4. 1) together with *grāma* (village) and *nagara* (town).* So we must either admit that the Ābhīras migrated to India before Patañjali or there were other cowherds who lived in *ghoṣas* before the advent of the Ābhīras. The admission of either of these alternatives render the theory of the Christian origin of the cult of Gopāla untenable. That there were Ābhiras in India even when Kātyāyana, Patañjali's predecessor, wrote, is evident from his Vārttika on Pāṇini IV. 1. 4 where the word *mahā-śūdrī* is excluded from the operation of the rule. *Mahāsūdrī*, according to Amara, means *ābhīrī*, cowherdess. According to Kāśikā "the word mahāśūdra denotes a man of *ābhīra* caste."† The

* कः पुनरार्यनिवासः । ग्रामो घोषो नगरं संवाह इति

† महाशूद्रशब्दो ह्याभीरजातिवचनः ।

author of *The Periplus of the Erythrean Sea* (§ 41), who wrote about A.D. 60, places Abiria, the land of the Ābhīras, between Scythia (Śaka-Kṣatrapa dominions) and the coast land called Syrastrene (Saurāṣtra), thus corresponding to the area assigned to the Ābhīras in the Harivaṃśa (5161-5163). If, therefore, the legend of Gopāla grew among the Ābhīras, as it very probably did, it grew independently of Christian influence.

The dramatic representation of *Kaṃśavadha* or slaughter of Kaṃśa by Kṛṣṇa, referred to in the Mahābhāṣya of Patañjali (on Pāṇini III: 1. 26) indicates that these legends are older than Christianity. Professor Keith truly observes, "But surely the existence of standing enmity between Kṛṣṇa and Kaṃśa, his uncle, of which the Mahābhāṣya presents the most conclusive proof, essentially presupposes the existence of a legend of the youthful Kṛṣṇa. The relationship would normally be accompanied by friendship and protection: when the reverse is found, and the nephew slays the uncle, the similar legends found elsewhere justify us in thinking that tradition must have told some tale of the efforts of the uncle to remove from his path the unwelcome nephew. It can hardly be supposed that it was left for Christianity, as Mr. Kennedy seems to suggest, to find a justification for the killing of Kaṃśa in the massacre of the Innocents."*

Journal of the Royal Asiatic Society, 1908. p. 173.

In Bhasa's *Bālacarita** we actually possess an old drama of which Kaṃśavadha or the slaughter of Kaṃśa is the theme. Kālidasā, in his *Mālavikāgnimitra*, calls Bhāsa 'far-famed' (*prathita vaśas*) and 'ancient' (*purāṇa*). This indicates a considerable distance of time between Kālidāsa and Bhāsa. A comparison of the Prākṛt used by Bhāsa and by Aśvaghoṣa leads Sten Konow to place Bhāsa a century after Aśvaghoṣa, that is to say, in the third century A.D.† The wish expressed in the concluding stanza of the Bālcaritā (*bharatavākya*) that the King might be the sole ruler from sea to sea between the Himālaya and the Vindhya does not necessarily imply that Bhāsa's royal patron was the sole ruler of Northern India and a poet whom Kālidāsa calls *purāna* can not very well be placed later than the third century A.D. But whatever be the date of Bhāsa, comparison of the *Bālacarita* and *Harivaṃśa* shows that in Bhāsa's play we have an independent version of the story of child Kṛṣṇa. Bhāsa's story differs in certain points from the story as told in the Harivaṃśa. In the Harivaṃśa Nārada warns Kaṃśa that he will be killed by the eighth issue of his sister Devakī, while, according to *Bālacarita*, a Ṛṣi named Madhuka cursed Kaṃśa that he would come by his end in that way. But the difference in the accounts of the *hallīśa* sport

* *Bālacarita* of Bhāsa, edited with notes by Gaṇapati Śāstrī, Trivandrum, 1912.

† *Indian Antiquary*, 1914.

is very remarkable. It forms the subject matter of *adhyāya* 77 (4078-4098) of the *Harivaṃśa*. Herein *halliśa krīḍā* is treated as synonymous with *ratī*, or sexual enjoyment, and we are further told that the boy Kṛṣna spent night after night in the company of young *gopa* girls who were forbidden to do so by their parents and brothers.* But in Bhāsa's play *hallīśaka* is the name of an innocent village dance. I shall reproduce Bhāsa's account in translation:—

"*Saṃkarṣaṇa*. Dāmaka, are all the *gopa* girls here?

Dāmaka. Yes, sir, all are assembled here.

Dāmodara (Kṛṣṇa). O Ghoṣasundarī, O Vanamālā, O Candrarekhā, O Mṛgākṣī, perform the Hallīśaka dance which well suits a *ghoṣa*.

All. As your lordship commands.

Saṃkarṣaṇa. O Dāmaka, O Meghanāda, play on the musical instruments.

Both. Very well, sir.

Old cowherd. Sir, you play the *hallīśaka*; what shall I do?

Dāmodara. Be a spectator.

Old cowherd. Very well, sir (*all dance*) Ho! Ho! very good music! very good dance! I shall also dance. But I am tired. (Act III)."

In Act IV of Bālacārita, Kṛṣṇa, after subduing Kāliya, comes out of the Yamunā (Jumna) with some flowers and presents them to the *gopa* girls.

* ता वार्यमाणाः पितृभिर्भ्रातृभिर्मातृभिस्तथा ।
कृष्णं गोपाङ्गना रात्रौ मृगयन्ते रतिप्रियाः ॥

Bhāsa's play contains no reference to Kṛṣṇa's love-making with the Ābhīra maidens, a theme which is so well-suited to dramatic treatment, and therefore seems to be older than chapter 77 of the Harivaṃśa in its present form.

As regards the antiquity of the cult of Gopāla it may be observed that Indians are extremely conservative in religious matters and refuse to adopt any cult unless it can be recognized as *sanātana* or coming from time immemorial. Consequently absence of archæological or literary evidence can not be construed as a conclusive proof of the non-existence of the cult before the time of Bhāsa or Harivaṃśa. Farnell's observation relating to the history of Greek cults holds good of Indian cults as well. He writes, "The chronologic statement is embarrassed by the absence of any record of date for the institution and diffusion of most of the cults, and for the growth of certain religious ideas; nor can we safely date a religious fact by the date of the author who first mentions it; a detail of ritual, a myth, a religious concept attested only by Pausaniaus or a late scholiast may descend from an age far anterior to the Homeric." * Sir Rāmkṛṣṇa Bhāndārkar holds that the cult of Rāma "must have come into existence about the eleventh century," because Madhva or Ānandatīrtha is said to have brought an image of Rāma from Badarikāśrama and sent a disciple to Jagannātha

* *Encyclopædia of Religion and Ethics*, Vol. vi, p. 394*b*.

about the year A.D. 1264 to bring what was called the original idols of Rāma and Sītā.* But he has overlooked the fact that Varāhamihira, who died in A.D. 587, gives the measurements of the image of Rāma in his *Bṛhatsaṃhitā*. "The image of Rāma, son of Daśaratha, and Bali, son of Virocana, should be made one hundred and twenty aṅgulas (LVII. 30)". A deity called Rāma-devatā is named in the *Avadānaśataka* which is assigned to about A.D. 100 by Speyer and was translated into Chinese in the first half of the third century.† The Nānāghāt cave inscription wherein Vāsudeva and Saṃkarṣaṇa of the lunar race (*canda-suta*) are invoked is assigned to the first century B.C. by Sir Rāmakṛṣna and to an earlier epoch by Bühler. "For about five hundred years after this," Bhandarkar writes, "there are no epigraphical or sculptural traces of any Brāhmanic religious system; and they reappear about the time when the Guptas rose to power in the first quarter of the fourth century."‡ But the Sanskrit Buddhist texts of this period, to say nothing of the plays of Bhāsa, contain clear references to the cults of Viṣṇu, Śiva and other Brāhmanic gods. In Avadāna 7 of the *Avadānaśataka* it is said that before the birth of Bhagavān (Buddha) King Prasenajit

* *Vaiṣṇavism*, etc., p. 47.

† "सोऽपुत्रः पुत्राभिनन्दी शिववरुणकुबेरशक्रब्रह्मादीनन्यांश्च देवताविशेषा-नायाचते । तद्यथा रामदेवता वनदेवताश्चत्वरदेवताः शृङ्गाटकदेवता बलिप्रति-ग्राहिकदेवताः सहजाः सहधार्मिका नित्यानुबद्धा अपि देवता आयाचते ।" *Avadānaśataka* (Bibliotheca Buddhica III), Vol. I, p. 195.

‡ *Vaiṣṇavism*, etc., pp. 42-43.

of Srāvastī worshipped the "Tīrthika gods" with flowers, incense, sweet-smelling garlands, etc. One day a gardener came to Śrāvastī with nine lotus flowers for Prasenajit and was met by a Tīrthika (heathen) worshipper who wanted to buy the flowers. They came to where Anāthapiṇḍada was, who offered double the price offered by the Tīrthika. Then both of them went on bidding more and more till it came up to 100,000. The gardener now asked the Tīrthika, "For whose sake you offer higher price?" He replied, "I offer higher price for the sake of Bhagavān Nārāyaṇa."* In Avadāna 23 it is said that the young wife of a merchant of Rājagṛha (in Magadha) who had gone to the sea was very anxious for his safe return. Then "prostrating herself before Nārāyaṇa she promised, 'if my husband return shortly, I shall make an offering of a golden wheel'." When her husband returned safe and successful, she had a golden wheel made, and surrounded by her maid-servants, set out with the wheel and incense and flowers for the Devakula or the temple of Nārāyaṇa.† The few early epigraphic records which relate to the worship of Vāsudeva contain nothing that preclude the possibility of the existence of the cult of child Kṛṣna in those days. The earliest one, assigned to about 200 B.C., at Ghasundi in Rajputāna, records the erection of a pujā stone at the Nārāyanavāta for *bhagavat*

* "अहं भगवतो नारायणस्यार्थे इति।" *Avadānaśataka*, Vol. I, p. 37.

† *Ibid*. I, p. 129.

Saṃkarṣaṇa and Vāsudeva.* The next in point of time is the Besnagar pillar inscription dating from about 140 B.C., which records the erection of a Garuḍadhvaja of Vāsudeva the god of gods, by the Bhāgavata Heliodora, a native of Taxila and a Yona (Yavana) ambassador from Maharāja Aṃtalikita.† The third epigraph, the Nānāghāt cave inscription referred to above, which opens with an invocation of Saṃkarṣaṇa and Vāsudeva of the lunar race, also indicates that at the time of this inscription Saṃkarṣaṇa and Vāsudeva were believed to have been born on this earth in the lunar race and must have passed through childhood. Instead of pushing *argumentum ad silentio* too far, it is, therefore, more reasonable to recognize the cult of child Kṛṣṇa as a necessary appanage of the cult of elder Kṛṣṇa-Vāsudeva than as an offshoot of Christianity.

The orthodox view regarding the origin of the cult of Vāsudeva (known as Bhāgavata, Pāñcarātra, or Sātvata system) held by scholars like Hopkins, Garbe, Grierson, Jacobi and Bhandarkar, is that it was founded by a Kṣatriya teacher named Kṛṣṇa Vāsudeva, who was later on identified with Bhagavat under which name the Bhāgavatas worshipped the Supreme Being. This view has been disputed by the champions of comparative anthropology. Professor Berridale Keith, referring to a passage in the Mahābhāṣya (on

* Lüder's *List of Brāhmi Inscriptions*, No. 6.

† Lüder's *List*, No. 669.

Pāṇini III, 1, 26), writes, "The Mahābhāṣya tells us that in the Kaṃśavadha the Granthikas divided themselves into parties, the one, followers of Kaṃśa, the other, followers of Kṛṣṇa, and that the former were *kālamukhāḥ* and the latter *raktamukhāh*. Weber was naturally puzzled to find that Kṛṣṇa's friends were red in colour, but the whole thing explains itself when we regard the contest as one of the many old nature rituals where two parties join in mimic strife, the one striving to rescue, the other to capture, the sun. . . . . . The supporters of Kṛṣṇa as identified with the sun, Viṣṇu, naturally wear the red colour of the luminary as an act of sympathetic magic."* Professor Keith has restated this theory in his two essays on the origin of Indian drama and *ākhyāna*.† In the second of these essays he observes, "It is true that Indian tradition tells us that Kaṃśa was Kṛṣṇa's uncle, and that we can, if we like, insist that this is a piece of history, but such euhemerism is, if at present again fashionable, hardly likely to remain long in vogue." Professor Keith's theory has found an adherent in Mr. N. Macnicol, who considers the passage in the *Mahābhāṣya* "perhaps the most conclusive evidence in support of the explanation of the Kṛṣṇa cult as originally that of a vegetation spirit."‡ Kaṃśavadha described by Patañjali was a "vegetation masque," "a play in

---

* *Journal of the Royal Asiatic Society*, 1908, pp. 172-173.

† *Ibid.*, 1911, p. 1008; *Ibid.*, 1912, p. 416.

‡ *Ibid.* 1913, p. 149.

which the struggle of the spring with the winter is represented and sympathetically aided.''

This "most conclusive evidence" regarding the significance of Kaṃśavadha is based on a misunderstanding of the text of Patañjali.* The question that is discussed in this obscure passage is, why present tense is used in such sentences as, 'He causes Kaṃśa to be killed', 'He causes Bali to be bound', instead of past tense, for Kaṃśa was killed and Bali was bound long long ago. According to Kaiyaṭa those who explain the acting of the actors are called Śaubhikas. The Śaubhikas cause Kaṃśa to be killed and Bali to be bound (by the actors) in the presence of the audience. So present tense is used in connection with the acting of the actors in the dramatic performance of *Balibandha* and *Kaṃsavadha*. The same may be said in connection with the pictorial representation of *Kaṃsavadha*. The next question raised is, how can present tense be used in

---

* इह तु कथं वर्त्तमानकालता कंसं घातयति बलिं बन्धयतीति। चिरहते च कंसे चिरबद्धे च बलौ। अत्रापि युक्ता, कथम्। ये तावदेते शौभिका [शोभनिका K] नाम एते प्रत्यक्षं च कंसं घातयन्ति प्रत्यक्षं च बलिं बन्धयन्तीति। चित्रेषु कथम्। चित्रेष्वपि उद्गूर्णा निपातिताश्च प्रहारा दृश्यन्ते कंसस्य हन्यस्य च [कंसकर्षण्यश्च K]। ग्रन्थिकेषु कथम्। यत्र शब्दग्रन्थनमात्रं [शब्द गडुमात्रं K] लक्ष्यते। तेऽपि हि तेषामुत्पत्तिप्रभृत्याविनाशाद् बुद्धीर्व्याचक्षाणाः [वृद्धीर्व्याचक्षाणाः K] सतो बुद्धिविषयान् प्रकाशयन्ति। आतश्च सतः। व्यामिश्रिताश्च [व्यामिश्रा हि K] दृश्यन्ते। केचित् कंसभक्ता भवन्ति केचिद्वासुदेवभक्ताः। वर्णान्यत्वं खल्वपि पुष्यन्ति। केचिद्रक्तमुखा भवन्ति केचित् कालमुखाः।"

Benares edition of *Mahābhāṣya* (variants adopted by Keilhorn noted within square brackets).

connection with the *Granthikas*. By a *Granthika* is meant a *Kathaka* or narrator of sacred legends. The meaning of the question is, how can present tense be used in connection with the story of *Kaṃsavadha* narrated by a *Kathaka* by the combination of words only, without the aid of actors or pictures. Patañjali's answer is thus summed up by Bhatṛhari (*Vākyapadīya* III.5.5):—" Kaṃśa and others who are given shape by means of words that describe them and are perceived by the mind are considered as moving under the eyes of the audience."* Helarāja, commenting on this stanza, writes, " The narrator (*Kathaka*) creating faith in the bodily forms of Kaṃśa and others in the hearers, causes Kaṃśa, existing in the mind (imagination) only, to be slain by Vāsudeva existing in imagination."† Haradatta, in his *Kāsikāpadamañjari*, explains the whole passage as follows:—

" The narrators who narrate *Kaṃśavadha* from a book tell the story of Kaṃśa and others from their birth to their death. They (Kaṃśa and others), being described, appear as if visible in the minds of the audience. The minds of the audience are occupied by them. Therefore they (the audience) take different sides, some turn partisans of Kaṃśa and others become partisans of Vāsu-

* "शब्दोपहितरूपांस्तु बुद्धेर्विषयतां गतान् ।
प्रत्यक्षमेव कंसादीन् साधकत्वेन मन्यते ॥"

† "तथा च कथकः श्रोतरि कंसाद्याकारप्रत्ययजननात् बुद्धि वासुदेवो बुद्धि कंसं घातयतीति प्रयोजकस्य समारोपात् प्रयोगोपपत्तिः ।"

deva. They assume different colours also, some are red-faced, some are dark-faced.'' *

So, according to the Indian interpreters of Patañjali, it was not the *granthikas* or narrators who divided themselves into two parties, but the audience, some of whom sided with Kaṃśa and others with Kṛṣṇa, the partisans of the former becoming pale with grief and the partisans of the latter beaming red with joy on the triumph of their hero. The *granthikas* still narrate *Kaṃśa-vadha* and other episodes in the life of Kṛṣṇa from the Bhāgavata Purāṇa in the villages of India. But they never do so divided in parties or with faces coloured. We are, therefore, hardly justified in assuming that they did so in the time of Patañjali.

Perhaps the earliest account of the doctrines of the Bhāgavatas is found in Brahma Sūtras II, 2. 42-45, as explained by both Śaṅkara and Rāmānuja. The doctrine of the four *vyūhas* or 'divisions' of the Supreme Being is the corner-stone of the system. The *vyūhas* are, Vāsudeva, Saṃkarṣaṇa, Pradyumna and Aniruddha. From Vāsudeva, who is the highest Brahman and the highest cause, there originates the individual soul called Saṃkarṣaṇa ; from Saṃkarṣaṇa, the inter-

* "येऽपि ग्रन्थं वाचयन्तः कंसवधमाचक्षते काथिका नाम तेऽप्युत्पत्तिप्रभृत्याविनाशात् कंसादीन् वर्णयन्ति येऽपि वर्ण्यमानाः श्रोतॄणां बुद्धिस्थाः प्रत्यक्षवद्भवन्ति चित्तमपि तेषां तदात्मकमिव भवति, ततएव व्याश्रिताश्च भवन्ति, नानापक्षसमाश्रयो व्याश्रयः केचित् कंसभक्ताः केचिद्वासुदेवभक्ताः वर्णान्यत्वं खल्वपि पुष्यन्ति, केचित् रक्तमुखाः केचित् कालमुखाः।"

nal organ called Pradyumna; and from Pradyumna, the principle of egoity called Aniruddha. The root of Vaiṣṇavism lies buried in this theory of the four *vyūhas*. Grierson seems to hold that this theory is but a Bhāgavata adaptation of Saṃkhya-yoga. For, speaking of the process of creation, he writes, "The principles according to which creation is held to have developed resemble those of Sāṅkhya-yoga, but, owing to the assumed necessity of connecting the immaterial Vāsudeva with the material world, are more complicated."* Bhandarkar traces the root of the four *vyūhas* to Bhāgavadgītā. He writes:—

"But the Bhāgavadgītā contains no allusion to the vyūhas or forms of the supreme, Saṃkarṣaṇa and others, while the latter form a characteristic of the Bhāgavata school. The Gītā, however, mentions as the Prakrtis of Vāsudeva the five elements, the mind, Buddhi or knowledge, and egoism as well as Jīva (VII, 4.5). The last is identified with Saṃkarṣaṇa in the Bhāgavata system, egoism with Aniruddha, and mind, with which probably Buddhi is associated, with Pradyumna. What appears to be the fact is this: The Bhāgavadgītā was composed before the doctrines of the Bhāgavata school were reduced to a system, and it was then that the three of the Prakṛtis of the supreme were personified into Saṃkarṣaṇa, Pradyumna and Aniruddha, who were members of the family of Vāsudeva."†

* *Encyclopædia of Religion and Ethics*, II, p. 543*b*.

† *Vaiṣṇavism*, etc., pp. 12-13.

The personification of abstract ideas into minor historical personages seems rather strange, and the theory itself is based on a confusion of the twofold nature (Prakṛti) of the Supreme Being as defined in the Bhāgavadgītā (VII, 4-6) wherein we are told, "Earth, water, fire, air, ether, mind, intellect, egoity—thus eightfold is my nature divided. Lower is this nature; other than this and higher know that nature of mine which has become the individual soul by which this world is supported. Remember that all beings spring from this; I am the origin and the dissolution of the Universe."* Śaṅkara in his *bhāṣya* takes the eightfold lower nature (*aparā prakṛti*) of the Supreme Being as illusion-force (*māyā-śakti*) and the *parā prakṛtī*, 'higher nature', as pure. Vāsudeva himself (*mamātmabhūtām*), and Kṣetrajña or one who knows the body. Commenting on Brahmasutras II. 2. 42, Śaṅkara observes regarding the four vyūhas, "Among them Vāsudeva is the *parā Prakṛti*." Sir R.G. Bhandarkar ignores the fundamental distinction between *parā* and *aparā* prakṛtis of the Gītā when he places Jīva in the same category with mind, *buddhi*, and egoism. The vyūhas, Saṃkarṣaṇa or individual soul, Pradyumna or the internal organ (mind), and Aniruddha or egoism of the Bhāgavatas do not constitute the Prakṛti or Māyā of Vāsudeva, but are evolved from him in a causal chain—the individual soul (Saṃkarṣaṇa) originating from Vāsudeva,

* Thibaut's translation.

the internal organ (Pṛadyumna) from the individual soul and the principle of egoity (Aniruddha) from the internal organ. But both the Pṛakṛtis of the Gītā—*parā* and *aparā*—are without beginning. We are told in XIII. 19, "Know thou both Prakṛti and Puruṣa to be without beginning."

Professor Garbe's view regarding the chronological position of the Gītā in the history of Vaiṣṇavism appears to be more in accordance with facts. Summing up his views, Professor E. W. Hopkins writes:—

"About two centuries before Buddha, the warrior chief of the Yādava clan, who was also a religious teacher, but not of the Brāhmanic schools, founded a moral religion of monotheism, God being in his system called simply Bhagavat. This religiously-minded chieftain was the 'son of Devakī,' and his religion was at first confined to his own clan. But as time went on, the teaching of Krishna extended beyond tribal limits, and at the same time the founder of the religion was himself identified with the god he taught, so that the 'son of Vasudeva' became god by virtue of the same euhemerism that changed Buddha into God. This was the form of the Vāsudeva religion recognized in the fourth century B.C. by Pāṇini, and the doctrine of *bhakti* belonged to it as early as this time. But for a century or more after this Krishnaism still lay outside the Brahmanism. During this period, till c. 300 B.C., the religion of Krishna was united with Sāṃkhya-yoga philosophy. After this, in the second period, from

300 B.C. till the Christian era, Krishna was identified with Vishnu, as the religion became Brahmanized, and in this same period arose the original Gītā."*

Professor Garbe's view that Kṛṣṇaism or Vāsudevism in its original form lay outside the pale of Brāhmanism is historically correct. The orthodox followers of Vedism and Vedāntism recognize the Bhāgavadgītā as authoritative, but condemn the Bhāgavata or Pāñcarātra system as un-Vedic or heterodox. Kumārila, in his *Tantravārtika*, refers to Kṛṣṇa as "a great law-giver," "who is always cited as an example of righteous conduct," and quotes Gītā IV. 11†; but he includes Pāñcarātra among *smṛtis* or systems, such as Bauddha, Sāṃkhya, Yoga, Pāśupata and Nigrantha, that are "opposed to Veda" and "are not honoured by those who know the Vedas."‡ Śaṅkara, who in the introduction to his *bhāśya* on the Gītā calls it "the quintessence of the meaning of all the Vedas (*samasta-vedārthasāra-saṃgrahabhūtam*)," proves the un-Vedic character of the Pāñcarātra by reproducing, in his *bhāśya* on the Brahmasūtras II. 2. 45, this text,—"Śāndilya is said to have promulgated the Pāñcarātra doctrine because he did not find a sure basis for the highest welfare of man in the Veda and its auxiliary disciplines." According to the Purāṇas, like Bud-

* *Journal of the Royal Asiatic Society*, 1905, pp. 385—386.

† *Tantravārtika*, translated by Prof. Gaṅgānath Jhā, p. 194.

‡ *Ibid.*, p. 165.

dhism and other similar systems, Pāñcarātra was deliberately promulgated for misleading wicked men. Purusottama in his *Bhāṣyaprakāśa* on Ballabhācārya's *Anubhāṣya* (II. 2. 42) quotes from Kūrma Purāṇa (I 16. 115-116), "O Vṛṣadhvaja (one with a bull as his emblem on the banner), we shall make *śāstras* (sacred books) for protecting (*rakṣaṇārthāya*) those who are outside the Vedic pale (*Vedabāhyānām*) and for misleading sinners. Thus addressed by Viṣṇu, Śiva, and so also Viṣṇu advised in turn by Śiva, promulgated misleading systems such as Kāpāla, Lāguḍa, Vāma, Bhairava —eastern and western, Pāñcarātra, Pāśupata and thousand others."* Purusottama also. quotes from Sāmba Purāṇa,—"The husband of Laksmī (Viṣṇu) promulgated the *tantra* (system) called Pāñcarātra, Bhāgavata or Vaikhānasa for those who have strayed from the Veda."† But Appaya Dīkṣita writes in his *Vedāntakalpatarupariṃala*,— "As it is un-Vedic, so Pāñcarātra has been declared as unworthy of acceptance by those who follow the Veda in the Vaikhānasa-śāstra thus,

* "तथाहि वेदबाह्यानां रक्षणार्थाय पापिनाम् ।
विमोहनाय शास्त्राणि करिष्यावो वृषध्वज ॥
एवं सम्बोधितो रुद्रो माधवेन मुरारिणा ।
चकार मोहशास्त्राणि केशवोऽपि शिवेरितः ॥
कापालं लागुडं वामं भैरवं पूर्वपश्चिमम् ।
पाञ्चरात्रं पाशुपतं तथान्यानि सहस्रशः ॥"

† "पाञ्चरात्रं भागवतं तन्त्रं वैखानसाभिधम् ।
वेदभ्रष्टान् समुद्दिश्य कमलापतिरुक्तवान् ॥"

Śrīmadanubhāṣyam. Benares Sanskrit Series, Vol. I, p. 674.

'Āgneya Pāñcarātra, together with Tāntrik initiation, is un-Vedic, therefore the god of gods (Viṣṇu) should be worshipped according to Vaikhānasatantra which is agreeable (*saumya*) and based on the Veda (*Vaidik*).' "* These texts show that Pāñcāratra was considered un-Vedic by the orthodox; and this could hardly have been the case had it been based upon Bhāgavadgītā.

The un-Brāhmanic Vāsudevism or Pāñcarātra was probably first confined to the Yādava clan of Kṣatriyas to which Kṛṣṇa-Vāsudeva himself belonged. As we have already seen,† the Yādavas or Sātvatas were originally settled in Saurāṣtra or the Kāthiāwaḍ Peninsula and then spread to Mathura. Kriṣṇa-Vāsudeva (or Keśava) the son of Vasudeva of the Yādava or Sātvata clan and of his wife Devakī, was born in Mathura and afterwards migrated to Dvārakā in Saurāṣṭra. The Pāñcarātra system is called *Sātvata-bidhi* evidently after the Sātvata clan. Epic, Purāṇic, Bauddha and Jaina traditions agree in bearing testimony to the existence of Kṛṣṇa-Vāsudeva and Baladeva or Saṃkarṣaṇa as historical persons. If the identity of Kriṣṇa-Vāsudeva with Kriṣṇa, son of Devakī, mentioned in the Chāndogya Upaniṣad III. 17.6,

---

* "एवमवैदिकत्वादेव वैदिकापरिग्राह्यत्वं पाञ्चरात्रस्योक्तं वैखानससमाख्ये,"—

"आग्नेयं पाञ्चरात्रं तु दीक्षायुक्तं च तान्त्रिकम् ।
अवैदिकत्वादनन्तं ततो वैखानसेन तु ॥
सौम्येन वैदिकेनैव देवदेवं समर्चयेत् । इत्यादिना ।"

Vedāntakalpataru-Parimala, Vizianagram Sanskrit Series, p. 453.

† Chapter I, pp. 28-29.

is once admitted, all difficulties of tracing the evolution of the Bhāgavata religion disappear. Dhṛtarāṣṭra, son of Vicitravīrya, is mentioned in the Kāṭhaka Saṃhitā, the Kauravya King Parīkṣit in the Atharvan, and Parīkṣita's son Janamejaya in the Brāhmaṇas. If Kṛṣṇa Vāsudeva is a historical person, he was born in the same epoch in which these undoubtedly historical Kuru sovereigns flourished; that is to say, at the time of the composition of the later Saṃhitās and the Brāhmaṇas, but before the Upaniṣads—before the development of the monism of the Upaniṣads and the dualism of the Sāṃkhya-Yoga The Chāndogya Upaniṣad III. 17. 6 tells us what Kṛṣṇa learnt from his teacher. This text is very clearly explained by Professor Hopkins in the following passage:—

"Krishna, son of Devakī, was taught by his teacher, Ghora Āngirasa, that sacrifice may be performed without objective means; that generosity, kindness, and other moral traits are the real signs of sacrifice; and it is then said: "The priest Ghora Āngirasa having said this to Krishna, the son of Devakī—and the latter was thereby freed from (thirst) desire—said: "When a man is about to die let him resort to this triad; 'the imperishable art thou,' 'the unmoved art thou'; 'breath's firmness art thou'; in regard to which are these two verses in the Rig-Veda (VIII. 6. 30; I. 50. 10): 'till they see the light of the old seed which is kindled in the sky,' and 'perceiving above the darkness the higher light, the sun, god among gods, we come to the highest light.'" Krishna thus learned the abolition of sacrifice, and the worship of the sun, the highest light (Vishnu), as true being,—for this is the meaning of the philosophical passage taken with its context.''*

Perhaps the great Sātvata chief—great in war and policy as well as in philosophy and religion —taught what he had learnt from his teacher—practice of morality as the true sacrifice and worship of Viṣṇu as 'god among gods' (monotheism)—to men of his own clan whose guide, friend and philosopher he was. But Epic, Purāṇic, Jaiṅa and Bauddha traditions agree in telling us that destruction overtook the Sātvatas of Dvārakā in the life-time and under the very eyes of this mighty hero and teacher who also met with a tragic end. In the Mahābhārata, Book XVI, we are told that some hot-headed Yādava warriors played pranks with three great Brāhman sages, Viśvāmitra, Kaṇva and Nārada, and brought on a fearful curse on their whole clan which resulted in destructive internal dissensions. After witnessing the extermination of his kith and kin in deep sorrow, Vāsudeva retired to a forest where he was shot dead through mistake by a hunter named Jarā. The story is thus told in the *Antagaḍa-Dasāo* of the Jainas in the shape of a prophecy by Ariṣṭanemi, the twenty-second Tīrthaṃkara: "Verily, Kaṇhe, thou shalt be sent

* Hopkins' *Religions of India*, p. 465.

forth by thy mother and father's behest from the city of Bāravaī when it shall be consumed by reason of strong waters, fire, and the wrath of Divāyane; ...... and in the Kosamba forest, underneath a goodly nyagrodha tree, upon a daïs of earthen-block, thy body covered with a yellow robe, thou shalt be wounded in the left foot by a sharp arrow shot by Jarākumāra from his bow."* Here Divāyane or Dvaipāyana is named in place of the three sages of the Mahābhārata. The story of the destruction of the Andhakas and the Vṛṣṇis as told in the Ghata Jātaka (No. 454) resembles the epic version in many points. Here also it is stated that Vāsudeva was shot dead by an old huntsman named Jarā, and the sage whose curse caused the catastrophe is called Kaṇhadipāyana (Kṛṣṇa-Dvaipāyana). In the Kumbha Jātaka (No. 512) occurs this *gāthā* (stanza):—

> "'Twas after drinking this, I ween,
> The Andhakas and Vrishni race,
> Roaming along the shore, were seen
> To fall, each by his kinsman's mace."

Again in the Saṃkicca Jātaka (No. 530):—

> "Assailing black Dipāyana the men of Vrishni race
> With Andhaka sought Yama's realm, each slain by other's mace."

In the Arthaśātra of Kauṭilya I. 6 (3) also the destrucion of the Vṛṣṇis is connected with Dvaipāyana.

These legends preserved by three rival sects do

* *Antagaḍa-dasāo*, translated by L. D. Barnett, Chapter V.

not seem to be baseless. The Saurāṣṭras, classed as men of mixed origin by Baudhāyana, and the Ābhīras, called Mlecchas in the Mahābhārata (XVI. 7. 63), became dominant in Western India after the fall of the Yādavas. In the Harivaṃśa (94, 5161) the Yādava Kingdom called Ānarta is described as "mostly inhabited by the Ābhīras (*ābhīra-prāya-mānuṣam*)." The Ānarta country and its inhabitants were called Surāṣṭras or Saurāṣṭras, probably after the Raṭṭas (Rāṣṭras), akin to the Rāṣṭikas of Asoka's rock edicts, now represented by the Mahārāṣṭras or Marāṭhas. These Saurāṣṭras and Ābhīras, from whom the Gujaratis of our day have evidently sprung, were Aryan in speech and belonged to the Indo-Afghan stock. The monotheistic religion that Kṛṣṇa Vāsudeva taught to the men of his own clan was handed on by the Sātvatas (Yādavas) to the Saurāṣṭras and the Ābhīras, who gave it the un-Vedic turn. Vāsudeva, his brother Saṃkarṣaṇa, his son Pradyumna, and his grandson Aniruddha were probably deified by these Outlanders who lay outside the pale of Vedism.

The doctrines underlying the Sātvata religion of the Saurāṣṭras and Ābhīras were probably first reduced to system by a teacher named Śāndilya Kāśyapa. According to the Mahābhārata (Bhīṣma Parvan, 66. 40) the religion of Vāsudeva was preached by Śaṃkarṣaṇa in accordance with the Sātvata system (*vidhi*) at the end of the Dvāpara and in the beginning of the Kali Age. In a Pāncarātra text named Īśvara-Saṃhitā (I. 38-41) the initiation of Śāndilya to Bhāgavatism is thus described:—"In days past, in Totādri peak, Śāndilya, the great sage, sat fixed in severe austerities (*tapas*) for many, many years. In the end he obtained from Śaṃkarṣaṇa—in the interim between the Dvāpara Age and Kali Age—the Veda going by the name of *Ekāyana*, and taught them well to Sumantu, Jaimini, Bhṛgu, Aupagāyana, and Mauñjāyana."* The Vṛddha-Hārita-Saṃhitā contains this legend about un-Vedic Vaiṣṇavism originally taught by Śāndilya. In ancient time there was a noble Brāhman of the Kāśyapa family named Śāndilya who was learned in all the sacred literature. He promulgated a religious code (*dharma-saṃhitā*) for the worship of Viṣṇu drawn up in un-Vedic spirit. Adopting his (Śāndilya's) system some of the great sages (*maharṣayah*) worshipped Keśava in un-Vedic manner. Men performed religious rites in a way not ordained in the *śāstra* (Veda) and the earth was deprived of *svāhā*, *svadhā*, and *vaṣatkāra*. Angered at this Viṣṇu condemned Śāndilya to live in hell. Śāndilya was struck with terror and bowing repeatedly prayed, "O Lord, I am a sinner; save me." Viṣṇu took pity on him and thus modified his curse, "O Brāhman, after suffering the tortures of hell for hundred years according to the calculation of gods you will be born in the family of Bhṛgu and will be known as Jamadagni. There again worshipping me according to rules laid down in the Veda,

* *Journal of the Royal Asiatic Society*, 1911, p. 942.

you will attain, O best of sages, my pure world." Śāṇḍilya did as advised by Viṣṇu when he was again born on the earth and ultimately entered the world of Hari. The author of the Vṛddha-Hārita-Saṃhitā draws this moral from the legend, "Therefore un-Vedic religion should be avoided from a distance and Hari should be worshipped with devotion in accordance with rules laid down in the Veda. Drawing the wheel (emblem of Viṣṇu) on the upper part of both arms according to the rule of the Sruti and the *ūrddhapundra* mark (on the forehead) Hari should be worshipped with pure heart according to proper rules.''*

कश्चित्पुरा द्विजश्रेष्ठ काश्यपो ब्राह्मणोत्तमः ।
शाण्डिल्य इति विख्यातः सर्वशास्त्रविशारदः ॥
स तु धर्मप्रसङ्गेन विष्णोराराधनं प्रति ।
अवैदिकेन विधिना कृतवान् धर्मसंहिताम् ॥
अवलम्ब्य मतं तस्य केचिच्च नराधमाः ।
अवैदिकेन मार्गेण पूजयन्ति स्म केशवम् ॥
अशास्त्रविहितं धर्मं सर्वं कुर्वन्ति मानवाः ।
स्वाहा स्वधा वषट्कारवर्जितं स्वाध्यायवर्जितम् ॥
ततः क्रुद्धो जगन्नाथः शङ्खचक्रगदाधरः ।
इदमाह मुनिश्रेष्ठं शाण्डिल्यममितौजसम् ॥
दुर्बुद्धे मामकं धर्मं परमं वैदिकं मतम् ।
अवैदिकक्रियायुक्तं प्रागज्ञात् कृतवानसि ॥
यस्मादवैदिकं धर्मं प्रवर्त्तयसि त्वं द्विज ।
तस्मादवैदिकं लोकं निरयं गच्छ दारुणम् ॥
तस्य दैवस्य वाक्यात्तु शाण्डिल्योऽभूद्भयाकुलः ।
स्तुवन् प्राह जगन्नाथं प्रणिपत्य पुनः पुनः ॥
त्राहि त्राहीति लोकेश मां विभो त्वां पराधीनम् ।
ततः स कृपया विष्णुर्भगवान् भूतभावनः ॥
दिव्यं वर्षशतं विप्र भुक्त्वा निरययातनाम् ।
उत्पत्स्यसे भृगुवंशे जमदग्निरितीरितः ॥

What was the un-Vedic method of worshipping Viṣṇu originally taught by Śāndilya we are not told in the Vṛddha-Hārītā-Saṃhitā. The Nārāyaṇīya section of the Śānti Parvaṇ (Chaps. 336-353) of the Mahābhārata contains the earliest exposition of the Pāñcarātrā in its Brāhmanized form. It may be possible to distinguish the different stages— the pre-Brāhmanic and the Brāhmanic—in the evolution of Vaiṣṇavism by analysing this document. About the origin of the Pāñcarātra we are told (Chap. 337),—"This supreme scripture was compiled and uttered by the seven Citraśikhandin Ṛṣis (Marīci, Atri, Aṅgiras, Pulastya, Pulaha, Kratu and Vaśiṣṭha) and (Manu) Svāyambhuva, after worshipping Hari Nārāyaṇa for a thousand years of heaven. They then read it to Nārāyaṇa, who praised it and certified it to be in complete accord with the four Vedas."* This of course refers to the Nārāyaṇīya

तथाराध्य पुमर्थं तु वैदिकेनैव धर्मतः ।
गच्छ तस्मिन् मुनिश्रेष्ठ समलोकं सुनिर्मलम् ॥
इत्युक्त्वा भगवान् विष्णुस्तत्रैवान्तरधीयत ।
शाण्डिल्यः नित्यं प्राप्य पुनस्तस्य भूतले ॥
वेदोक्तविधिना विष्णुमर्चयित्वा सनातनम् ।
विष्णुप्रसादात् संप्राप्तवान् परमं हरेः ॥
तस्मादवैदिकं धर्मं दूरतः परिवर्जयेत् ।
वैदिकेनैव विधिना भक्त्या संपूजयेद्धरिम् ॥
श्रौतेन विधिना सम्यं स्नात्वा वै पाञ्चरात्रयोः ।
धृतोर्ध्वपुण्ड्रः प्रयतात्मा विधिनैवार्चयेद्धरिम् ॥

Vṛddha-Hārita Smṛti, XI, 180–194 (included in *Smṛtīnāṃ Samuccaya*, Anandāśrama Series, No. 48, p. 348).

* Sir George Grierson's abstract, *Indian Antiquary*. XXXVII (1908), p. 375.

section wherein Śāndilya-Kāśyapa is not recognized as a teacher. The philosophical doctrine of the successive origination of the four 'vyūhas' which is declared 'impossible' by Bādarāyana in his Brahma Sūtras II. 2 . 42 both according to Śaṅkara and Rāmānuja, finds a place in the Nārāyaṇīya side by side with the orthodox view that the four 'vyūhas' are the four different manifestations of the Supreme Being and not originating in succession. "It was my fourth form (Vāsudeva)," we are told, "that created Śeṣa or Saṃkarṣaṇa. He produced Pradyumna, and in turn Pradyumna produced Aniruddha. From the lotus sprung from Aniruddha's navel was produced Brahmā."*

The Nārāyaṇīya also contains evidences of a living cult of the four 'Vyūhas.' The way in which a devotee attains final emancipation or union with the Supreme Being is thus described (Chap. 346), "The place, where he dwells, with Wisdom (*vidyā*) for His companion is named by the Veda 'Sat,' the existing, the productive cause of things created (*bhūta*). The perfect who are free from actions, whether good or bad (*puṇya-pāpa-vivarjita*), go thither. The first enter the sun (*āditya*) as the door. There their bodies are consumed and they become atomic entities (*paramāṇubhūta*). Thence they enter that god, and then, freed from him, they stand in the body (*tanu*) of Aniruddha. Then having become men-

* *Ibid.*, p. 377.

tal entities (*manobhūtā*) they enter Pradyumna. Freed from Pradyumna, the best Brāhmans and Sāṃkhyas, with the Bhāgavatas, enter Saṃkarṣaṇa who is living soul. Thence, void of the three constituents (*traiguna-hīna*), they instantly enter the Supreme Self (*paramātman*), the Kṣetrajña, himself without constituents, who is Vāsudeva, the abode of all things (*sarvāvāsa*)."* The vyūhas were worshipped in different groups. "By some Hari is worshipped under one manifestation (vyūha, i.e. Aniruddha), by some under two (i.e., Aniruddha and Pradyumna), by some under three (i.e., Aniruddha, Pradyumna and Saṃkarṣaṇa), and by some under four (i.e., Aniruddha, Pradyumna, Saṃkarṣaṇa and Vāsudeva)."†

Side by side with the cult of the four 'vyūhas,' the Nārāyaṇīya reveals to us another phase of Vaiṣṇavism, the cult of the incarnations (*avatāra*) of Viṣṇu. It contains (Chap. 341) brief accounts of the six incarnations of Viṣṇu, viz. the boar, the man-lion, the dwarf, Paraśurāma, Rāma, son of Daśaratha and Kṛṣna, also called Sātvata. This is followed by a list of ten incarnations wherein Haṃsa is substituted for Buddha of our modern standard list and placed at the top Bhandarkar considers this stanza containing the list of the ten incarnations as a later interpolation.‡ The theory of the incarnations is Vedic

* *Indian Antiquary*, XXXVII (1908), p. 381.

† *Ibid.*, p. 384.

‡ *Vainavism*, &c , pp. 39–40.

in origin. It is found in an embryonic stage in the Ṛgveda. In one stanza of the Ṛgveda (VII. 100. 6) reference is made to a form of Viṣṇu different from his ordinary one in the following words: "Do not assume this form, since thou didst assume another form in battle." Professor Macdonell traces the roots of four of the incarnations of Viṣṇu—the tortoise, the fish, the dwarf and the boar—in the Vedic literature and concludes, "Thus we see that when the doctrine of the Avatārs of Viṣṇu became established in Hinduism through the fusion with him of the popular deity Kṛṣṇa, four mythological conceptions derived from the Veda were ready to be appropriated as incarnations of Viṣṇu in his character as Preserver and Benefactor of the world."* The man-god Kṛṣṇa-Vāsudeva worshipped by the Sātvatas, the Saurāstras and the Ābhīras was evidently brought into line with the gods of the Vedic pantheon by being recognized as an incarnation of Viṣṇu and thereby Pāncarātra was Brāhmanized.

The Īkṣvāku hero Rāma was probably recognized as an incarnation of Viṣṇu at a later period in imitation of Kṛṣṇa-Vāsudeva. "It is not likely," writes Jacobi, "that the theory of incarnation was first suggested by the story of Rāma; in all probability there was already another similar incarnation of Viṣṇu acknowledged by the people of India. This must have been his

---

* *Journal of the Royal Asiatic Society*, 1895, p. 188.

incarnation as Kṛṣṇa, since the preceding incarnations, as appears from our remarks on them, seem to have had little importance as far as popular religion was concerned."* It has long been recognized by scholars that those parts of the Rāmāyaṇa (Bks. I and VII) wherein Rāma is recognized as an incarnation of Viṣṇu did not form part of the original epic of Vālmīki, but are later additions and interpolations.† The opening canto of the Rāmāyaṇa indicates that in the original version of the poem Rāma was represented as a mere man and not an incarnation of Viṣṇu. Vālmīki asks Nārada to name the man who was then the greatest and the best of men—who was the most perfect man then living. Hearing this Nārada, who is described as "one knowing the three worlds" (heaven, earth and the nether world) said, "The manifold virtues described by you are difficult to meet with (in one person). (However) hear, O Muni, I shall speak to you of the man (*naraḥ*) possessing those (virtues) whom I remember."‡ Nārada then goes on to give an account of Rāma's person, character and career from his proposed installation as heir-apparent to his attaining *brahmaloka* or the world of Brahmā (not Vaikuntha the world of Viṣṇu) after a reign of 11,000 years. In this narrative no reference is made to Rāma's identity with Viṣṇu; on the

* *Encyclopaedia of Religion and Ethics*, VII. p. 195*a*

† *Ibid.*, 1915, p. 326.

‡ बहवो दुर्लभाश्चैव ये त्वया कीर्त्तिता गुणाः ।
मुने वक्ष्याम्यहं बुद्ध्वा तैर्युक्तः श्रूयतां नरः ॥ (I. 1. 7).

contrary it is said, that "(he was) equal in valour to Viṣṇu," thereby indicating that he was not yet recognized as Viṣṇu. Episodes like those of Kavan dha and of the Śramaṇī (nun) Śavarī described in Book III, cantos 69-74, afforded the poet suitable opportunities of declaring Rāma as the incarnation of Viṣṇu, had he been aware of it. Kabandha was a hideous demon with a mouth in his belly and a pair of long arms. Rāma and Lakṣmaṇa cut off his two arms that rendered him helpless. Then Kabandha narrated his story. He was an asura as handsome as Indra, Sun-god and Moon-god. Sometimes he used to assume the terrible form in order to frighten the Ṛṣis. One day a great sage named Sthūlaśirā cursed him that he would retain that hideous form permanently Kabandha then sought to appease the sage who said, "When Rāma, cutting off your arms, will burn you in a deep forest, then you will regain your huge and handsome form (71. 6-7)." Kavandha performed great penances and propitiated Brahmā who granted him long life. Emboldened by this he attacked Indra who destroyed his knees and turned him into a Kavandha with two long arms. Indra also said, "You will go to heaven when Rāma and Lakṣmaṇa will cut off your arms in battle (71. 15-16)." Kavandha requested Rāma to burn his body in a funeral pyre and said that when his body would be burnt he would be able to know who had abducted Sītā and how she was to be recovered. When Kavandha's body was placed on a pyre, a beautiful being rose out of it in the sky, and getting into a *vimāna* or aerial chariot advised Rāma to seek the assistance of Sugrīva and on his way to Sugrīva's place visit the Sramaṇī named Śavarī. "O Rāma, seeing you who is worthy of being saluted by all creatures and who is like a god, Savarī, who is ever devoted to her pious duties, will go to heaven."* If the poet who wrote this stanza recognized Rāma to be the incarnation of Viṣṇu, he could not have resisted the temptation of referring to that fact here. Again when Rāma and Lakṣmaṇa reached the hermitage of Śavarī, she welcomed Rāma in a speech wherein she called him "*devavara*," "foremost of gods," "bull among men (*puruṣarṣabha*)," "tiger among men (*puruṣavyāghra*)," but not as Bhagavat or Nārāyaṇa. Śavarī told Rāma that when he was at Citrakūṭa the sages of the hermitage whom she had served all her life, when about to depart for heaven in aerial chariots, said to her, "Rāma will come to your very holy hermitage. Entertain that guest with Lakṣmaṇa. Seeing him you will go to the highest eternal world (74. 15-15)."

In Book VI of the epic we are told, when Rāvaṇa was killed and Sītā was brought before Rāma, he refused to take her back on the ground that she had lived too long in Rāvaṇa's city to remain chaste. Hearing these cruel words, Sītā determined to put an end to herself and entered

* त्वां तु धर्मे स्थिता नित्यं सर्वभूतनमस्कृतम् ।
दृष्ट्वा देवोपमं राम स्वर्गलोकं गमिष्यति (73 27) ।

a pyre prepared for her by Lakṣmaṇa. When she did so Vaiśravana, the Pitṛs, Yama, Indra, Varuṇa, Śiva, Brahmā and other gods appeared before Rāma and said that though he (Rāma) was the creator of the worlds and omniscient, why did he forget himself and refused to take back Sītā like an ordinary man. Rāma inquired in reply, "I know myself to be a man named Rāma, son of Daśaratha. Tell me, O Bhagavat (Brahmā), who am I and whence am I?"* Brahmā told him in reply that he was Nārāyaṇa, Viṣṇu, Kṛṣṇa and Sītā was Lakṣmī. This seems to indicate that there was a time when Rāma was not recognized as an incarnation of Viṣṇu.† Even as it is, this canto appears to be out of place and a superfluity in the poem. Brahmā's speech reminding Rāma of his identity with Viṣṇu-Kṛṣna evidently produced no impression upon him. The next following canto (118) opens thus, "Hearing this auspicious speech uttered by Brahmā (*pitāmaha*), Agni (*Vibhāvasu*) arose [from the pyre] with Vaidehī (Sītā) in his lap."‡ Agni then speaks to Rāma in a quite different tone. He does not refer to the fact that Sītā was the incar-

* "आत्मानं मानुषं मन्ये रामं दशरथात्मजम् ।
सोऽहं यश्च यतश्चाहं भगवांस्तद्ब्रवीतु मे ॥ (VI. 117. 11).
Rāmāyana, Bombay, 1902.

† See Jacobi's remarks, *Encyclopædia of Religion and Ethics*, VII, p. 194*a*.

‡ "एतच्छ्रुत्वा शुभं वाक्यं पितामहसमीरितम् ।
अङ्केनादाय वैदेहीमुत्पपात विभावसुः ॥"

nation of Lakṣmī. All that Agni says is, Sītā is chaste and requests Rāma to take her back without scruple (VI. 118. 5-10). So cantos 117 and 118 of the Rāmāyaṇa Book VI can not be recognized as the composition of the same authors, but are the work of two different authors belonging to two different ages. In the abstract of the epic as given in the opening canto of Book I the episode of Sīta's entering the pyre and Rāma's recognition of her innocence on the testimony of Agni is referred to, but nothing is said about the intervention of Brahmā or the very important revelation made by him (I. 1. 81-83).

These evidences indicate that in the original Rāmāyaṇa, probably the work of a single poet, Vālmīki, who flourished before 500 B.C. according to Jacobi, and in the fourth century B.C. according to Keith, Rāma was depicted as a man and not as an incarnation of Viṣṇu. The portions of the Rāmāyaṇa wherein Rāma is represented as an Avatāra (incarnation) were probably added at the time when the Māhābhārata was reduced to its present Kṛṣṇaite form about 200 B.C.

The cult of the avatāras of Viṣṇu taught by the Brāhmanic epics and the Purāṇas proved a formidable rival to the older Pāñcarātra or Bhāgavata cult of the four vyūhas and ultimately ousted it. The orthodox Vaiṣṇavas of course could not persuade themselves to believe that the Pāñcarātra was really un-Vedic and found a way out of the difficulty by interpreting the theory of the Vyūhas in a different way. Rāmānuja writes in his *Śrībhāṣya* (II. 2. 42): "The criticism that the Bhāgavatas teach an inadmissible origination of the individual soul, is made by people who do not understand that system. What it teaches is that the highest Brahman, there called Vāsudeva, from kindness to those devoted to it, voluntarily abides in a fourfold form, so as to render itself accessible to its devotees." The identification of all the four Vyūhas with the highest Brahman proved injurious to the old cult. The way in which the orthodox Vaiṣṇavas endeavoured to reconcile these rival cults is thus explained by Rāmānuja in the *Śrībhāṣya* (II. 2. 42):—

"That highest Brahman, called Vāsudeva, having for its body the complete aggregation of the six qualities, divides itself in so far as it is either the 'Subtle' (*sūkṣma*), or 'division' (*vyūha*), or 'manifestation' (*vibhava*), and is attained in its fulness by the devotees who, according to their qualifications, do worship it by means of works guided by knowledge. 'From the worship of vibhava-aspect one attains to the vyūha, and from the worship of the vyūha one attains to the "Subtile" called Vāsudeva, i.e. highest Brahman' —such is their doctrine. By the 'vibhava' we have to understand the aggregate of beings, such as Rāma, Kṛṣṇa, etc., in whom the highest Being becomes manifest; by the 'vyūha,' the fourfold arrangement or division of the highest Reality, as Vāsudeva, Saṃkarṣaṇa, Pradyumna, and Aniruddha; by the 'Subtle' the highest Brahman itself, in so far as it has for its body the mere aggregate of the six qualities—as which it is called Vāsudeva.''*

The following passage of the *Sātvata Saṃhitā*, quoted by Bhandarkar, is very significant:—

''When the pure Brahman, which is the aim and end of the creation, exists in the heart of qualified Brāhmaṇas, who worship Vāsudeva, the highest Śāstra, which is the great Upaniṣad of Brahman, springs forth from it for the redemption of the world and confers discrimination; it contains divine methods and has for its fruit final deliverance. I will then explain that to you which is of various kinds. This Śāstra, along with Rahasya, is fruitful to those who have gone through Yoga with its eight parts and whose soul is devoted to mental sacrifice. The Yogins, who are Brāhmaṇas guided by the Vedas and who have given up the mixed worship, are competent for the worship of the single one, dwelling in the heart. The three orders, Kṣatriya and others, and those who are *prapanna* or have resorted to self-surrender are competent for the worship of the four Vyūhas accompanied by mantras, and also unaccompanied by them, so far as regards the series of ceremonies concerning the four Vyūhas as well as the actions and the collection of mantras concerning the Vibhavas.'' †

Here the worship of Vāsudeva as ''the single

* Thibaut's translation, S.B.E. XLVII, p. 525.

† *Vaiṣṇavism*, etc., pp. 39-40.

one" is assigned to Brāhmans "guided by the Veda" and "have given up the mixed worship"; and the worship of the four Vyūhas with or without mantras to three other orders (castes) who were evidently addicted to mixed, that is to say, Vedic as well as un-Vedic, worship. The worship of the Vyūhas unaccompanied by mantras was of course un-Vedic. In practice the worship of the Vibhava forms or incarnations on the one hand, and of 'the single form' Vāsudeva, Nārāyaṇa or Viṣṇu on the other, threw the worship of the Vyūhas in the background and finally ousted it. Amarasiṃha in his lexicon gives the synonyms of Saṃkarṣaṇa, Pradyumna and Aniruddha (I. 23-27) after those of Vāsudeva (I. 18-22). Varāhamihira in the chapter (XLVII) on characteristics of images of his *Bṛhatsaṃhitā* makes no reference to Aniruddha vyūha, but gives directions for making the images of Baladeva (Saṃkarṣaṇa), Pradyumna and Śāmba. "Baladeva should be made with plough in one hand, drunken eyes, adorned with one ear-ring and body as white as conch shell, moon and lotus-stem."* "Śāmba (should be made) with a club in one hand; Pradyumna (should be made) handsome and holding a bow. The wives of these two deities should be made holding shield (*kheṭaka*) and sword."†

---

* बलदेवो हलपाणिर्मदविभ्रमलोचनश्च कर्त्तव्यः ।
बिभ्रत् कुण्डलमेकं शङ्खेन्दुमृणालगौरतनुः ॥ ३९ ॥

† शाम्बश्च गदाहस्तः प्रद्युम्नश्चापभृत् सुरूपश्च ।
अनयोः स्त्रियौ च कार्ये खेटकनिस्त्रिंशधारिण्यौ ॥ ४० ॥

Thus though there is literary evidence of the survival of the worship of all the four Vyūhas up to the sixth century A.D., archæological evidences regarding the cults of Pradyumna and Aniruddha (or Śāmba according to Varāhamihira) are non-existent and evidences of the worship of Baladeva (Saṃkarṣaṇa) along with Vāsudeva are very rare. This latter form of worship appears to have been quite common before the Christian era. Kauṭilya in his *Arthaśāstra* (XIII. 3) refers to "ascetics with shaved head or braided hair and pretending to be the worshippers of god, Saṃkarṣaṇa" and to their "sacrificial beverage.*" In the Ghasundī inscription already referred to, the construction of a wall round the hall of worship of Saṃkarṣaṇa and Vāsudeva is mentioned. Under Pāṇini II. 2. 34 Patañjali notices "a verse in which it is stated that certain musical instruments are sounded in a gathering in the temple of Dhanapati, Rāma and Keśava. Here Rāma and Keśava are Balarāma and Vāsudeva-Kṛṣṇa, and it is clear that there were festive gatherings at their temples in Patañjali's time."† I have already referred to the Nānāghāt cave inscription, wherein Saṃkarṣaṇa is invoked along with Vāsudeva. But in the archæological remains of the Gupta period when there was evidently a revival of Vaiṣṇavism under the patronage of the Gupta

* English translation by R. Shamasastry, Bangalore, 1915, p. 485.

† *Vaiṣṇavism*, etc., p. 13.

emperors, some of whom are called *paramabhāgavata* on their coins, traces of Saṃkarṣaṇa worship are practically absent. Sir R. G. Bhandarkar, in section XII of his work where later traces of the Bhāgavata school and general Vaiṣṇavism are described, is able to refer only to one piece of sculpture found in a temple at Osia in Rajputana bearing a representation of Saṃkarṣaṇa.* The only well-known instance of the survival of the worship of Balarāma (Saṃkarṣaṇa) along with Vāsudeva (Jagannātha) up to our own time is found in the temple of Purī in Orissa. Some features of the worship of Jagannātha, Balarāma, and Subhadrā at Purī, such as the non-observance of the caste rules in connection with the *mahāprasāda* or cooked food offered to the gods, and the presence of a class of priests called Daitas, who are said to be of aboriginal Śavara descent, may perhaps be the last remnants of the primitive un-Vedic Pāñcarātra ritual.

* *Ibid.*, pp. 45-46.

CHAPTER IV.

Race and Cult—Śāktism.

The Indian cult of Śakti or the cosmic energy personified as a female is far more primitive than the cult of Kṛṣṇa-Vāsudeva. Female deities play very minor parts in the Vedic pantheon and Vedic polytheism culminated in the monotheistic conception of Prajāpati on the one hand, and the pantheistic conception of Brahman-Ātman on the other. But some of the names of the Śakti of the Śākta occur in the latest works of the Vedic literature. These references are thus summarised by Jacobi:—

"Ambikā is called Rudra's sister in the *Vājasaneya Saṃhitā*, but in the *Taittirīya Āranyaka* X. 18, she has already become the spouse of Rudra, just as in later times. In the same work X. 1, we find an invocation of Durgā Devī, who is there styled Vairochanī, daughter of the Sun or Fire; and in X. 1, 7, among verses addressed to Agni, we meet with two more names of Durgā (here called Durgī), viz. Kātyāyanī and Kanyākumārī. Umā, daughter of Himavat, is mentioned in the *Kena Upaniṣad*, III. 25, as a heavenly woman conversant with Brahma, on which account the commentator regards her as a personification of the Brahmavidyā; but in *Taitt. Ār* X. 18 (according to the Draviḍa text) Rudra is invoked as Umāpati, 'husband of Umā.' Kālī and Karāli, two names of Durgā, occur in the *Mundaka Upaniṣad* 1, 2, 4, among names of the seven tongues of Agni.''*

The epithet 'Haimavatī' or 'daughter of Himavat' indicates that the goddess Umā was originally worshipped by the dwellers in the Himālayan region. As Rudra is *Giriśa*, 'lord of the mountains,' according to the Śatarudrīya of the *Yajurveda*, so Umā Haimavatī is his consort. Jacobi writes about Umā:—"Apparently she was originally an independent goddess, or at least a kind of divine being, perhaps a female mountain ghost haunting the Himālayas, and was later identified with Rudra's wife.''† Etymologically *Ambikā* means 'mother,' and *Durgā* means 'one who is approached with difficulty.' Bhadrakālī is named in the *Sānkhyāyana-grīhysūtra* II. 15, 14 in connection with the Vaiśvadeva rite which a a householder was required to perform daily; " 'Adoration to Śrī'—(thus) in the bed at the head, 'to Bhadrakālī' at the foot." So also Manu III. 89, "Near the head (of the bed) he shall make an offering to Śrī (fortune), and near the foot (of the bed) to Bhadrakālī.''

Ambikā, Durgā, Umā, Kātyāyanī and Bhadrakālī of the later Vedic literature are obscure minor divinities who can hardly be accepted as the proto-types of the Devī (goddess) or the Śakti of the Śākta. The Devī is first revealed in

* *Encyclopædia of Religion and Ethics*, Vol. V, p. 217b.

† *Encyclopædia of Religion and Ethics*, Vol. II, p. 813a.

her true character in two hymns of the epic, *Mahābhārata*. In one of these hymns (VI. 23) she is addressed as Siddhasenānī (generaless of the Siddhas), the dweller on Mandara, Kumārī (maiden), Kālī (black or time as destroyer), Kapālī (wearer of skulls), Bhadrakālī, Mahākālī, Candī (angry), Candā (angry), Tārinī (deliveress), Karālī (frīghtful), Vijayā (victory), Jayā, "younger sister of the chief of cowherds [Kṛṣṇa], eldest born in the family of the cowherd Nanda, delighting always in Mahiṣa's blood," Kauśikī, Umā, Śākambharī, "destroyer of Kaitabha," Vedaśruti, she "who dwellest continually near Jambu, mountain-precipices, and sepulchres," "the great sleep of embodied beings," "mother of Skanda," "divine Durgā," "dweller in wildernesses," Svāhā, Svadhā, Sarasvatī, Sāvitrī, 'mother of' the Vedas, and the Vedānta," Mahādevī, Jambhanī, Mohinī, Māyā, Hrī, Srī, and Sandhyā. In the other hymn (IV. 6) the goddess is described as "born in the womb of Yaśodā," "the favourite of Nārāyaṇa," "who rose to the sky when thrown on a piece of stone," "holding sword and shield," "four-armed," "four-faced," "consort of Nārāyaṇa," she "who destroyed the demon Mahiṣa to save the three worlds," "whose perpetual abode is in the Vindhyas, the best of the hills," and "who is fond of spirituous liquor, flesh, and sacrificial victims."

The legends alluded to in the epithets younger sister of the chief of the cowherds, daughter of

Nanda and Yaśoda, etc., are narrated in the *Harivaṃsa* (58). Therein we are told that Viṣṇu descended to the nether world (*pātāla*) and asked sleep in the form of destroying time (*nidrā kāla-rupinī*) to put the six demons named *saḍgarbhas* into the womb of Devakī in succession, to transfer the seventh child of Devakī from her womb to that of Rohinī, and then herself be born as the ninth child of Yaśodā, wife of Nanda, the Gopa chief, on the same night on which he himself was to be born as the eighth child of Devakī, to baffle the designs of Kaṃsa. Viṣṇu told her that she would be carried to Devakī, and when seizing her by her feet Kaṃsa would be ready to throw her on a piece of rock, she would rise to the sky; then Indra would assign the Vindhya mountains as her perpetual abode wherein, meditating on Viṣṇu, she would slay the two demons, Śumbha and Niśumbha. These legends seem to indicate that the nomadic Ābhīras of Western India were originally worshippers of a goddess who was later on identified with the mountain deity presiding over the Vindhya hills conceived as a female and worshipped by the hill tribes. Jacobi writes, "A similar mountain-goddess had her home in the Vindhyas; she was of cruel character, as might be expected from a goddess of the savage tribes living in those hills. Her name is Vindhya-vāsinī, and she too is identified with Siva's wife."* In a hymn of the goddess given in the *Harivaṃsa*,

* *Encyclopædia of Religion and Ethics*, Vol. II. 813a.

59, it is said of her, "You are worshipped by the Śavaras, Barbbaras (savages), and Pulindas (*śavarai rbbarbbarai ścaiva pulindaiśca supujitā* 3234)." In the Prākṛtā poem *Gauḍavaho* of Vākpati, a contemporary of Bhavabhuti, the goddess is addressed as Śavarī (v. 305), 'Śavara woman.' In the Varāha Purāṇa (28, 34) she is addressed as Kirātinī, 'Kirāta woman,' and in the *Abhidhānacintāmaniparisiṣṭā* of Hemacandra Kirātī is given as one of her names. One of the rites ordained in connection with the annual autumnal worship of Durgā is called *Śāvarotsava.* From a text reproduced by Śūlapāṇi in his *Durgotsava-Viveka* from the *Kālikapurāṇa* it appears that this *śāvarotsava* was a licentious revel and was performed at the time of throwing the image of the goddess into the water.* In the *Merutantra* one of the five subdivisions of *vāmamārga*, the 'left-hand path' of worshipping the goddess, is called *śāvara*, 'relating to the Śavaras'.†

The well-known legend of Dakṣa's sacrifice indicates that the orthodox followers of Vedism did not acknowledge the right of Siva as Devī's

---

* विसर्ज्जनं नवम्यान्तु [? दशम्यान्तु] कुर्य्याद्वै शावरोत्सवैः ।
धूलिकर्द्दमविक्षेपैः क्रीडाकौतुकमङ्गलैः ॥
भगलिङ्गाभिधानैश्च भगलिङ्गप्रगीतकैः ।
भगलिङ्गक्रियाभिश्च क्रीडयेयुरलञ्जनाः ॥

† कौलिकोऽकुलतां प्राप्तो वामः श्यामार्गोत्तमः ।
चीनमार्गो मध्यमः स्यात् सिद्धान्तीयोऽपरो भवेत् ॥
कनिष्ठः शावरो मार्गः इति वामस्तु पञ्चधा ।
Purascaryārṇava, Benares, 1901, p. 22.

consort, to say nothing of Devī herself, to a share of the sacrificial food along with the Vedic gods. The earliest version of the legend is given in the Mahābhārata XII. 284-285. Herein it is said that Dakṣa, son of Pracetas, began a horse sacrifice (Aśvamedha) at Hardwar at the foot of the Himālayas. All the gods with their wives, Ṛṣis, Dānavas, Gandharvas and all other classes of beings attended the sacrifice. A sage named Dadhici happened to notice that Mahādeva (Rudra), the consort of Pārvatī, was not present in the assembly and asked the reason why. Dakṣa replied, " In this world there are eleven Rudras with matted hair and holding spear; but I do not know who is Maheśvara among them."* In Kailāsa, the mountain-abode of Śiva, the Goddess Pārvatī was much grieved because her husband had not been invited by Dakṣa and offered an adequate share of the sacrificial food. Instigated by her, Śiva created the fierce Bīrabhadra out of his own mouth to destroy Dakṣa's sacrifice. Fierce-looking Mahākālī, also called Bhadrakālī, born of Devī's wrath, followed Bīrabhadra to the place of Dakṣa's sacrifice. They destroyed all the sacrificial materials. This brought Dakṣa to his senses, who was advised by Bīrabhadra to propitiate Śīva. Dakṣa prayed to Śīva who issued out of the fire and conferred on him the desired boon. Then Dakṣa repeated

---

* "सन्ति नो बहवो रुद्रा शूलहस्ताः कपर्दिनः ।
एकादशस्थानगता नाहं वेद्मि महेश्वरम् ॥

a long hymn containing the thousand and eight names of Śiva. Highly pleased with the hymn Śīva thus advised Dakṣa (XII. 185, 122-127):—

"'The Devas and Dānavas, extracting it (the Pāśupata religion) with the help of arguments addressed to reason from the Vedas, the six auxiliary sciences (of the Veda) and Sāṃkhya and Yoga, practised for long very hard penances; it is transcendental (*apūrva*) and productive of benefits of all sorts; it is open to men of all castes and orders; it leads to final emancipation; it may be mastered in several years or by restraining the organs of sense; it is esoteric, and it is censured by the unwise only; it is opposed to the rules laid down for the observance of castes and orders and agrees with them in certain points only; those who know the true logical conclusions have really grasped it; it is intended for those who are above the four orders. This excellent Pāśupata religion was created by me, O Dakṣa, in days of yore. He who practises it obtains full recompense. Let that recompense be thine, O very fortunate one, and cast off thy grief.' Saying so Mahādeva, who possessed immeasurable prowess, disappeared from the view of Dakṣa with his wife and attendants." *

* वेदात् षडङ्गादुद्धृत्य सांख्ययोगाच्च युक्तितः ।
तपः सुतप्तं विपुलं दुश्चरं देवदानवैः ।
अपूर्वं सर्वतो भद्रं विश्वतोमुखमव्ययम् ।
अब्दैर्दशाहैः संयुक्तं गूढमप्राज्ञनिन्दितम् ॥
वर्णाश्रमकृतैर्धर्मैर्विपरीतं क्वचित् समम् ।

It should be noticed that the Śiva whom Dakṣa ignored in his sacrifice was not the Vedic Rudra, but the Siva worshipped by the monotheistic Pāśupatas. This legend of Dakṣa's sacrifice indicates that the Pāśupata conception of Rudra or Śiva as the Supreme Being arose outside the pale of Vedism and the orthodox followers of the Veda could not persuade themselves to acknowledge him readily. No share of the sacrificial food is claimed on behalf of Śiva's consort, Durgā.

The legends relating to the destruction of the demons Mahiṣa, Sumbha, and Niśumbha, alluded to in the epic hymns, form the theme of the well-known *Devī-māhātmya* of the *Mārkandeya Purāṇa* (*Cantos* 81—93). In this poem the Devī is thus described:—"She exists eternally, embodied as the world. By her this universe was stretched forth. Nevertheless her origin is in many ways; hear it from me. When she reveals herself in order to accomplish the purpose of the gods, *it is* then *said* in the world that she is born; she is also named the Eternal One (81. 47—48)." * She is the creator of Brahmā, Viṣṇu and Siva. Brahmā is made to say (81. 65):—"Since Viṣṇu, I and Śiva have been made by thee to assume bodies, who

---

गतां तैरध्वरस्थितमत्यान्तमिदं मतम् ॥
मया पाशुपतं दक्ष शुभमुत्पादितं पुरा ।
तस्य चीर्णस्य तत् सम्यक् फलं भवति पुष्कलम् ॥
तथास्तु वै महाभाग त्वय्युक्तो मानसो ज्वरः ।
एवमुक्त्वा महादेवः सपत्नीकः सहानुगः ।
अदर्शनमनुप्राप्तो दक्षस्य मितविक्रमः ॥

* Pargiter's translation (*Mārkandaya Purāṇa*, Bib. Ind.).

9

then may be powerful *enough* to extol thee?" She is the "mother of the whole world," the "queen of the universe," the "gem of the universe" She is addressed as, "Thou art not known! Even by Hari, Hara and the other *gods thou art* incomprehensible (84. 6)." The demon Mahiṣa, and, afterwards, Sumbha and Niśumbha, deprived Indra and other gods like Agni, Vāyu, Varuṇa, Candra, Yama, Kuvera of their possessions and their portions of the sacrifice. The goddess Candikā slaughtered these demons and restored the gods to their dominions and shares of sacrifices. This incarnation of the goddess "to accomplish the purpose of the gods," who are the Purāṇic representatives of the Vedic nature gods, is but a fiction to connect Vedic polytheism with Śākta monotheism. The legends relating to Devī's slaying the demons are evidently nature myths. In the *Devī-māhātmya* she is made to say:—"When the twenty-eighth age has arrived, in the Vaivasvata Manvantara, two other great Asuras shall be born, Śumbha and Niśumbha. Then born as the offspring of Yaśodā's womb in the cowherd Nanda's house, *and* dwelling on the Vindhya mountains, I will destroy them both (92. 36—37)." Again, "Next, O ye gods, I shall support (i e. nourish) the whole world with the life-sustaining vegetables, which shall grow out of my own body, during a period of heavy rain. I shall gain fame on the earth then as Śākambharī ('herb-bearing or herb-nourishing'); and in that very period I shall slay the great Asura named Durgama (92. 43—44)." Durgā as Sākambharī is the vegetation spirit or corn-mother, and demons Mahiṣa and Śumbha and Niśumbha are demons of drought. According to the *Devīmāhātmya* (92. 11) and even now in Bengal her "great annual worship" "is performed in autumn time," which is the time when the crops are ripening and the harvest is near. The *śāradīya pujā* or the autumnal worship of Durgā is analogous to the service of the Greek goddess Demeter Chloe that took place on the sixth of Thargelian. "This sacrifice," writes Farnell, "was probably one of atonement, a propitiation of the goddess whose fruits were about to be gathered. We have now evidence from all parts of the world and other evidence from Attica itself, of the harvest process being regarded as a dangerous act, which must be rigidly guarded by many prior piacular ceremonies."* The goddess is also worshipped in spring.

An important aspect of Durga-worship, called *navapatrikā* or the worship of the nine plants (lit. 'leaves'), also clearly shows that the goddess was conceived as the personification of the vegetation spirit. These nine plants are,—*rambhā*, 'plantain tree', *kacvī* (Arum colocasia), *haridrā*, 'turmeric plant', *jayantī*, 'barley', *bel* or *bilva*, 'wood-apple', *dārima*, 'pomegranate', *aśoka*, *māna*, and *dhānya*, 'paddy.'† The form of the

* *Cults of the Greek States*, III, p. 34.

† "रम्भा कच्वी हरिद्रा च जयन्ती बिल्वदाड़िमौ।
अशोकमानकश्चैव धान्यञ्च नवपत्रिका॥"

goddess presiding over the plantain tree is called Brahmāṇī, over the *kacvī* is called Kālikā, over the turmeric plant is called Durgā, over *jayantī* is called Kārttikī, over the wood-apple tree is called Sivā, over the pomegranate tree is called Raktadantikā ('she with blood-red teeth'), over the *aśoka* tree is called Śokarahitā ('she without sorrow caused by bereavement'), over the *māna* plant is called Cāmnudā, and over the paddy plant is Lakṣmī (the goddess of fortune).* After praying severally to the deities of the nine plants, the votary concludes, "Om, O leave (*patrike*), O nine forms of Durgā, you are the darling of Mahādeva; accept all these offerings and protect me, O queen of heaven. Om, adoration to Durgā dwelling in the nine plants." This worship of *navapatrikā* is but a survival of the agrarian phase of Durgā-worship. Durgā is now worshipped in her image as a war-goddess riding on a lion, holding various weapons in her ten, sixteen or eighteen arms, and engaged in killing the demon Mahiṣa. This hymn is recited on the eve of her worship:—"In days of yore Brahmā performed the invocation ceremony of the goddess untimely (in autumn) for bringing about the death of Rāvana and favouring Rāma. I invoke thee in the evening of the sixth day (of the bright half) of Āśvina. Śakra (Indra) also obtained dominion in the abode of the gods by invoking

* *Puraścharyārṇava*, Part III (Benares, 1904), pp. 1034-1035.

thee. Therefore I invoke thee for obtaining wealth, dominion, and influence; as the ten-headed (Rāvana) was killed by Rāma, so may I destroy my enemy."*

The legend referred to here connecting the worship of Durgā in autumn with Rāma's slaying Rāvana is unknown to the *Rāmāyaṇa* of Vālmīki. According to the *Rāmāyaṇa* VI. 105, Rāma worshipped Sūrya, the sun-god, and not Durgā, at the instance of the sage Agastya, before his last encounter with Rāvana which ended in the death of the mighty demon. This legend, therefore, was evidently invented to explain the transformation of Durgā as the vegetation spirit to the war-goddess and bring her worship in line with epic Brāhmanism. The Devī named in a sacred formula (*mantra*) quoted by Kauṭilya in connection with sowing seeds in his *Arthaśāstra* (II. 24) is probably the prototype of Durgā as the corn-spirit. Kauṭilya writes:—" Always when sowing seeds, a handful of seeds bathed in water with a piece of gold shall be sown first and the following mantra recited:—' Salutation to God Prajāpati Kāśyapa. Agriculture may always flourish and

* रावणस्य वधार्थाय रामस्यानुग्रहाय च ।
अकाले ब्रह्मणा बोधो देव्यास्त्वयि कृतः पुरा ॥
अहमप्याश्विने षष्ठ्यां सायाह्ने बोधयामि वै ।
शक्रेणापि च सम्बोध्य राज्यं प्राप्तं सुरालये ॥
तस्मादहं त्वां प्रतिबोधयामि विभूतिराज्यप्रतिपत्तिहेतोः ।
यथैव रामेण हतो दशास्यस्तथैव शत्रुं विनिपातयामि ॥

the goddess (may reside) in seeds and wealth. Chaṇḍavāṭa ho.' '' *

Another phase of the Devī closely related to her as Śākambharī is Annadā, 'the giver of food', or Annapūrṇā, 'she who is full of food.' Annadā is thus described by Bhāratacandra in his *Annadāmaṅgala* :—" In her left hand she holds a cup made of precious stones and filled with primordial ambrosia; a spoon made of precious stones containing rice fried in ghee (*saghṛta palānna*) is in her right hand. How beautiful are her two arms! Serving in different fashions food of various tastes for chewing, sucking, licking, drinking, and therewith feeding Kṛttivāsa (Śiva), she watches Maheśa's dance and smiles a sweet smile. Gods, Asuras, Rakṣas, Apsarases, Kinnaras, Yakṣas, Gandharvas, serpents, human beings, Sidhyas, Sādhyas, Vidyādharas, the nine planets and the guardians of the ten cardinal points, all eat food of various tastes...... Vidhi (Brahmā), Viṣṇu, the three-eyed god (Śiva) and other gods and Ṛṣis sing around her. Āgama (*Tantra*), Purāṇa and Veda do not know thy secret; thou, O Goddess, art (both) Puruṣa and Pradhāna (Prakṛti).'' †

---

* *Kauṭilya's Arthśāstra*, English translation, pp. 145-146.

† বামকরতলে ধরি   কারণ অমৃত ভরি   পানপাত্র রতন নির্ম্মিত ।
রত্নহাতা ডানি হাতে   সঘৃত পলান্ন তাতে   কিবা দুই ভুজ সুললিত ॥
চর্ব্ব্য চূষ্য লেহ্য পেয়   নানারস অপ্রমেয়   বিবিধ বিলাসে পরশিয়া ।
ভুঞ্জাইয়া কৃত্তিবাস   মধুর মধুর হাস   মহেশের নাচন দেখিয়া ॥
দেবতা অসুর রক্ষ   অপ্সর কিন্নর যক্ষ   সবে ভোগ করে নানা রস ।
গন্ধর্ব্ব ভুজঙ্গ নর   সিধ্য সাধ্য বিদ্যাধর   নবগ্রহ দিক্‌পাল দশ ॥
*   *   *   *   *   *
বিধি বিষ্ণু ত্রিলোচন   আদি দেব ঋষিগণ   চৌদিকে বেড়িয়া করে গান
আগম পুরাণ বেদ   না জানে তোমার ভেদ   তুমি দেবী পুরুষ প্রধান ।

Another aspect of Śāktīsm that demands notice in this connection is the worship of the *kula* trees. The very first duty enjoined upon a Śākta on rising from bed very early in the morning is the salutation of the *kula* trees with the formula "*Om kulavṛkṣebhyo namah.*"* According to the *Kulacuḍāmaṇi*, "the worshipper should salute the *kula* tree whenever he sees it." † The author of the *Śāktānandataraṅginī* reproduces two different lists of *kula* trees, *viz.*, Aśoka (Jonesia Asoka), Keśara (Bakula), Bel (wood-apple), Karṇikāra, Cūta (the mango tree), Nameru (Rūdrākṣa tree), Piyāla, Sindhuvāra (Niśundha), Kadamba, Marubaka (Jhintikā), and Campaka. Another list of eight *kula* trees contains these additional names:—Slesmātaka (Vaheḍā tree), Karañja, Nim, Asvattha (ficus religiosa). The *Tantrāsāra* gives a list of ten *kula* trees also including Vaṭa (the fig-tree), Udumvara (ficus glomerata), Dhātrī (āmalaka tree), Ciñcā (the tamarind tree). It is said of *kula* trees:—"The *Kula Yoginīs* always dwell in all these *kula* trees. No one should sleep under the *kula* trees nor injure them." ‡ The Kula Yoginīs dwelling in *kula* trees were probably originally minor vegetation spirits. The

* 'ब्राह्मे मुहूर्त्ते उत्थाय "ॐ कुलवृक्षेभ्यो नमः" इति कुलवृक्षं नमस्कृत्य गुरुं ध्यायेत्' *Tāra-rahasya-vṛttikā*, Patala I.

† "यदि पश्येत् कुलतरुं प्रणमेत् साधकस्सदा" *Śāktānandatāraṅginī*, p. 112.

‡ तिष्ठन्ति कुलयोगिन्यः सर्व्वेष्वेतेषु सर्व्वदा ।
न स्वपेत् कुलवृक्षाधो न चोपद्रवमाचरेत् ॥

Śāktānandatāraṅginī, p. 112.

worship of *kula* tree may also be regarded as a remnant of primitive totemism, for *kula* also denotes family and *kulataru* may be translated as 'totem tree.' Trees are still worshipped as family gods by the Marāṭhās of the Deccan. "Marāṭhā families have *devaks* or sacred symbols, which appear to have been originally totems, and affect marriage to the extent that a man cannot marry a woman whose *devak* reckoned on the male side is the same as his own. They are totems, worshipped during marriage and other important ceremonies."* Among the *devaks* of the Marāṭhā families occur the names of the following *kula* trees:—Vad (Ficus Indica), Pimpal (Ficus Religiosa), Kadum (Nanclea Cadamba), Umbar (Ficus Glomeratā), Nāgacampā (Mesua ferrea) and Rudrāksh (Elaeocarpus ganitrus).

The form of the Devī that has got the largest number of votaries in Bengal is Kālī. Kālī's annual worship takes place in autumn in the night of the new moon when the *dīpālī* or 'lamp festival' is held. She is also the object of worship of the village *bāroāri pujā* or public worship held annually almost in every village in Bengal with funds raised from public subscriptions. Kālī is also worshipped as Raksā Kālī or 'protectress Kalī' whenever cholera breaks out in an epidemic form. In her *dhyāna* (directions for meditation) in the *Satantratantra* reproduced by Kṛṣṇānanda in his *Tantrasāra* Kālī is described as:—

* *Census of India*. 1901, Vol. I, *Ethnographical Appendices*, Calcutta, 1904, p. 99.

"The goddess resembling a mountain of black pigment; having a frightful face; Śivā; adorned with several garlands made of heads; with dishevelled hair; smiling face; resting on the lotus-like breast of Mahākāla; having fleshy breast; addicted to sexual union with Śiva in the reverse order; having terrible teeth; decorated with a nāga (serpent) encircling her as a sacred thread; having the crescent moon on her forehead; having all sorts of ornaments; adorned with garlands of heads; with a girdle round her loin consisting of thousands of hands of dead persons; sky-clad; attended by thousands of kotis of Śivās and Yoginīs; having her lotus-like mouth filled with blood; drunk with wine; having Agni, Sun and Moon for her eyes; with blood-red face; wearing as her earrings the dead bodies of two infants; her body covered with blood falling from the cluster of heads round her neck; dwelling in the midst of the fire of the cremation ground; worshipped by Brahmā and Keśava (Viṣṇu); (with two of) her lotus-like hands holding a head just severed, and a sword, and (with two others) offering blessings and protection." *

अञ्जनाद्रिनिभां देवीं करालवदनां शिवां ।
मुण्डमालावलीकीर्णां मुक्तकेशीं स्मिताननां ॥
महाकालहृदम्भोजस्थितां पीनपयोधरां ।
विपरीतरतासक्तां घोरदंष्ट्रां शिवैः सह ॥
नागयज्ञोपवीताढ्यां चन्द्रार्द्धकृतशेखरां ।
सर्व्वालङ्कारसंयुक्तां मुण्डमालाविभूषितां ॥
शवहस्तसहस्रैस्तु बद्धकाञ्चीं दिगम्बरां ।
शिवाकोटिसहस्रैस्तु योगिनीभिर्व्विराजितां

In a Tāntrik text quoted in the *Purascaryārṇava* (p. 728) Kāli (Kālikā) is called *kālarūpinī*, 'embodiment of Time'; and in the *Vṛhaddharmapurāṇa* (I. 23. 13) *, *saṃhāranividadhvāntakāyā* 'having a body deep black like the darkness of the time of destruction.' These epithets and the abode assigned to her, the fire of the cremation ground (*śmaśāna*), make it quite clear that in the Tāntric image of Kālī is pictured forth the Indian or rather the Bengali conception of the all-destroying Time. The picture, though hideous, is vivid and must be recognized as one of the masterly creations of imagination. Time spares neither young nor old. Human heads make up the necklace of Kālī and the corpses of infants her earrings. She is four-armed. In her one hand she has a bleeding human head and with the other she is bestowing blessings; in her third hand she holds the sword and with her fourth hand she assures safety.

Another well-known form of the Devī is Tārā or Tārinī, 'savioures' or 'deliveress.' The modern cult of Tārā seems to be a Brāhmanic Śākta adaptation of the Mahāyāna Buddhist cult of Tārā. Tārā of the modern Śākta, also called Ugra-Tārā

रक्तापूर्णमुखाम्भोजां मद्यपानप्रमत्तिकां ।
वक्त्रार्कवह्निनेत्राञ्च रक्तविस्फारितानना ॥
विगतासु किशोराभ्यां कृतकर्णावतंसिनीं ।
कण्ठावसक्तमुण्डाली गलद्रुधिरचर्चितां ॥
श्मशानवह्निमध्यस्थां ब्रह्मकेशववन्दितां ।
सद्यःछिन्नशिरः खड्ग वराभीतिकराम्बुजां ॥

* Bibliotheca Indica.

"because she saves from great (*ugra*) danger,"* Ekajatā (she who has but one chignon), and Nila (blue) Sarasvatī is practically the same as Blue Tārā, Ekajaṭā or Ugra-Tārā of the Mahāyānists. The Ugra-Tārā of the Mahāyānists is thus described:—

"She has from four to twenty-four arms, and is generally standing and stepping to the right on corpses. She has the third eye, is laughing horribly, her teeth are prominent, and her protruding tongue, according to the *sādhanā*, is forked. Her eyes are red and round. Her hips are covered by a tiger skin, and she wears a long garland of heads. If painted, her colour is blue, and her chignon is red. She is dwarfed and corpulent. Her ornaments are snakes. If she has but four arms her symbols are, sword, knife, blue lotus, and a skull-cap, or she may carry the bow and arrow instead of the last two symbols." †

---

* उग्रापत्तारिणी यस्मादुग्रतारा प्रकीर्त्तिता, *Tantra-sāra*, Calcutta, Śakābda, 1821, p. 251.

† Getty's *The Gods of Northern Buddhism*, Oxford, 1914, p. 111. Foucher in his *Iconographie Bouddhique*, Part 2, quotes this description of *Ekajatā* from the *Mahācīnakrama-Tārā-sādhanā*:—

"ततो ऊँ-कारजां पश्येत् कर्त्तृकां बीजभूषिताम् ।
कर्त्तृं परिणतं ध्यायादात्मानं तारिणीमयम् ॥
प्रत्यालीढ़पदां घोरां मुण्डमालाप्रलम्बिताम् ।
खर्वलम्बोदरां भीमां नीलनीरजराजिताम् ॥
त्र्यम्बकैकमुखीं दिव्यां घोराट्टहासभासुराम् ।
सुप्रहृष्टां शवारूढ़ां नागाष्टकविभूषिताम् ॥
रक्तवर्त्तुलनेत्रां च व्याघ्रचर्मावृताकटिम् ।
नवयौवनसम्पन्नां पञ्चमुद्राविभूषिताम् ॥

This description and the *sādhanā* quoted by Foucher are in substantial agreement with the *dhyāna* of Tārā reproduced from the *Fetkārīya Tantra* in the *Tantrasāra*.* One notable feature of this goddess, the Akṣobhya on her head (*maulāvakṣobhyabhūṣitām*), is also reminiscent of Mahāyanism. Aksobhya is the second of the five Dhyāni-Buddhas, a small image of which deity is often placed in the head-dress of Tārā, Prajñāpāramitā and Mañjuśrī.† Though the Akṣobhya on the head-dress of the Śākta Tārā, as distinguished from her Mahāyana prototype, is a "Nāga in form (*nāgaı ūpadhṛk*)," still it cannot but be recognised as a link in the chain

ललज्जिह्वां महाभीमां सदंष्ट्रोत्कटभीषणाम् ।
खड्गकर्त्तृकरां सव्ये वामोत्पलकपालधाम् ॥
पिङ्गोग्रैकजटां ध्यायान् मौलावक्षोभ्य भूषिताम् ।"

ततो ॐ-कारजां पश्येत् कर्त्तृकां नीलभूषिताम् ।
कर्त्तृकोपरिगतां ध्यायेदात्मानं तारिणीमयम् ॥
प्रत्यालीढपदां घोरां मुण्डमालाविभूषिताम् ।
खर्व्वां लम्बोदरीं भीमां व्याघ्रचर्म्मावृतां कटौ ॥
नवयौवनसम्पन्नां पञ्चमुद्राविभूषिताम् ।
चतुर्भुजां लोलजिह्वां महाभीमां वरप्रदाम् ॥
खड्गकर्त्तृसमायुक्त-सव्येतरभुजद्वयाम् ।
कपालोत्पलसंयुक्तसव्यपाणियुगान्विताम् ॥
पिङ्गोग्रैकजटां ध्यायेन्मौलावक्षोभ्यभूषिताम् ।
बालार्कमण्डलाकार-लोचनत्रयभूषिताम् ॥
ज्वलच्चितामध्यगतां घोरदंष्ट्रां करालिनीम् ।
स्वावेशस्मेरवदनां स्त्र्यलङ्कारविभूषिताम् ॥
विश्वव्यापकतोयान्तःश्वेतपद्मोपरिस्थिताम् ।"

† Getty's *The Gods*, etc., p. 35.

connecting the Śākta with the Bauddha phase of the goddess. Another important link is the legend of Buddha and Vasiṣṭha told in the *Rudrayāmalatantra* XVII, *Brahmayāmalatantra* I-III, and *Mahācīnācāratantra*, and referred to in several other Tantras.* The legend runs :—

"The great sage Vasiṣṭha, son of Brahmā, practised the most severe austerities for a long time meditating upon a *mantra* received from his father. He practised *Yoga* as it was then taught by the orthodox teachers, who enjoined self-denials of all sorts upon their disciples. Vasiṣṭha discovered that he derived no benefit from the practices, and so he repaired to his father to ask for another *mantra*. He was, however, advised to continue with his *mantra* for a further period and to follow the *yogamārga* for the worship of the *Devī* called Buddheśvaṛī, according to a *sākhā* of the Atharvaveda. Vasiṣṭha now repaired to the sea-shore according to *Rudrayāmala* or to the Kāmākhyā hills (near Gauhati in Assam) according to the *Brahmxyāmala* and once again applied himself to the strict observance of the orthodox methods of *Yoga*. As he did so for a long time without any result, he cursed the *Devī* in a fit of anger. The Devī thereupon condescended to appear before him to say that he had adopted an altogether wrong path. Her worship, said the

* See *Tārātantram* (*Gauḍagranthamālā* 2) with Appendix, edited by Giriśa Candra Vedāntatīrtha with an English Introduction by A. K. Maitra. Published by the Varendra Research Society, Rajshahi, 1914.

Devī, was unknown to the Vedas; it was known only in the country of *Mahācīna*, a country of Buddhistic practices, and Vasiṣṭha would gain his object, if he received instructions from Viṣṇu now residing there in his incarnation as Buddha. So Vasiṣṭha repaired to *Mahācīna*. But here he was amazed to find that Buddha was drinking wine in the company of women. His doubts were soon dispelled by Buddha, who ultimately initiated him into the mysteries."

Tārā was evidently admitted to the Mahāyāna pantheon from the older Śākta pantheon. The earliest reference to a Buddhistic worshipper of Tārā is found in this phrase of Subandhu's *Vāsavadattā*: "As a female (Buddhistic) ascetic is devoted to Tārā and wears red garments (*bhiksukī 'va tārānurāgaraktāmbaradhāriṇī*)." * Subandhu wrote after Uddyotakara and before Bāṇa in the latter half of the sixth century. Tārā is recognised by the Buddhists as the 'mother of all the Buddhas and Bodhisattvas' and the consort of Avalokiteśvara. I reproduce below a few stanzas from a Tibetan hymn in Tārā's praise, very popular amongst Lāmaist people in Tibet, Sikhim, etc., translated by Waddell.†

> "Hail O Tārā! quick to save!
> Lotus-born of pitying tear
> Shed down by the Three-World-Lord,
> Grieving sad for sunken souls.

* Gray's *Vāsavadattā*, New York, 1913, p. 97.

† *Journal of the Royal Asiatic Society*, 1894, pp. 71-74.

Hail to Thee with grand piled-up hair,
Shrining there Tathāgata,
Victor of the universe.
Thou a saintly victor too!

Hail! adored by mighty gods,
Indra, *Brahmā*, Fire and Wind,
Ghostly horde and *Gandharvas*
All unite in praising Thee!

Hail! with moon as diadem,
Amitā, the Boundless Light,
Seated midst thy plaited hair
Ever shedding glory bright."

Like Viṣṇu and Śiva, Śakti or Devī as Durgā or Kālī is worshipped from two different standpoints. From the non-sectarian polytheistic standpoint she is worshipped as one of the divinities of the Hindu pantheon; and from the sectarian monotheistic Śākta standpoint she is worshipped as the Supreme Being, the Ādyā Śakti, primordial energy, conceived as a female. Of late there has appeared a tendency among educated Hindus and European students who depend upon the former for their information, to minimise the importance of Hindu sectarianism which has even led Census authorities to give up the attempt of collecting statistics about sects. Sir Edward Gait reproduces in his Census of India, 1911, Report (p. 115) this testimony of a well-known Bengali scholar and writer:—"I fast on the *Śivarātri* day because it is sacred to Śiva, and

I fast on *Ekādaśi* day because it is sacred to Vishnu. I plant the *bel* tree because it is dear unto Śiva, and the *tulsi* because it is dear unto Vishnu. The bulk of Hindus are not sectaries. Though the sects write much and make the most noise, they are only a small minority." But this learned person appears to have withheld one important information. Has he received *dīksā* or initiation from a *guru*? If so, what is the deity (*devatā*) of the *mūla-mantra* or the root formulā? The root formula that the *guru* secretly communicates to the *śiṣya* (disciple) contains the name of one single deity only and determines the sect of the *dīkṣita* or the initiated person. If the *mūla-mantra* contains the name of Vāsudeva or Nārāyaṇa, he is a Vaiṣṇava; if it contains the name of Śiva, he is a Śaiva; and if the deity of the *mūla-mantra* is Dūrgā, Kālī, Tārā, or Tripurasundarī, he is a Śākta. The initiated Hindu may be personally free from sectarian narrowness, still he must be classed as a sectary. If "the bulk of the Hindus are no longer sectaries," it is because the bulk of the Hindus have ceased to be Hindus in the sense in which their ancestors were Hindus, that is to say, they no longer care to receive *dīkṣā* from the *guru*. In all the ancient land-grants inscribed on copper plates the sect to which the donor and his ancestors belong is scrupulously stated. As an illustration I shall refer to a grant of Vināyakapāla, the Pratihāra king of Kanauj, dated Samvat 988 (A.D. 931). In this record seven predecessors of

Vināyakapāla are thus named along with their sects:—

1. *Paramavaiṣṇava* (devout Vaiṣṇava) Mahārāja-śrī-Devaśaktideva.
2. His son *paramamāheśvara* (devout Śaiva) Mahārāja-śrī-Vatsarājadeva.
3. His son *paramabhagavatībhakta* (devout worshipper of Bhagavatī, i.e., a Śākta) Mahārāja-śrī-Nāgabhata.
4. His son *paramādityābhakta* (devout worshipper of Āditya, i.e., a Saura) Mahāraja-śrī-Rāmabhadradeva.
5. His son *paramabhagavatībhakta* (devout Śākta) Mahārāja-śrī-Bhojadeva.
6. His son *paramabhagavatībhakta* (devout Śākta) Mahārāja-śrī-Mahendrapāladeva.
7. His son *paramavaiṣṇava* (devout Vaiṣṇava) Mahārāja-śrī-Bhojadeva (II).
8. His brother *paramādityabhakta* (devout Saura) Maharāja-śrī-Vināvakapāladeva (Mahīpāladeva).*

Though the bulk of the modern Hindus may not be sectaries, their ancestors were, and it is yet possible to collect statistics relating to the geographical distribution of sects twenty-five to fifty years before. For without such statistics the scientific study of Hinduism is not practicable.

The sectarion Sākta conception of Sakti is thus defined in the opening verse of Brahmā-

* *Indian Antiquary*, XV, pp. 140-141.

nanda's *Śaktānandataraṅginī*, 'the stream of Śākta's joy':—"After saluting Prakṛti (Nature), Nityā (Eternal), and she who is Parmātman, *Śāktānandataraṅginī* is compiled for the enjoyment (of worldly happiness) and final emancipation (*mukti*)."* The author then quotes this definition of *Prakṛti* from Yāmala:—"Sattva, Rajas, and Tamas are the three *guṇas* (constituents of primitive matter); when these (*guṇas*) are in a state of equilibrium it is known as undifferentiated Prakṛti; she is Mūla-Prakṛti (primordial substance), Pradhāna as well as Puruṣa."† Here Śaktī is identified with both Prakṛti and Puruṣa of the Sāṃkhya philosophy. The Śakta or Tāntrik conception of Prakṛti is very clearly defined in a hymn to Prakṛti in the *Prapanchasāra Tantra*, XI, 48-67. I shall reproduce a few stanzas of this hymn in Arthur Avalon's translation:—‡

"Be gracious to me, O Pradhānā,
Who art Prakṛti in the form of the elemental world.
Life of all that lives. [Our Lady,
With folded hands I make obeisance to Thee
Whose very nature and will it is to do
That which we cannot understand. (1).

---

* प्रणम्य प्रकृतिं नित्यां परमात्मस्वरूपिणीम् ।
तन्यते भुक्तिमुक्त्यर्थं शाक्तानन्दतरङ्गिणी ॥

† सत्त्वं रजस्तम-इति गुणत्रयमुदाहृतम् ।
साम्यावस्थितिरेतेषामव्यक्तिं प्रकृतिं विदुः ॥

‡ *Prapancharāra Tantra* (Tāntrik Texts, Vol. III), Introduction, pp. 29-37.

Even Aja (Brahmā), Adhokshaja (Viṣṇu) and
Trīkshaṇa (Śiva)
Know not Thy Supreme form which is Māyā,
But pray to Thee in Thy gross form as Ruler.
Therefore so must I pray to Thee. (3).

Thou art Antarātmā,
Who by the Sun upholdest all living creatures,
And Who by the Moon ever nourishes them,
Again assuming the appearance of Fire the
carrier of oblations Thou burnest:
O Mahādevī, verily do these three lights and
fires issue from Thee. (7).

Assuming the form of Brahmā with active
quality,
The four-headed one seated on a shining white
swan,
Thou dost create the world
Of which Thou becomest the Mother.
Who is there indeed, Oh Supreme Ruler,
Who can imagine Thy supreme state? (8).

Adorned with crown,
Resplendent with conch and discus
As Nārāyaṇa with quality of manifestation
(*sattvaguṇa*),
Thou dost maintain the world;
For He also is part of Thee. (9).

Again in the form of the three-eyed Rudra
Carrying axe and a rosary,
On whose matted hair are moon, serpent and
Ganges,

He with the quality which veils (*tamoguṇa*)
Thou dost at the end of the Kalpa destroy the whole universe,
And then alone shinest. (10)."

The author of *Śāktānandataraṅginī* quotes this description of *Nityā* from *Śaktīyāmala* :—"She from whom and according to whose will Brahmā, Viṣṇu, Śiva and others come into being and in whom again they disappear is called Nityā, 'the Eternal one." *

From this sketch of the traits of the goddess it is possible to distinguish two different strata—one primitive and the other advanced. The primitive form of Durga is the result of syncretism of a mountain-goddess worshipped by the dwellers of the Himalaya and the Vindhyas, a goddess worshipped by the nomadic Abhīra shepherds, the vegetation spirit conceived as a female, and a war-goddess. As her votaries advanced in civilisation the primitive war-goddess was transformed into the personification of the all-destroying time (Kālī), the vegetation spirit into the primordial energy (Adyā Sakti) and the saviouress from *sāmsāra* (cycle of rebirths), and gradually brought into line with the Brāhmanic mythology and philosophy.

For a conception of the god-head analogous to that of the Śākta conception of the Devī we should travel beyond countries dominated by the

---

* ब्रह्मविष्णुशिवादीनां भवो यस्यां निजेच्छया ।
पुनः प्रलीयते यस्यां नित्या सा परिकीर्त्तिता ॥

Vedic Aryans and the Avestic Iranians to Asia Minor, Syria, Egypt and other countries bordering on the Mediterranean. Hogarth writes, "In regard to the Ægean *Divine spirit* itself, personified in the iconic age as a goddess and a young god, the student of comparative religion finds himself on very familiar ground. A goddess with a young subordinate god is known in early times, in every coast of the Mediterranean which looked towards Crete. In Punic Africa she is Tanit with her son; in Egypt, Isis with Horus; in Phoenicia, Ashtaroth with Tammuz (Adonis); in Asia Minor Cybele with Attis; in Greece (and especially in Greek Crete itself), Rhea with the young Zeus. Everywhere she is παρθένος, i.e. *unwed*, but made the mother first of her companion by immaculate conception, and then of the gods and all life by the embrace of her own son. In memory of these orginal facts her cult (especially the most esoteric mysteries of it) is marked by various practices and observances symbolic of the negation of true marriage and obliteration of sex. A part of her male votaries are castrated; and her female votaries must ignore their married state when in her personal service, and often practise ceremonial promiscuity." *

It should be noted in this connection that the Aryan-Hellenic invaders of Greece were not Śāktas. "We know now that they found in many centres a culture superior to their own and a religion of

* *Encyclopædia of Religion and Ethics*, I, p. 147a.

an advanced theistic type with elaborate, though mainly aniconic, ritual, devoted pre-eminently to a great goddess, by whose side a god was only the subordinate partner. It has then been pointed out that, where we find in historic Greece the goddess-cult predominant and especially the prevalence of a virgin-goddess, we should recognise the Minoan-Mycenæan (Ægean) tradition in antagonism to the Aryan, the latter invariably maintaining the predominance of god.'' * From the Śākta world of the West should also be excluded the Sumerians and their successors, the Babylonians and the Assyrians. Ishtar, the most prominent female deity in the Babylonian pantheon, corresponding to Ashtarte (Astarte) or Ashtoreth of the other Semites, occupied a subordinate place as compared to Anu, the heaven-god, Enlil, the earth-god, Ea, the water-god, Sin, the moon-god; and Shamash, the sun-god.

As there is a strong resemblance between the Indian Śākta conception of Śakti and the Śākta ritual of the followers of *bāmācāra* and *kulācāra*, who practised ceremonial promiscuity, on the one hand, and the Semitic conception of Ashtart (Astarte), the Egyptian conception of Isis, and the Phrygian conception of Cybele on the other, it may be assumed that Śāktism arose in India under the same social conditions as those under which Astarte was conceived in Syria, Cybele in Asia Minor, and Isis in Egypt.

* *Ibid.* VI, p. 396a.

Regarding the origin of Astarte Professor Paton writes:—

"There is a large body of evidence to show that the Semites before their separation passed through a matriarchal stage of society. The tribe was a group of people inhabiting a particular oasis in the Arabian desert. It was made up of mothers and their brothers and children. The fathers were men of other tribes, dwelling in other oasis, who contracted only temporary unions with the mothers. Descent was traced through the mother, and she was the head of the clan in peace and in war. In such a society the chief deity of the tribe must have been conceived as a counterpart of the human matriarch. Male divinities might exist and be known as 'maternal uncle' but they would not be called 'father,' and would play so unimportant a part that they would survive only sporadically in later religion. This view is confirmed by the fact that all those traits which are oldest and most permanent in the character of Ashtart-Ishtar are those which for other reasons we must predicate of the ancient Semitic tribal mother." *

In Asia Minor, the home of the cult of the Great Mother Cybele, matriarchate, mother-right or mother-kin, a social system which traces descent and transmits property through women and not through men, "lingered in Lycia down to historical period; and we may conjecture that in former

* *Ibid.* II. p. 115b.

times it was widely spread through Asia Minor.''* In Egypt, the home of Isis, "the archaic system of mother-kin, with its perference for women over men in matters of property and inheritance, lasted down to Roman times.''† To this is traced another strange Egyptian custom, the marriage of full brothers with full sisters. "Such unions were the rule, not the exception, in ancient Egypt, and they continued to form the majority of marriages long after the Romans had obtained a firm footing in the country.'' ‡ The explanation of this custom offered by the Egyptologists and anthropologists is thus summed up by Sir James Frazer:—

"It would be doubtless a mistake to treat these marriages as a relic of savagery, as a survival of a tribal communism which knew no bar to the intercourse of the sexes. For such a theory would not explain why union with a sister was not only allowed, but preferred to all others. The true motive of that preference was most probably the wish of brothers to obtain for their own use the family property, which belonged of right to their sisters, and which otherwise they would have seen in the enjoyment of strangers, the husbands of their sisters .... This simple and perfectly effective expedient for keeping the property in the family most probably explains the custom of brother and sister marriage in Egypt.'' ‡

* Frazer's *Adonis Attis Osiris*. London, 1907, pp. 394-395.
† *Ibid.*, p. 395. ‡ *Ibid.*, p. 397.

The Śākta conception of the Devī as Ādyā Śākti 'the primordial energy' and Jagadambā, 'the mother of the universe' also very probably arose in a society where matriarchate or mother-kin was prevalent. The most important question in connection with Śāktism is, among what division of the Indian people did it originate? A Sanskrit stanza in *anustup* metre recited by the Śākta Paṇḍits of Bengal affords the traditional answer to this question. In this stanza we are told:—"The cult (*vidyā*) was revealed in Gauḍa (Bengal), popularised (*prabalīkṛtā*, lit. 'strengthened') by the Maithilas, it here and there prevails in Mahārāṣṭra, and has disappeared in Gujarat."* Bengal is still the stronghold of Śāktism, and there are Śāktas in Mithilā (North Bihar), the Maraṭhā country and Gujarāt. Here, with the questionable exception of Mithilā, all other countries belong to the Outer Indo-Aryan belt. Did Śāktism then originate among the Indo-Aryans of the Outer countries? If evidences were forthcoming to prove that mother-kin at one time prevailed among them, the traditional view regarding the origin of Śāktism could be accepted as a working hypothesis. An overwhelming majority of the higher caste Hindus of

* "गौड़े प्रकाशिता विद्या मैथिलैः प्रबलीकृता ।
क्वचित् क्वचिन् महाराष्ट्रे गुर्ज्जरे प्रलयं गता ॥"

This stanza has been communicated to me by Pandit Bāmanadāsa Vidyāratna, Principal, Rānī Hemanta Kumārī Sanskrit College, Rajshahi.

Bengal—the Brāhmans, the Kāyasthas, and the Vaidyas—are Śāktas. There is no evidence to show that these castes ever passed through a mother-kin stage in course of their history. But a usage that still survives among some sections of the Marāṭhā Brāhmans indicates the existence of mother-kin among them at one time. Mandlik writes:—"The question of marriage of a man with the daughter of his mother's brother was once considered debatable by some writers. Usage has however sanctioned such marriages amongst the Dekkani Brāhmans of various denominations. Thus among various sections of the Deśastha-Brāhmans and among the Karhādas such connections are very frequent; and it is said that if a man can get such a bride, he will often have no other.'' * The marrying of maternal uncle's daughter is an old custom. Baudhāyana refers to it in his *Dharma-sūtra*. Kumārila (who flourished in the seventh century A.D.) writes in his *Tantravārtika*: "The people of the south are happy when they get a chance of marrying the daughter of their maternal uncle." † This custom, called *menarikam* in the Tamil country, is evidently a survival of the mother-kin stage. When property was transmitted through woman a man would be naturally happy to see his daughter married to his sister's son, the heir to the family property. The Mahā-

* Rao Saheb V. N. Mandlik's *Hindu Law or Mayukha, Yājñavalkya*, Bombay, 1880, p. 415.

† English Trans., p. 184.

bhārata contains positive evidence of the prevalence of mother-kin among one division of the Outlandic Indo-Aryan folk, the Āraṭṭa-Vāhīkas. In Book VIII, 45. 13, we are told, "O Salya, for this reason among the Āraṭṭas the nephews and not the sons inherit the property." * In the *Ambaṭṭha Sutta* and the *Mahāvastu Avadāna* we are told that the Ikṣvāku princes, who were banished by their father and took shelter on the slope of the Himalayas, and from whom the Sākyas traced their descent, married their own sisters in order to maintain the purity of their line. Dr. D. B. Spooner, in his recently published paper on *The Zoroastrian Period of Indian History*, argues that this indicates the Zoroastrian or Magian affinities of the Śākyas, for the next-of-kin marriage was one of the points insisted by Zoroaster, and his patron Vishtasp married his sister Hutos.† Both the Buddhist and the Brāhmanic (Purānic) authorities agree in tracing the descent of the Śākyas from the Ikṣvākus of Kośala. The name of Ikṣvāku occurs in the Ṛgveda and there is evidence to show that the Ikṣvāku line was originally a line of princes of Purus.‡ Therefore an un-Vedic custom like sister-marriage can not be ascribed to the Śākyas. But the legend indicates that the men among whom it grew up, presumably the Buddhist monks of Eastern India, were

* तस्मात्तेषां भागहरा भागिनेया न सूनवः ।

† *Journal of the Royal Asiatic Society*, 1915, p. 440.

‡ *Vedic Index*, I, p. 75.

familiar with the custom. In the *Dasarathajātaka* Sitā is represented as the sister as well as the wife of Rāma, son of Dasaratha of the Ikṣvāku line. The *Rāmāyana*, the kernel of which can not be later in date than the *Dasarathajātaka*, leaves no doubt about the fact that the story of sister-marriage on the part of Rāma was an invention of the Buddhist author or authors of the Jātaka. But probably sister-marriage was at one time practised in Magadha, the early centre of Buddhism. According to the Ceylonese *Mahāvaṃsa*, it was at one time practised in Bengal. In this work we are told (VI. 36) that Sihabāhu, King of Vaṅga and Rāḍhā (Lāḷa), married his sister Sihasīvalī. These Buddhist stories of sister-marriage indicate the existence of mother-kin in Eastern India. From these evidences we may infer that mother-kin was at one time universal among the Indo-Aryans of the Outer belt and led to the growth of Śāktism among them. Mother-kin still prevails among certain Malayāli-castes of Malabar and was evidently universal among the Draviḍas at one time; and so it may be argued that Śāktism might as well have originated among the Dravidas and was borrowed from them by their Indo-Aryan neighbours. One strong objection to this view is the absence of Śāktism among the Tamils. The Draviḍas very probably fell under the influence of Vedic culture before they had advanced to the monotheistic stage of spiritual development independently.

Dr. Spooner, in the above-mentioned paper, traces the origin of the conception Śakti to a Persian (Magian) origin. He writes:—"And is not the great Ishtar, perhaps the most popular divinity among the Persians, peculiarly associated with the Asuras or Dānavas? Witness the compounds *asuraguru*, 'teachers of the Asuras' and '*dānavapūjitā*,' 'worshipped by the Dānavas,' both of which are Sanskrit names for Venus, well-attested." *

Bhagdatta, King of Prāgjyotiṣa [Kāmarupa], is called *Yavana* and *asura* in the Mahābhārata. From this Dr. Spooner derives the "undoubted truth that Bhagadatta was a Persian, and Prāgjyotiṣa a Magian settlement" and proceeds:—"Let us remember further that the most popular of goddesses among these Persians was the goddess Ishtar, whose peculiar associations with the Magians in India has been noted above (p. 81). Are not the Tāntrik system and the Śākta cult a development on Indian soil of the sympathetic magic rites in connection with this goddess as the symbol of fertility which Jastrow tells of? This unravels for us the whole mystery to which Wilson calls attention [i.e., 'that Assam, or at least the north-east of Bengal, seems to have been, in a great degree, the source from which the Tāntrik and Śākta corruptions of the Religion of the Vedas and Purāṇas proceeded'], and furthermore explains the 'curious fact' mentioned to me by

* *Journal of the Royal Asiatic Society*, 1915, p. 81.

Mahāmahopādhyāya Haraprasād Shāstrī, that, according to his own researches, the Śākadvīpin Brāhmans were specially associated with this cult. This is a valuable bit of confirmatory evidence, for which I am much obliged to the Mahāmahopādhyāya.'' *

The first point to be noted in this connection is that Ishtar was not a Persian or Magian, but a Babylonian, divinity, and she became Persian by her identification with the truly Persian divinity Anāhita. "After the conquest of Elam by the Indo-European Medes and Persians the old goddess [Innana of Erech] was identified with Anāhita, and under this name enjoyed extensive homage.'' † Cumont's description of the Avestic Anāhita is reproduced here:—

"Ardvī Surā Anāhita, that is, undoubtedly, 'the high, powerful, immaculate one' is a goddess of fertilising waters, and more particularly of a supernatural spring, located in the region of stars, from which all the rivers of the world flow (Darmasteter). The fertility which the divine water caused in the earth was extended to the animal kingdom, and, according to the Avesta, Anāhita purifies the seed of males and the womb and milk of females' (*Vendīdād*, VII, 16; *Yašt* V, 5), and is invoked by marriageable girls, and by women at the time of child-birth (*Yašt* V). At the same time she is thought of as a goddess of

---

* *Ibid.*, p. 435.

† *Encyclopædia of Religion and Ethics*, VII, p. 433a.

war, who rides in a chariot drawn by four white horses (*Yaśt* V, 11-13), which are wind, rain, cloud, and hail (*Yaśt*. v, 120), and she bestows victory on the combatants, and gives them sturdy teams and brave companions. The Avestan hymn, after enumerating all the heroes of the past who sacrificed to Anāhita, including Zoroaster, whom she instructed in her worship, concludes with a very exact description of her appearance and her dress (*Yaśt* V, 126 ff.). 'She is a beautiful maiden, powerful and tall, her girdle fastened high, wrapped in a gold-embroidered cloak, wearing earrings, a necklace, and a crown of gold, and adorned with thirty otter skins.'' *

The cult of Anāhita spread from Iran to the west, ''but she was always regarded as the goddess of sacred waters.'' In Iran, ''under the influence of the Chaldeean star-worship, Anāhita had become the planet Venus.'' † But one great fact that distinguishes the Śakti of the Indian Śākta and the Persian Anāhita is that while in the Avestan pantheon Anāhita occupies a position subordinate to Ahura Mazda, in the Sākta pantheon Śakti is above all, the mother of all, the creator even of Brahmā, Viṣṇu and Śiva. The Śakti of the Śākta really resembles the Great Mother Cybele worshipped by the Lydian neighbours of Persians and not the Persian Anāhita.

* *Encyclopædia of Religion and Ethics*, I, p. 414b.

† *Ibid.*, p. 415b.

If Cybele could be conceived by the Lydians independently of Mazdaism, it is not necessary to assume a Mazdayasnian origin of Śakti on the ground of sex. The Hindu divinity who is identified with Venus is not the goddess Durgā but the god Sukrācārya, the preceptor of the Asuras. Dr. Spooner does not indicate the source from which Mahāmahopādhyāya Haraprasād Śāstrī learnt that "the Śāka-dwīpin Brāhmans were specially associated with this [Śākta] cult." The Śakadvīpin Brāhmans in Bengal are represented by the Gaṇakas. According to the *Vṛhaddharmapurāṇ* (*Uttarakhanda*, XIII, 52) the Gaṇaka was born of Śākadvīpī father and Vaiśya mother.* The Gaṇaka Brāhmans of Bengal are specially associated with the worship of the *grahas* or planets and the Brāhmans who are specially associated with Śakti worship are the Rāḍhīya, Vārenda and Vaidika Brāhmans. The authentic history of the Śākadvīpīya, Bhojaka, or Maga Brāhmans, so far as it is known to us, shows that they have ever been specially associated with the worship of the sun and stars. Varāhamihira, who died in A.D. 587, says in his *Bṛhatsaṃhitā* (60, 19), that the installation and consecration of the images and temples of the sun should be caused to be made by the Magas. Bāṇa in his *Harśacarita* (Chap. IV) introduces us to an astrologer

* शाकद्वीपात् सुपर्णेन चानीता यः स देवलः ।
शाकद्वीपी द्विजः सोऽभूद्विभुवे धरणीतले ।
देवलाद्गणको जातो वैश्यायां वाद्दकोऽपि च ॥

called Tāraka the Bhojaka (Maga) who is thus described, "Hundreds and hundreds of times he had shown supernatural insight by announcing facts beyond the ken of man, a calculator, deeply read in all the treatises on astronomy, extolled and liked among all astrologers, endowed with the knowledge of three times."* In the Deo-Baranak inscription of Jīvitagupta II of Magadha, who flourished in the eighth century A.D., recorded with the object of continuing the grant of a village to the Sun under the name of Varuṇavāsin, several generations of Bhojakas are referred to; *viz.* Bhojaka Sūryamitra, who was evidently patronised by Bālāditya (*c.* A.D. 485 to 535), Bhojaka Haṃsamitra patronised by the Maukhari King Sarvavarman (*c.* A.D. 575 to 600), Bhojaka Ṛṣimitra patronised by king Avantivarman, and Bhojaka Durdharamitra, who obtained the assent of Jīvitagupta II to the enjoyment of the village.†

* Cowell and Thomas, English translation, pp. 109, 110; text (Bombay, 1912), p. 128.

† Fleet's *Gupta Inscriptions*, pp. 213-218.

CHAPTER V.

RACE AND CASTE—THE BRĀHMANS OF THE OUTER COUNTRIES.

Religion is universal and universal also is the minister of religion or priest. But hereditary priesthood independent of and claiming superiority to the king is a peculiarly Indian institution. Castes making up the Hindu laity are known by different names in different ethnic regions of India, and are organised on different models. But Hindu priests all over India are known by the same designation, Brāhman, and all Indian Brāhmans trace their descent from the same Ṛṣis first known from the Ṛgveda—the eight founders of the Brāhmanic *gotras*, viz., Viśvāmitra, Jamadagni, Bharadvāja, Gotama, Atri, Vasiṣṭha, Kaśyapa, Agastya, and others.* This Brāhmanic claim to Midlandic origin offers a difficulty to the ethnic classification of Indo-Aryans proposed in Chapter II. Physically the Brāhmans of the Outer countries—of Gujarat, of the Marāṭhā country, and of Orissa and Bengal—are more closely related to their non-Brāhman neighbours than to the Brāhmans of the Midland. The head form of the Outlandic Brāhman does not support his claim to be the pure-blooded descendant of the Midlandic Vedic Ṛṣis, but indicates his close physical rela-

* See above, p. 19.

tionship to his non-Brāhman neighbours classed as Śūdras and *antyājas* or outcastes. The wide difference in the head form of the Kānvakubjīya Brāhmans of the United Provinces and the Maithila Brāhmans of Bihar on the one hand, and the Nāgar Brāhmans of Gujarat and the Rāḍhīya, Vārendra, and Vaidika Brāhmans of Bengal on the other, cannot be explained by miscegenation alone, but indicates that the Brāhmans of the Outer countries are at base Outlandic in stock, and have not absorbed Midlandic elements in larger proportions than their non-Brāhman clients (*yajmāna*). This may perhaps lead some to doubt the value of the head form as indicated by the cephalic index as a test of race. But there are not wanting traditions and legends that confirm the data of cephalometric measurements, whereas traditions and legends pointing to the contrary view seem to be baseless.

Among the Outer countries inhabited by men of mixed origin according to Baudhāyana, Bihar, comprising the ancient Videha, Aṅga and Magadha, now contains a population wherein the Midlandic elements predominate.* This is partly due to the mingling of the descendants of those invaders from the holy land watered by the Sarsvatī who, according to the legend of Māthava, the Videgha, narrated in the Satapatha Brāhmaṇa,† settled in and Brāhmanised Videha, with the natives of Magadha and Aṅga, and partly to a larger influx of immigrants from the Midland

* See above, p. 60. † See above, pp. 51—52.

later on than was possible elsewhere. The Maithila Brāhmans of Bihar evidently represent the invaders from the region of the Sarsvatī who Brāhmanised Videha in the Vedic period, and the Kanaujia Brāhmans and Rājputs of Bihar represent later immigrants But even in Bihar, which is now ethnographically only a province of the Midland, it is yet possible to recognise the representatives of those Brāhmans or *brahmabandhus* of Magadha * who were originally the priests of the primitive Vrātya or un-Vedic cults of Magadha.

One such group of Bihāri Brāhmans are the Gayāwals of Gayā. In the *Gayāmāhātmya* of the *Vāyupurāṇa* (112, 1-6) we are told that when at the end of the great sacrifice performed by King Gaya the gods requested him to ask for a boon, Gaya prayed, "Let those Brāhmans who were cursed by Brahmā in days of yore be purified and worshipped in sacrifice, and let this city be called Gayā after my name and become [as holy as] the city of Brahmā." † The story of

* See above, p. 39.

† यज्ञं चक्रे गयो राजा बह्वन्नं बहुदक्षिणम् ।
यत्र द्रव्यसमूहानां संख्या कर्तुं न शक्यते ॥
सिकता वा यथा लोके यथा वा दिवि तारकाः ।
तथा रत्नसुवर्णाद्यैरसंख्यातास्तु दक्षिणाः ॥
नैवेह पूर्वे ये केचिन्न करिष्यन्ति चापरे ।
प्रशंसन्ति द्विजास्तुष्टा देवी देवी सुपूजिताः ॥
गयं विष्ण्वादय स्तुष्टा वरं ब्रूहीति चाब्रुवन् ।
गयस्तान् प्रार्थयामास अभिशप्ताश्च ये पुरा ॥

the great sacrifice performed by the royal sage (*rājarṣi*) Gaya, son of Amurtarayas, in the vicinity of the *akṣaya* (immortal) Vata (Ficus Indica) and the Gayaśira hill, is also referred to in the *Mahābhārata* (III. 95).

Another Bihar caste in which we may recognise the representatives of the primitive Brāhmans of Bihar are the Bābhans or Bhuiñhār Brāhmans. According to the Census returns of 1901 Bābhans in Bihar (1,108,438) exceeded in number all sub-castes of Brāhmans put together (1,094,500). Bābhan is peculiarly a Bihar caste. In the United Provinces Bābhans numbered only 205,951 in 1901. MM. H. P. Sāstrī has called attention to the fact that the term *bābhan* occurs in the inscription of Asoka "as a corruption of the word *brāhmaṇa*" * In the Manserha and the Shahbazgarhī versions of the Rock Edicts of Asoka Brāhmaṇa is written as *Brahmaṇa*, and in the Girnar version as *Bāmhana* with the exception of Edict IV. wherein the Sanskrit form *Brāhmaṇa* is retained. In all other versions of the Rock Edicts that are written in a dialect—the old Māgadhī Prākṛt—that differs from both the divergent dialects of Girnar and Shahbazgarhī, two alternative forms, *Baṃbhana* and *Bābhana*,

---

ब्रह्मणा वै द्विजाः पूताः भवन्तु क्रतुपूजिताः ।
गया पुरीति सन्नाम्ना ख्याता ब्रह्मपुरी यथा ॥
एवमस्तु वरं दत्त्वा ततश्चान्तर्दधुः सुराः ।
गयश्च भोगं सम्भोग्य विष्णुलोकं परं ययौ ॥

* *Journal of the Asiatic Society of Bengal*, 1902, Part I, p. 61.

are met with. *Baṃbhana* is uniformly used in the Kalsi version of the edicts. *Baṃbhana* is used twice (III and IV) and *Bābhana* thrice in the Dhauli version, and both the forms are met with in the Jagauda version as far as it has been read. *Bābhana* also occurs in the Delhi-Sivalik Pillar Edict VII$_2$. *Baṃbhana* is evidently the same as *Bābhana* with *ā* shortened and nasalised in accordance with the phonology of a sub-dialect. In the spoken language of Western Bengal, Brāhman is called *Bāmun* and in that of Eastern Bengal, *Bāman*. We may, therefore, conclude that in the dialect spoken in Magadha in the third century B.C. Brāhmans were called *Bābhans*, and the modern Bābhans are the representatives of the ancient local Bābhans who have been deprived of their priestly functions by the Brāhman immigrants from the Midland. MM. H. P. Sāstrī holds, "that the Bābhans were Brāhman-Buddhists who lost their caste and position in Hindu society." But in the Rock Edicts of Asoka the *Bābhana* (and its equivalents, *Bamhana* retained in the later literary Prākṛts, and *Bramaṇa*, of Girnar and the north-western versions respectively) is mentioned side by side with the Samana or Śramaṇa. There is nothing in the Edicts to show that the Bābhans or Brāhmans of Magadha of the time of Aśoka were all Buddhists. The Aśoka of the Edicts is not an orthodox Buddhist himself, for the goal that he holds out to his subjects who are commanded to follow his sacred law (*dhamma*) is not nirvāna but paradise. If the modern Bābhans were the representatives of the Buddhist Brāhmans of old then we should have found them not only in Bihar but also in Bengal and other parts of India where Buddhism lingered as long. The indigenous Brāhmans of Magadha were called Bābhans probably because they spoke Prākṛt and were distinguished from the Sanskrit-speaking Brāhman immigrants from the Madhyadeśa by their Prākṛt name. We do not hear of Bābhans elsewhere, because elsewhere in the Outer countries there had never been such a large influx of Brāhmans from the Madhaydeśa as in Bihar. The Brāhmans of the other Outer countries—of Bengal, Orissa, the Deccan and Gujarat—are mostly Bābhans in blood, that is to say, descendants of the native Prākṛt-speaking primitive priests, though known by the Sanskrit form of the name.

Quite opposed to this view of the origin of the Outlandic Brāhmans are the evidences furnished by the *Kulapañjikās* or the genealogical works of the Rāḍhīya, Vārendra and Pāścatya Vaidika Brāhmans of Bengal that represent them as pure-blooded descendants of immigrants from the Madhyadeśa. All the Rāḍhīya and the Vārendra Brāhmans be'ong to five *gotras* or clans tracing their descent from the following five Ṛṣis, *viz.*, Sāṇdilya, Kaśyapa, Bharadvāja, Vatsa and Sāvarṇa. The genealogists, not content with the remote connection with the Brāhmans of the Madhyadeśa indicated by the names of these Ṛṣi ancestors, further assert that all the Rāḍhīya and Vārendra Brāhmans of Bengal making up nearly 80 per cent of the total Brāhman population are the descendants of five Brāhmans belonging to the five above-named gotras who came from Kanauj to Bengal with their wives on the invitation of a king named Ādiśūra, thirty to thirty-five generations before. Epigraphical evidences bear witness to the existence of a Śūra line of kings in Southern Bengal in the eleventh century A.D., and evidences are not also wanting to show that in those days Brāhmans belonging to one or other of these gotras were freely migrating to Bengal from the Madhyadeśa of which the city of Kanauj or Kānyakubja was then the capital. Thus the donee of the Belāba grant of Bhojavarman issued from Vikramapura, a Brāhman named Rāmadevaśarman, belonging to Sāvarṇa *gotra*, and a student of the Kāṇva recension of the White Yajurveda, is described as "the great-grandson of Pitāmbara-devaśarman, a native of Siddhalagrāma in Uttara-Rādhā who came from Madhya-deśa (*madhyadeśa-vinirgata*)." * So of course it is quite possible that a king named Ādiśūra, from whom, according to the Vārendra genealogists, Ballālasena (about A.D. 1150-1169) is said to have been ninth in descent through his mother Vilāsadevī, might have imported Brahmans from Kanauj, then the capital of the Gurjjara Pratihāra kingdom, for performing certain Vedic rites. In an unpublished grant of the 33rd year of King

* *Epigraphia Indica*, Vol. XII, p. 39.

Vijayasena issued from Vikramapura it is said that his chief queen, Vilāsadevī, the mother of the heir-apparent, Ballālasena, came of the Sūra family. But the story of the descent of all the Rāḍhīya and Vārendra Brahmans from five immigrants from Kanauj imported by Adiśūra appears to be a much later invention. It finds no place in the genealogical tables that were drawn up in the tenth, eleventh, twelfth and even fifteenth centuries. The earliest genealogical table of evidently a Vārendra Brāhman family belonging to the Śāṇḍilya *gotra* is embodied in the so-called Badal Pillar inscription of the time of Nārāyaṇapala, still standing in a village called Haragauri in the district of Dinajpur in the Vārendra country. Herein we are told that in Sāṇḍilya's race was Viṣṇu (?), in his lineage Vīradeva, in his family Pāñcāla ; from him was born Garga, the minister of Dharma, or Dharmapāla, "the regent of the east." Garga's son was Darbhapāṇi, 'distinguished by his knowledge of the four Vedas', who was the minister of Devapāla. Darbhapāṇi's son was Someśvara, from whom was born Kedāramiśra who filled "the circle of the quarters with the abundant (sacrificial) fires." "At the sacrifice of him, the image of Bṛhaspati, the illustrious Prince Śūrapāla, having destroyed the forces of his enemies, often attended of his own accord, like Indra himself, the destroyer of the demon Vala ; and ever desirous of the welfare of the earth, girt by the several oceans, he there with bent head received the pure water, his soul being bathed in the water of faith." Kedāramiśra's son was Guravamiśra, the minister of King Nārāyaṇapāla, who "expounded the Vedas in books of moral tales, which excited a thrill of joy and showed that he was a born Vālmiki of the Kali age." *

A stone inscription † assigned to the eleventh century discovered at Selimpur in the district of Bogra in the Vārendra country gives the history of a Vārendra Brāhman family belonging to the Bhāradhvāja *gotra*. In this record it is said that a place called Tarkāri, forming a part of Śrāvastī, was the original home of the Brāhmans of the Bhāradvāja gotra. In the Puṇḍra country there was a village called Bālagrāma which was "the ornament of Varendri." Between Bālagrāma and Tarkāri lay Sakatī. Mr. Rādhāgovinda Basāk, who discovered this inscription and has edited and translated it,‡ regards Sakatī as the name of a river and places Śrāvastī of the record within Puṇḍra (Varendrī). In the early Sanskrit literature we meet with two cities called Srāvastī—one founded by Lava, son of Rāma (*Rāmāyaṇa* VII.) and another by Srāvasta in Gauḍadeśa (*Matsya Purāṇa*, XII. 30). Cunningham regarded both the Srāvastīs as identical and identi-

---

* *Epigraphia Indica*, Vol. II, pp. 164-166.

† The stone bearing the inscription has been presented to the Varendra Research Society by Babu Vijayagovinda Basu Chaudhury, Zeminder of Khalsi.

‡ See the Bengali Magazine *Bhāratavarṣa* of 1322, pp. 1044—1055.

fied Gauḍa-deśa with the Gonḍa district of Oudh. But in all other texts and records Gauḍa is applied to Varendra in Bengal or to Bengal as a whole. So it seems more reasonable to identify the Gauḍa of the Purāṇa with Varendra or Bengal, and recognise in the Śrāvastī of Srāvasta an ancient city in Bengal which was separated from Bālagrāma of this record by Sakatī. Brāhmans belonging to the Bhāradvāja gotra migrated from Srāvastī to Bālagrāma, and one family of Bālagrāma again migrated to the neighbouring Sīamva. In this family was born Paśupati. His son was Sāhila; Sāhila's son was Manoratha; Manoratha' son was Sucarita. From Sucarita was born Taponidhi, from Taponidhi Kārttikeya, and from Kārttikeya and his wife Kaliparvva (daughter of Aṅgada, grand-daughter of Ajamiśra, and the great grand-daughter of Viṣṇu belonging to the Kutumbapalli family) was born Prahāsa, who was well-versed in Tarka (the Nyāya philosophy), Tantra, and the Dharmaśāstra or sacred law and caused this inscription to be recorded. It is also said in this record (v. 22) that Prahāsa refused to accept a donation of 900 gold coins and a grant of land yielding one thousand a year from Jayapāla, King of Kāmarupa.

A record of the twelfth century, the Bhuvaneśvara inscription of Bhavadeva, surnamed Bālabalabhībhujaṅga (the paramour or lord of Bālabalabhī) gives the genealogy of a Rāḍhīya Brāhman family belonging to Sāvarṇa gotra and Siddhalagrāma whither Pitāmbara, the great grandfather, as we have already seen, of the donee of Bhojavarman's grant, also belonging to the Sāvarṇa gotra, migrated from the Madhyadeṣa. The contents of this inscription is thus summed up by Keilhorn :—

"Of the villages granted to, and the homes of, Brāhmans learned in the Vedas who are born in the family of the sage Sāvarṇa, a hundred may adorn the land of Aryāvarta; but foremost among all is Siddhala which is the ornament of the country of Rāḍhā. At that village prospered a family to which belonged a certain Bhavadeva [I] whose elder and younger brothers were Mahādeva and Attahāsa. He, to whom the King of Gauḍa granted the village of Hastinībhītta, had eight sons, the chief (or eldest) of whom was Rathāṅga. From Rathāṅga sprang Atyaṅga; and his son was Budha, surnamed Sphurita. From him Ādideva was born, who became minister of peace and war of the King of Vaṅga. His son was Govardhana, distinguished as a warrior and a scholar. He married Sāṅgokā, the daughter of a Bandyaghatīya Brāhman and begat on her the person in whose honour this *praśasti* was composed, Bhavadeva [II], whom the poet glorifies as a divine being, while he indicates his worldly position by telling us that, aided by his council (the king) Harivarmadeva long exercised the government, and that his policy rendered prosperous the reign of the king's son also."*

* *Epigraphia Indica*, Vol. VI, p. 205.

One section of the Vārendra Brāhmans belonging to the Kāśyapa gotra are known as *Karañjagāiñ* from a village named Karañja. Caturbhuja, who composed his Sanskrit poem, the *Haricaritam*, at Rāmakeli in the district of Maldah in the Varendra country in Śakavarṣa 1415 (A.D. 1493), was a Brāhman of the Karañjagāiñ. In the concluding stanzas of the *Haricaritam* Caturbhuja gives this account of his ancestors. There was a village in Varendrī named Karañja where many learned Brāhmans lived. Svarṇarekha, the foremost man among the Brāhmans, obtained the whole of that village as a grant from King Dharmapāla. Bhundu was born in his family. Bhundu's son was Divākara, "the Sun of the Kāśyapa clan" (*Kāśypagotrabhāskara*). In his line was born Nityānanda Kavīndra ('king of poets'), who compiled the *Smṛtikaumudī*. From Nityānanda was born Śivadāsa whose youngest brother was the poet Caturbhuja, the author of *Haricaritam*.* We know of only one Dharmapāla who ever ruled over Varendra. This was the second king of the Pāla dynasty who flourished in the first half of the ninth century A.D. Attempts have been made by some Bengali writers to identify the Dharmapāla named by Caturbhuja with a Dharmapāla who, according to tradition, reigned in Kāmarupa on the one hand, and with Dharmapāla of Daṇḍabhukti, who, according to the Tirumalai rock inscription

* M.M. H. P. Śāstrī's *A Catalogue of Palm-leaf and selected Paper MSS. in the Darbar Library, Nepal*, pp. 134-135.

of King Rajendra Chola I, "was destroyed in a hot battle" by that Chola conqueror between A D. 1020 and 1024.* This Dharmapāla of Daṇḍabhukti was evidently a vassal of King Mahipāla I of the Pāla dynasty who recovered Varendra from a usurper of the Kamboja family. So the grant of a village in Varendra on the part of Dharmapāla of Daṅḍabhukti is inconceivable. The history of Varendra from the time of Dharmapāla, the second King of the Pāla dynasty, to the invasion of Muhammad Bakhtiyar (from about A.D. 800 to 1198) is too well-known from contemporary sources to admit of the foisting of a second Dharmapāla within this epoch. It may be said that Caturbhuja who wrote more than six centuries after Dharmapāla cannot be accepted as an authority for the history of Dharmapāla's time. But it is probable that Caturbhuja derived his information that his ancestor Svarṇarekha obtained the grant of Karañja-grāma from Dharmapāla either from the copper-plate grant itself or from a genuine family tradition based on the deed. In any case, the absence of the name Suṣeṇa, who, according to the genealogical works, was the Brāhman belonging to the Kāśyapa-gotra who is said to have been imported by Ādisūra from Kanauj, and to whom every Vārendra Brāhman of Kāśyapa gotra of our day traces his descent, in the family history of a learned Brāhman of the Kāśyapa-gotra and Karañjagāiñ written by himself, shows that

* *Epigraphia Indica*, IX, pp. 232-233.

the story of Suṣeṇa's coming was unknown in A.D. 1494 when Caturbhuja wrote, and was invented by the genealogists later on.

Not only does Suṣeṇa find no mention in the history of the Kāśyapá-gotrīya Brāhmans of Karañjagāiñ written by Caturbhuja, but the man who first lived in Karañja is represented as the great-great-grandson of a Svarṇarekha in the works of the genealogists. The genealogy of the Kāśyapa section of the Vārendra Brāhmans as given in these works is thus reproduced by the author of the Bengali work, *Gauḍe Brāhman* *—

1. Suṣeṇa (came from Kanauj on the invitation of Ādiśūra).

|

2. Brahmā Ojha.

|

3. Dakṣa.

|

4. Pitāmbar.

|

5. Hiraṇyagarbha.

|

6. Vedagarbha.

|

7. Jigni Mahāmuni.

|

8. Svarṇarekha (in his time King Ballālasena is said to have divided the Brāhmans into Rāḍhīya and Vārendra subcastes and he was included in the latter group).

|

* *Gauḍe Brāhman* by Mahimā Candra Majumdar, second edition.

9. Sindhu Ojhā.

10. Kratu (founder of the Bhāduri family, created Kulin by Ballālasena).

10. Maitra (founder of the Maitreya family, created Kulin by Ballālasena).

11. Saṃkarṣaṇa.

12. Bhallukācārya.

13. Divākara (lived in Karañja and became the founder of the Karañjagāīn).

It may be noted in this connection that the well-known Bengali historian Mr. Akṣay Kumar Maitra, who first pointed out the wide divergence between the genealogy of the Vārendra Brāhmans belonging to Kaśyapa-gotra as given in the Haricaritam of Caturbhuja on the one hand, and that of the *Kulapañjikās* of the genealogists on the other, is himself a *kulin* (noble) Brāhman of the same gotra.*

One other obstacle to the credibility of the

* For further discussions of the historical value of the *Kulapañjikās*, the reader is referred to the author's articles 'Ādisūra' in the Bengali Magazine *Sāhitya* of 1321, pp. 751-759, and '*Bāṅgālār itihāser upādān*' in *Bhāratī of* 1322, pp. 941-952. The *Kulapañjikās* of the Pāścatya Vaidik Brāhmans are as valueless for the history of origins. See Mr. R. D, Banerji's *Bāṅgālār itihās*, pp. 135-131, and Mr. S. Kumār's article 'Earliest seat of the Senas,' in the *Indian Antiquary*, XLIV, pp. 270-274.

stories of the origin of the Bengali Brāhmans as given in the genealogical works of the Rāḍhīyas and Vārendras, is that it involves the assumption of the practical absence of Brāhmans in Bengal 30 to 35 generations, or say, eight to ten centuries, before. According to the genealogists of the Rāḍhīyas there were seven hundred Brāhman families in Bengal at the time of the coming of the five Brāhmans from Kanauj. But now-a-days representatives of the seven hundred families are nowhere to be met with, whereas the descendants of the five immigrants fill the whole country. Copper-plate grants, such as the Dhanaidaha grant of the time of the Emperor Kumaragupta I of A.D. 432,* a set of five grants of the time of Budhagupta and Kumara-gupta II recently discovered in the district of Dinajpur,† and the Faridpur grants of the time of Dharmāditya, Gopacandra and Samācāradeva,‡ bear witness to the fact that there were Brāhmans in Bengal well-versed in the Vedas in the fifth and the sixth centuries. The inclusion of the Karatoyā, the Lauhitya (Brahmaputra), and the place where the Ganges falls into the sea, among the *tīrthas* or holy places and rivers in the Mahābhārata (III. 85. 2—4), shows that Bengal was recognised as a seat of Brāhmanism even in the time of the composition of this part

* *Journal of the Asiatic Society of Bengal*, 1910.

† These plates have been sent to the Vārendra Research Society by Mr. Ezekiel, the Collector of Dinajpur, and are now being deciphered by Mr. Rādhāgovinda Basāk.

‡ *Indian Antiquary*, 1910, pp. 193-216.

of the epic, for there could not have been Brāhmanical *tīrthās* without a Brāhman population in the neighbourhood.

A legend narrated in the Vāyupurāṇa (104) giving a list of the *tīrthas* or holy places shows that at the time of the composition of this text Pauṇḍravardhana, the ancient capital of Puṇḍra or Varendra, was a well-known centre of orthodox Brāhmanism. Once upon a time doubts arose in the mind of Vyāsa, son of Satyavatī, as regards the meaning of a Vedic text. He then went to a cave of the Mount Meru to perform austerities in order to remove his doubts. After a lapse of three hundred years spent in the performance of severe penances, the four Vedas, crowned with matted hair, holding bunches of *kuśa* grass, and with deer-skin hanging over their shoulders, appeared before Vyāsa (67—70). Then—

"He found Mathurā, where Bhagavān Hari (Viṣṇu) himself incarnated, in their lotus-like hearts; Kāśī resembling Māyā (illusion) in a receptacle between the eye-brows; Kāñcī in the organ of generation; Avantī in the navel; Dwārakā in the throat; Prayāga in the breath of life; the rivers Gangā and Yamunā on their left and right; the Sarasvatī herself in the middle; Gayā in the face; the good place Prabhāsa between the jaw and the neck; the hermitage of Badarī in the aperture in the crown of the head; the *pīṭhas* Pauṇḍravardhana and Nepāla in the two eyes; the *pīṭha* called Pūrṇagiri on the forehead; Mathurā-*pīṭha* in the neck; Kāñcī-*pīṭha* in the loin; Jālaṇdhara-

pīṭha on the breast ; Bhṛgu-*pīṭha* in the ear ; and Ayodhyā in the nostril. Brāhmya (the cult of Brahmā) was in the aperture of the crown of their head, Śaiva (cult) in the parting of the hair, Śākta (cult) on the end of the tongue, Vaiṣṇava (cult) in the heart, Saura (cult) in the eyes and Bauddha (cult) was attached to their shadows.'' *

Owing to the existence of Brāhmanic *tīrthas* in the Outer countries the rule forbidding migration to them had thus to be modified:—" He who visits Aṅga, Vaṅga, Kaliṅga, Saurāstra and Magadha except on pilgrimage should be invested with the

---

* " अपश्यन् मथुरामेषां हृदयाम्भोजकल्पिताम् ॥
हरेर्भगवतः साक्षादाविर्भावस्थली हि सा ।
काशीमपश्यद् भ्रूमध्ये मायामाधारसंस्थिताम् ॥
लिङ्गदेशे ततः काञ्चीमवन्तीं नाभिमण्डले ।
कण्ठस्थां द्वारकामेषां प्रयागं प्राणगं तथा ॥
सव्यापसव्ययोस्तेषां गङ्गाऽपि यमुना नदी ।
मध्ये सरस्वती साक्षाद् गयाक्षेत्रं तथानने ॥
हनुग्रीवामध्यगतं प्रभासक्षेत्रमुत्तमम् ।
बदर्याश्रममेतेषां ब्रह्मरन्ध्रे ददर्श ह ॥
पौण्ड्रवर्धननेपालपीठं नयनयोर्युगे ।
पीठं पूर्णगिरिं नाम ललाटे समदृश्यत ॥
कण्ठे च मथुरापीठं काञ्चीपीठं कटिस्थितम् ।
जालंधरं तथा पीठं स्तनदेशेऽप्यदृश्यत ॥
भृगुपीठं कर्णदेशे अयोध्यां नासिकापुटे ।
ब्रह्मरन्ध्रे स्थितं ब्राह्मं शैवं सीमन्तसीमनि ॥
शाक्तं जिह्वाग्रविषयं वैष्णवं हृदयाम्बुजे ।
सौरं चक्षुःप्रदेशस्थं बौद्धच्छायानुसंगतम् ॥ "

Vāyupurāṇa (Ānandāśram Sanskrit Series, No. 49) *Adhyāya*, 104. 79-82.

sacred thread anew.'' * The incredible character of the stories of the genealogical works on the one hand, and the data of cephalometric measurements considered in the light of such injunctions in the Brāhmanic sacred books (*ante*, p. 40) on the other, point to the conclusion that the legend regarding the common origin of the (Bāleya) Brāhmans and the non–Brāhmans of Aṅga, Puṇḍra, Vaṅga, Suhma, and Kaliṅga narrated in the Harivaṃsa and the Purāṇas (*ante*, p. 69) is not baseless.

The legends relating to the origin of some of the important divisions of the Brāhmans of Mahārāṣtra and Gujarat appear to bear direct testimony to their local origin. About the Konkanasthas or Chittapāvans of Konkan we are told, "In the Sahyādri Khaṇḍa of the Skanda Purāṇa, —which bears marks of the composition or interpolation of some Deshastha of Kolhāpura (which city is much praised in it),—they are absurdly enough said to have been made by the Avatāra Paraśurāma (in want of Brāhmans to perform for him a śrāddha) from the *chitā*, or funeral pile, of sixty men, whom he consecrated or endowed with the Brāhmanhood, bestowing on them learning and beauty, and conferring on them fourteen *gotras*, and sixteen *upanāmas* (surnames).'' † Re-

---

* अङ्गवङ्गकलिङ्गेषु सौराष्ट्रे मगधेषु च ।
तीर्थयात्रां विना गच्छन् पुनः संस्कारमर्हति ॥

Quoted by Mitramiśra in the *Vīramitrodaya*.

† John Wilson's *Indian Caste*, Bombay, 1887, Vol. II, p. 19.

garding the Karhāda Brāhmans of Mahārāṣtra, "in the Sahyādri Khaṇḍa, which shows a spirit of violent hostility to them, they are said to have been made by Paraśurāma from camel's bones." * In themselves these legends are valueless and may disclose a spirit of violent hostility on the part of the author. But the absence of any rival tradition purporting to ascribe a nobler origin to the Karhādas and the Konkanasthas shows that they are based on a common belief that these Brāhmans are of local origin and not immigrants from Madhyadeśa.

Mr. Bhimbhai Kirparam in his work on the Hindus of Gujarat (*Bombay Gazetteer*, Vol. IX, Part I) divides the numerous sections of the Gujarati Brāhmans into three groups,—the early original Gujarat Brāhmans, the Brāhmans who migrated to Gujarat in the Middle Ages, and the modern or later immigrants. The first group includes these nine sub-castes :—the Anarvalās, the Bhārgavas, the Sajodras, the Jambus, the Kapils, the Khedavals, the Matālas, and the Nāgars. Of the Anarvalās the author writes, " According to local tradition, Rāma, on his return from the conquest of Ceylon, halted at a place called Pālārvāda in the hills called Bansda, about fifty-five miles south-east of Surat. Determining to hold a sacrifice he required the services of a large body of priests. He searched the country round, and failing to find priests enough collected eighteen

* *Ibid.*, p. 21.

thousand of the hill tribes and made them Brāhmans.'' A very similar legend is narrated in connection with the Sajodras, named after Sajod, a village in the Broach district. "The tradition is that Rāma made them Brāhmans to assist him in the performance of sacrifice and in a small mound near Sajod sacrificial ashes and burnt betelnuts are said still to be found."

No less than four legends are given by Mr. Kirparam in connection with the origin of the Nāgar Brāhmans of Gujarat. Two of them connect the origin of the Nāgar Brāhmans with the marriage of Śiva and Pārvatī. "Brahmā went to officiate [as priest] at Śiva's marriage with Pārvatī. He was smitten with Pārvatī's beauty and being unable to control himself left the marriage booth. Finding that there was nobody to officiate at the ceremony, Śiva threw down six grains of rice and from them arose six Brāhmans. There being no Brāhman girls, Śiva married these newly created Brāhmans to six Nāga girls to fit them to officiate as priests at the ceremony.'' The second legend is but a modification of this one, and the third connects the Nāgar Brāhmans with Śiva's sacrifice when that god was compelled to create a new set of Brāhmans. The fourth legend traces their origin from a Nāg (serpent) who assumed the form of a Brāhman, married a Brāhman girl, and had several children by her. Mr. D. R. Bhandarkar, following Sir George Campbell, holds that the Nāgar Brāhmans of Gujarat, the Gurjar Nāgars of Bulandshahar in the United Provinces, and the

Jāt Nagres come of the same stock and the Nāgar Brāhmans came to Gujarat from the north.* The Gujarātī language now spoken in Gujarat and Mārwārī spoken in Western Rajputana are traced by philologists to a common source called the old Western Rājasthānī which was a modification of the Śaurasena Apabhraṃśa, and this linguistic phenomenon is explained by the ethnological theory that Rājputāna and Gujarat were colonised by the Gurjaras who came from the ancient Sapādalakṣa (comprising the hilly country extending from Chamba on the west to Western Nepal on the east) imposing their language over the whole tract covered by their immigration.† Though the Gurjar invaders of Rājputāna and Gujarat might have imposed their language on the early inhabitants of Gujarat and Rājputāna, it is not possible to admit that they came in such large numbers as to modify the physical features of the natives of these areas in any appreciable degree. The typical Rajputs of Rājputāna are long-headed, and so also are the Sikh Jats and Gujars of the Punjab; ‡ but the Nāgar Brāhmans of Gujarat are broad or medium-headed. So we have as little reason for recognising the Gurjara invaders as an important factor in determining the physical type

* *Indian Antiquary*, Vol. XL, pp. 33-34.

† *Ibid.*, Vol. XLIII, pp. 22, and 164-166.

‡ Thirteen Gujars of the Punjab measured under the supervision of Sir Herbert Risley gave an average cephalic index of 72·4 and a maximum index of 78 and a minimum of 68; 80 Sikh Jats yielded—average 72·7, maximum 81, minimum 66.

of Western India as we have for the Śakas and Kushans.

Most of the other sections of the early group of Gujarāt Brāhmans are recognised as immigrants, not from the Madhyadeśa in the north, but from the south. "According to a legend the Motala Brāhmans were brought into Gujarat by Hanumāna from Kolhāpur." The Jambu and the Kapil Brāhmans are regarded as akin to the Motalas who came to Gujarat from the Deccan at about the same time. The Khedavals are believed to be immigrants from Sriraṅgam in Mysore. It was probably owing to a suspicion regarding their origin that it was enjoined that the Brāhmans of the Outer countries should not be fed at the funeral ceremony. Hemādri, who flourished in the Deccan in the thirteenth century, quotes this text from the *Saurapurāṇa* in his *Śrāddhakalpa*: "The Brāhmans of Aṅga, Vaṅga, Kaliṅga, Saurāṣṭra, Gurjara, Ābbīra, Koṅkaṇa, Draviḍa, Dakṣināpatha, Avantī, and Magadha should be avoided."* The Ābhīras are a class of Brāhmans of Maharāṣtra who are the priests of Ābhīra or Āhir herdsmen and cultivators and are probably themselves of Ābhīra origin. The broad, depressed noses of the Brāhmans of Southern India indicate that they are mainly Dravidian in blood like their neighbours.

* अङ्गवङ्गकलिङ्गांश्च सौराष्ट्रान् गुर्ज्जरांस्तथा ।
आभीरान् कौङ्कणांश्चैव द्राविड़ान् दक्षिणापथान् ।
आवन्त्यान् मागधांश्चैव ब्राह्मणांस्तु विवर्ज्जयेत् ॥
Chaturvargacintāmaṇi, *Śrāddhakalpa* (Bib. Ind.)

Among the non-Brāhman castes of the Outer countries, five exogamous sub-sections of the Vaṅgaja and the Dakṣiṇarāḍhīya Kāyasthas of Bengal, *viz.*, the Boses, Ghoṣes, Guhas, Mitras and Dattas, are said to be the descendants of five Śūdra attendants who accompanied the five Brāhman immigrants from Kanauj imported by Ādiśūra. It is also said that the ancestors of the Boses, Ghoṣes, Guhas and Mitras, when questioned by King Ādiśūra, admitted that they were the servants of the Brāhmans, but Puruśottam Datta is said to have declared, "Sir, listen to me; Datta is not the servant of anybody; he has only accompanied (the five Brāhmans); this is to be known about him."* The King, offended at the arrogance shown by this speech, deprived him of his claim to the noble rank (*kaulīnya*). The social life of the Vaṅgaja and Dakṣiṇarāḍhīya Kāyasthas of Bengal is still guided by an unquestioned faith in this story. But it is as baseless as the story of the descent of all the Rāḍhīya and Vārendra Brāhmans from the five Brāhmans of Kanauj who came to Bengal on the invitation of Ādiśūra of which it is but an appanage. There are two very strong reasons for disbelieving this story of the origin of these five sub-sections of the Kāyastha caste as told in the genealogical works. The Vārendra and Rāḍhīya Brāhmans of our day are mostly thirty to thirty-five generations re-

* দত্ত কারো ভৃত্য নয় শুন মহাশয়.
সঙ্গে আসিয়াছে মাত্র এই পরিচয়।

moved from the five Brāhmans who originally came from Kanauj, whereas the present generation of Boses, Ghoṣes, Guhas, Mitras and Dattas are mostly twenty-two to twenty-five generations removed from their five Śūdra companions or servants whose descendants are now known as Kāyasthas. This wide divergence shows that the so-called Kanaujia ancestors of the present generation of the Vaṅgaja and Dakṣiṇarāḍhīya *kulin* Kāyasthas could not have come with the five Brāhmans, but if they came at all, they came ten generations later. Some writers have endeavoured to reconcile the Brāhman and Kāyastha genealogical tables by assuming that the names of about ten generations have been dropped from the Kāyastha genealogy. But as the genealogical tables of the five sub-sections of the Kāyasthas fully agree among themselves there is hardly any room for such an assumption. Another serious objection to the current story of the origin of the Boses, Ghoṣes, Guhas, Mitras and Dattas is that in Kanauj and its neighbourhood—in what is now the United Provinces, and even in Bihar—we do not find Kāyasthas or other castes with such surnames, while men with the surnames of Ghoṣa and Mitra are met with in Bengal long before the coming of a Ghoṣa and a Mitra from Kanauj.

In the four Faridpur grants of the sixth century already referred to, officials bearing such surnames as Datta, Candra, Deva, Mitra, Sena, Ghoṣa, Kunda, Pālita and Nāga find mention. Traces of such surnames are also found in other

Outer countries. The copper-plate grants of the so-called Somavaṃśī kings of Trikaliṅga, who ruled over parts of Odra (Orissa) and [Southern] Kośala in the eleventh century A.D. contains the names of officials bearing Ghoṣa, Datta and Nāga titles. The writer of the grants of the third and sixth years of King Mahābhavagupta is, "Kāyastha Koighoṣa, son of Vallabhaghoṣa attached (*pratibaddha*) to the office of the minister of peace and war who was the son of Mallādharadatta."* A copper-plate grant of the eighth year of the same king "was written by Āllava, son of Kailāsa, who was attached to the office of Mahāsūndhivigrahi Rānaka Mallādatta, son of Dhāradatta"† The same minister is mentioned in a grant of the 31st year of Mhābhavagupta I as Malladatta.‡ A grant of the fifteenth regnal year of the next King, Mahāśivagupta, "was written by the Mahākṣapatalaka Śri Ucchava Nāga, son of Āllava Naga, who was known to Mahāsāndhivigrahika-rāṇaka Sri Cārudatta." § In a grant of the 28th year of the same king we are told that Siṃhadatta occupied the office of the minister of peace and war (*sāndhivigrahapada*) and the grant was written by the Kāyastha Suryasena attached to the office of the same Sāndhivigrahī of Kośala. || A grant of the third year of Mahā-Bhavagupta II, successor of Mahāśivagupta,

* *Epigraphia Indica*, XI, 95; *Ibid.* III, p. 344.

† *Ibid.* VIII, p. 140. ‡ *Ibid.* III, p. 350.

§ *Ibid.* XI, p. 98.

|| *Journal of the Asiatic Society of Bengal*, 1905, p. 23.

was written by Kāyastha Maṅgaladatta on the staff of the same minister Siṃhadatta. Mr. B. C. Mazumdar takes these officers surnamed Datta, Ghoṣa, and Nāga as Bengali Kāyasthas.* But these surnames were also once quite common among the Nāgar Brahmans of Gujarat. Mr. D. R. Bhandarkar writes:—

"Mr. Vallabhji Haridatt Achārya of Rajkot has kindly supplied me with a verse which sets forth what are called the 'Sarmans,' *i.e.*, name-endings, of the various *gotras* of the Nāgar Brāhmans. It has been found by him in three *MSS.* of the work *Pravarādhyāya* connected with the Nāgars. One of the *MSS.* is dated Samvat 1788 Vaiśākha Suda 8 Bhṛgu, and all distinctly and unmistakably state that the *gotras*, *pravaras*, etc., therein specified are those which were in existence before Samvat 1283. This verse, which is of great importance, runs as follows:—

"*Datta-guptau nanda-ghoṣau śarma-dasau ca varma ca.*
Nāga-datta-strāta-bhūtau mitradevau bhavastathā."

"Here is a list of thirteen 'Śarmans,' which were in use amongst the Nāgar Brāhmans nearly 700 years ago. Even now they are affixed to their names, when they perform the religious ceremonies.

* * * *

"No less than ten of these thirteen 'Śarmans'

* *Epigraphia Indica* XI, p. 104.

are found as family names among Kāyasthas in Bengal, corresponding to Datta, Gupta, Nandi, Ghoṣa, Śarma, Dās, Barmā, Bhut, Mitra and Dev. * * * The conclusion is, therefore, irresistible that at least ten of these 'Śarmanś' represent the names of families or tribes that were incorporated into the Nāgar Brāhman caste. This seems to point to a racial identity between the Kāyasthas of Bengal and the Nāgar Brāhmans of Gujarat." *

These surnames, called *paddhatis* in Bengal, seem to point not only to a racial identity between the Kāyasthas of Bengal and the Nāgar Brāhmans of Gujarat, but also indicate that all castes in Bengal having such surnames in common are of common origin. Nearly a hundred *paddhatis* or surnames are met with among the Kāyasthas. These are—

Aṅkura
Arṇa
Āic
Āg
Āḍhya
Āditya
Indra
Upamān
Om
Kīrtti
Kunda
Kṣām
Kṣem
Kṣur
Kṣom
Khil
Gaṇḍa
Guiñ
Guṇa
Guha
Gupta
Gauḍ
Ghoṣa
Candra (Chanda)
Caṇḍa
Jāma
Ḍhol
Tej
Toṣ
Datta
Dānā
Dāsa
Dāhā
Deva
Dūta
Dharani
Dhar
Dhanu

* *Indian Antiquary*, XL (1911), pp. 32-33.

Nandana	Bandi	Śani
Nandī	Bīṣṇu (Viṣṇu)	Śara
Nāga	Baiś	Śarmmā
Nāda	Brahma	Śāiñ
Nātha	Bhañja	Śānā
Pāla	Bhadra	Śīla
Pālita	Bhuiñ	Śuiñ
Pila	Bhūti	Śūra
Pūiñ	Manu	Sāma
Preta	Māhut	Siṃha
Bandhu	Mitra	Sen
Bardhana	Yaśa	Soma
Bal	Rakṣita	Hanu
Barmmā	Rāja	Hāti
(Varman)	Rāṇā	Hem
Bāna	Rājpūt	Heś
Binda	Rāhā·	Hui
Bīda	Rāhut	Hoḍ
Bīja	Rudra	Hom *
Baṅga (Vanga).	Lodha	
Basu (Bose)	Śakti	

The Baidya or Vaidya (physician) caste of Bengal shares thirteen of these *paddhatis*—Sena, Dāsa, Gupta, Datta, Dev, Kar, Rāj, Som, Nandī, Candra, Dhar, Kunda and Rakṣit—with the Kāyasthas. Some of the Kaẏastha-*paddhatis* are found among the Bārajīvīs, Tilis (Taulikas), Tāntis (Tantuvāyas), Tāmbulis and Suvarṇavaṇiks, and

* *Sambandha-nirṇaya*, by Lālmohan Vidyānidhi, 3rd edition, pp. 148-149.

are also to be met with among some other castes. In these *paddhatis* we should probably recognise the names of the primitive Alpine tribes who colonised all the Outer countries from Gujarat to Bengal. As the largest number of *paddhatis* survive among the Kāyasthas of Bengal, they should be considered, not merely as a functional caste like the writer castes of the other provinces of India, but as a caste of the national type, like the Marāthā caste of the Deccan, retaining an important feature of the organisation of the Aryan invaders from whom they are mainly descended. It should be noted that one of the Kāyastha *paddhatis* is Baṅga (Vaṅga). I know of a family belonging to the *Tantuvāya* (weaver) caste with this remarkable surname. One of the reproaches levelled against the Kāyasthas of Bengal by their opponents is that their organisation is not as rigid as that of the other castes, and men of lower castes, known by Kāyastha surnames, often get themselves admitted to its fold by contracting matrimonial alliances with stereotyped Kāyasthas. This allegation is not without foundation, and the comparative laxity of the Kāyastha organisation is due to the survival of primitive traits pertaining to a caste of the national type. Within the Kāyastha fold, the Kulins (nobles), that is to say, the Boses, Ghoṣes, Guhas and Mitras, view with suspicion the origin of Kāyastha families bearing other surnames and refuse to admit their claim to Kāyastha rank unless they are related to the Kulins by marriage As the status of the Kāyastha caste of

Bengal is now a subject of very keen controversy, I shall conclude this chapter with a brief reference to it.

The writers engaged in the Kāyastha controversy may be divided into two schools. One school, of which the most well-known representative is Paṇḍit Lālmohan Vidyānidhi, author of the *Saṃbandhanirṇaya*, regards the Kāyasthas in general, and the Bengali Kāyasthas in particular, as of Śūdra origin. For this view of the origin of the Kāyasthas they rely on the *Jātimālā* said to be attached to the *Agnipurāna* and the works of the Brāhman genealogists. I have already dealt with the testimony of the genealogical works. According to the *Jātimālā*, Śūdramaṇi sprung from the lotus feet of Brahmā; Śūdramani begat Hīma; Hīma begat Pradīpa; Pradīpa begat Kāyastha; Kāyastha begat three sons—Citragupta, Citrasena, and Vicitra. From Citrasena was born Bose (Basu), Ghoṣa, Guha, Mitra, Datta, Karaṇa, Mṛtyuñjaya, and Anukaraṇa. Of these brothers Karaṇa begat Nāga, Nātha, and Dāsa, and Mṛtyuñjaya begat Dev, Sen, Pālit, Siṃha, and many others.*

The other school traces the Kāyastha caste to Kṣatriya origins and advise those among the Kāyasthas who follow Śūdra usages to adopt Kṣatriya usages. The authorities relied on by this school are put in a nutshell in a *vyāvasthāpatra* or a paper containing the opinion of the

---

* *Ibid.*, p. 125.

leading Paṇḍits of Benares issued in 1873.* In this paper extracts are given from the *Padmapurāṇa* and the *Skandapurāṇa*, wherein we are told that the Kāyasthas are the descendants of two Kṣatriyas, Citragupta and Candrasena, who were degraded to the rank of writers by two sages, Māṇḍavya and Dālbhya, respectively. These texts can not be regarded as mere modern fabrications, for they are quoted in an authoritative compilation, the *Śūdradharmatattva* by Kamalākara, better known as *Śūdra-kamalākara*. But all these legends throw little or no light on the origin of the Kāyasthas. The only basis of fact that may be discerned in them is the reflection of the opinion of the contemporaries of the writers regarding the place of the Kāyastha caste in the Hindu society. The authors of the different legends probably had in view Kāyasthas of different provinces and the author of the *Jātimālā* evidently had in view the Kāyastha caste of Bengal, four sub-sections of which are said to have purchased the patent of *kulinism* by declaring themselves as Śūdra servants of Brāhmans. But *kulinism*, which involved the admission of Śūdra origin, was not recognised by two of the four sub-castes,—the Uttara Rāḍhīya and the Vārendra Kāyasthas. These Kāyasthas preferred to be known as members of the mixed Karaṇa caste than as pure-blood Śūdras.

---

* The Annual Reports of the *Vaṅgadeśīya Kāyastha-Sabhā* (in Bengali), second and third years, appendix *ca* (b).

All the Kāyasthas of Bengal were probably known as Karaṇas before the rise of *kulinism* in Vaṅga and Southern Rāḍha. In the accounts of castes given in the *Brahmakhaṇḍa* of the *Brahmavaivarta Purāṇa** and the *Bṛhaddharma Purāna* the Karaṇa occupies the place of the Kāyastha. The authors of both these accounts seem to disclose a familiarity with the caste system of Bengal and agree in assigning to the Karaṇa the place of honour in their list of the mixed castes. The legend relating to the origin of these mixed castes is narrated in the *Bṛhaddharma Purāṇa, Uttarkhaṇḍa* (chapter xiii). It is said that when Veṇa obtained the sovereignty of the earth he stopped the performance of sacrifices and other religious rites. The Brāhmans then approached him and said, "O king, if religious rites are not performed and Viṣṇu is not worshipped, anarchy will follow and mixed castes will spring up from the illicit connection of men and women of different castes." The wicked king took the hint and compelled men and women of unequal castes to procreate mixed castes. When mixed castes of the first degree had been created, Veṇa compelled them again to create other mixed castes. The names of the so-called thirty-six mixed castes, as given in the *Bṛhaddharma Purāṇa*, show how conversant the author was with the caste system of Bengal. I name them in the order in which they are mentioned in the text.

* Wilson's *Indian Caste*, Vol. I, pp. 439—441.

I. Twenty good mixed castes (*uttama saṅkarāḥ*) having Śrotriya Brāhmans as their Purohitas—Karaṇa (Kāyastha), Ambaṣṭha (Vaidya), Gandha Vaṇik, Kaṃsakāra (brazier), Śaṅkhakāra (shell-dresser), Ugra, Rājaputra (Rajput), Kumbhakāra (potter), Tantravāya (weaver), Karmakāra (blacksmith), Dāsa (Cāsi Kaivartta), Māgadha, Gopa (Goālā, milkman), Nāpita (barber), Modaka (Mayrā), Vārajīvī (Bārui, grower of betel leaves), Sūta, Mālākāra (gardener), Tāmbulī (seller of betel leaves), Taulika (seller of betel nuts, Tili traders).

II. Twelve *madhyama* or intermediate mixed castes—Takṣaṇ (wood-cutter), Rajaka (washerman), Svarṇakāra (goldsmith), Suvarṇavaṇik, Ābhīra, Tailakāraka (oilpresser), Dhīvara (fisherman), Śauṇḍika (wine-seller), Naṭa, Sāvāka or Śāvāra, Sekhara, Jālika (fisherman).

III. Aṇtyajas or outcastes—Malegrāhi, Kuḍava, Cāṇḍāla, Varūḍa, Carmakāra (Chāmār), Ghaṭṭajīvī (ferryman), Dolāvāhī, Malla.

Besides these thirty-six (really forty), the author names the Śākadvīpī or Devala Brāhmans and two other mixed castes, Gaṇaka and Vādaka. From the body of Veṇa also sprung Mleccha, Pulinda, Pukkasa, Khaṣa, Yavana, Suhma, Kamboja, Śavara, and Khara. When the Ṛṣis saw these castes born of sin they put Veṇa to death. Then they rubbed the arms of Veṇa and Pṛthu sprung up from them. Pṛthu restored religious rites, worshipped the Ṛṣis and requested them to assign to the mixed castes their occupations and duties. The Brāhmans asked the thirty-six mixed castes, also called Śūdras, what calling each of them would adopt according to which they should also be named. "When all of them were thus addressed by the Brāhmans versed in the sacred books, they began to speak, and Karaṇa first (*ādau*) spake thus, 'We are ignorant outcastes totally devoid of wisdom. Men like you are omniscient; please ordain for us what is fit.'" Then the Brāhmans said, addressing the King, "This is the Karaṇa; let him always prosper. He possesses humility and is well-behaved; he hath spoken well. He looks like one who is well versed in polity (*nītijña*) and he should do administrative work (*rājakārya*). He should worship the Brāhmans and gods. This (Karaṇa) is a Sat-Śūdra (good Śūdra); there is no doubt about it. Reverence for Brāhman, desire for worshipping gods, and good conduct, are the characteristics of a Sat-Śūdra." The Karaṇa then bowed his head before the Brāhmans who added, "Son, live on this earth, skilful in administrative work (*rājakārya-viśārada*) and expert in writing (*lipikarma-viśārada*)." *

* ब्राह्मणा ऊचुः । षट्त्रिंशज्जातयः शूद्रा यूयं भूतास्तु सङ्कराः ॥
कः किं करिष्यते कर्म्म च तद्भूतां समन्ततः ।
कर्म्मानुरूपानामानो यूयं सर्व्वे भविष्यथ ॥
व्यास उवाच । इत्युक्ता ये तदा सर्व्वे ब्राह्मणैः शास्त्रदर्शिभिः ।
वक्तुमारेभिरे विप्रांस्तत्रादौ करणोऽब्रवीत् ॥
करण उवाच । वयं मूर्खा जातिहीनाः प्रज्ञाशून्या विशेषतः
भवद्विधास्तु सर्व्वज्ञाः कुरुध्वं नो यथोचितम् ॥

The *Vṛhaddharma Purāṇa* is recognized in Bengal as one of the minor Purāṇas (*Upapurāṇa*) and has been printed more than once. The legend of Veṇa told in this Purāṇa is but an expansion of the older legend (*ante*, pp. 4—5) to explain the origin of the outlandish castes of Bengal. Historically it is of as little or as much value as other similar caste legends. It probably enshrines a true picture of the social organisation of Bengal before the Muhammadan conquest. The account of the Karaṇa or Kāyastha is in agreement with little that is known of the authentic history of the caste. This history shows that the Kāyasthas of Bengal were no mere clerks but administrators, scholars and enlightened patrons of learning, who really governed the country and took up arms in its defence whenever necessary.

Śrīdhara in his *Nyāyakandalī*, a widely known

व्यास उवाच । एवं श्रुत्वा तु वचनं तेषां वै मुनिसत्तमाः ।
प्रहृष्टवदना भूत्वा राजानमिदमब्रुवन् ॥
ब्राह्मणा ऊचुः । अयन्तु करणो नाम श्रीयुक्तो वर्त्ततां सदा ।
विनयाचारसम्पन्नो वचनं शृणु चोन्नवान् ॥
राजकार्य्यं करोत्वेष नीतिज्ञो ह्यथवे स्वयम् ।
ब्राह्मणे भक्तिमांश्चैव देवेष्वपि भवत्वपि ॥
एष एव हि सत्शूद्रो भवत्वेव न संशयः ।
ब्राह्मणे भक्तिमत्वन्तु देवताराधने मतिः ।
अमात्यत्वं सुशीलत्वमेतत् सत्शूद्रलक्षणम् ॥
व्यास उवाच । इत्युक्तवत्सु विप्रेषु करणो नाम सङ्करः ।
प्रणनाम च विप्राणां चरणात् भक्तिसंयुतः ॥
ब्राह्मणाश्च तमूचु वै सत्शूद्र तिष्ठेह भूतले ।
राजकार्य्येषु कुशलो लिपिकर्म्मविशारदः ॥

Vṛhaddharmapurāṇa, (Bib. Ind.) *Uttarkhaṇḍa*, 14, 28—38.

commentary on Praśastapāda's treatise on the Vaiśeṣika system of philosophy and called *Padārthadharma-saṅgraha*, introduces us to a learned Kāyastha of the tenth century who was also a liberal patron of learning. Śrīdhara was a Brāhman born in a village called Bhūrisṛṣṭi in Dakṣiṇa-Rāḍhā or South-Western Bengal. Srīdhara writes in the concluding stanza of his work, "Requested by Pāṇḍudāsa, Bhatta Śrīdhara wrote this *Nyāyakandalī* in the year 913 of the Śaka era."* Śrīdhara also refers to his patron in the body of the book thus, "Adorned with virtues resembling jewels, foremost of the Kāyastha race (*is*) Pāṇḍudāsa" † by way of example. Paṇḍudāsa could hardly have requested Śrīdhara to write a commentary on a difficult text dealing with a dry and abstruse system of philosophy had he not been himself a student of the system. In his *Nyāyakandalī* Śrīdhara refers to four other philosophical works written by himself. But among these only *Nyāyakandalī* has survived and must have enjoyed a wide circulation at one time as a standard work on Vaiśeṣika. It is referred to by Mādhava in the *Sarvadarśanasaṃgraha*. There is a sub-commentary on it called *Pañjikā* by a Jaina writer named Rajaśekhara. ‡ The printed edition

* त्र्यधिकदशोत्तरनवशतशकाब्दे न्यायकन्दली रचिता ।
श्रीपाण्डुदासयाचित भट्ट श्रीश्रीधरेणेयम् ॥
The Vizianagram Sanskrit series, No. 6, p. 331.

† गुणरत्नाभरणः कायस्थकुलतिलकः पाण्डुदास इत्यादिषु (p. 269).

‡ See the editor's preface to *Nyāyakandalī*.

of the *Nyāyakandalī* is based on manuscripts obtained from Kashmir, Poona and Benares. Pāṇḍudāsa, at whose request *Nyāyakandalī* was written, deserves a place in the history of Indian philosophy, and the Bengali Kāyasthas of the tenth century, of whom he was one, must have been very much advanced in wealth and culture.

A century after Pāṇḍudāsa flourished Sandhyākara Nandī, the author of the Sanskrit poem *Rāmacaritam*, wherein the story of Rāma of Ayodhyā, and the history of Rāmapāla, King of Gauḍa, are narrated in the same words yielding double meaning. Prajāpati Nandī, the father of Sandhyākara, who was the minister of peace and war of King Madanapāla, son of Rāmapāla, is described in the poem as the foremost of the Karaṇas (*karaṇyānāmagraṇī*).*

After the Muhammadan conquest the country was really ruled by semi-independent *chiefs* called *Bhuiñyās* (*Bhaumikas*, landholders). The number of these Bhuiñyās of Bengal is traditionally put down at twelve and the whole country was known as 'the dominion of the twelve Bhuiñyas' (*bāra bhuiñyār muluk*). All the Hindu Bhuiñyās known to us, who held sway in the fifteenth and the sixteenth centuries, were Kāyasthas. The principality of Bāklā Candradvīpa was founded by a Vaṅgaja Kāyastha named Danujamardana Deva early in the fifteenth century. Many of his silver coins

* *Rāmacaritam*, Memoirs of the Asiatic Society of Bengal, Vol. III. No. 1.

dated in Sāka 1339 (A.D. 1417), minted at Candradvīpa and Pāṇḍunagara, have been discovered in several districts of Bengal.* The principality of Bhuluā was founded by Biśvambhar Rāy, a Kāyastha of the Śūra family, probably at about the same time. The Bhuiñyās of Vikrampur and Jessore were Vaṅgaja Kāyasthas and the Bhuiñyā of Bhoosna was a Uttara-Rāḍhīya Kāyastha. The Bhuiñyā of Bāklā was overcome by Murād Khan, a general of Akbar, in A.D. 1574.† Ralph Fitch writes of south-eastern Bengal through which he travelled in 1582:—' They be all hereabouts rebels against their King Zebaldin Echebar [Jalaluddin Akbar], for here are so many rivers and islands that they flee from one to another, whereby his horsemen can not prevail against them.'' Kedār Rāy of Vikrampur died fighting against the imperial army under Mān Singh in A.D. 1603. Pratāpāditya of Jessore is said to have been defeated and carried to Delhi by the same Mān Singh in the reign of Jahangir. Mukunda Rāy of Bhoosna came into collision with Murad Khan, the conqueror of Bāklā, and, in order to get rid of him, invited him to a feast and murdered him, together with his sons. Mukunda Rāy's son Satrajit "gave Jahangir's governors of Bengal no end of trouble, and refused to send in the custom-

* R. D. Banerji's *Bāṅgālār Itihāsā*, pp. 130–132.

† *Journal of the Asiatic Society of Bengal*, 1878, Part I, p. 288. For details regarding the *Bāra Bhuiñiyās* see Dr. J. Wise's paper in *Journal of the Asiatic Society of Bengal*, 1874, Part I, pp. 199–214.

ary *peshkash* or do homage at the court of Dhākā. He was in secret understanding with the Rājāhs of Koch Bihār and Koch Hājo, and was at last, in the reign of Shāhjahān, captured and executed at Dhākā (about A.D. 1636)."* Sitārām Rāy, who revolted against Nawab Murshid Kuli Khan and perished in the struggle about A.D. 1712, was the last prince of the line of Mukunda Rāy. The struggle carried on by the Bhuīñyās of Bengal against the Mughul Emperors was no less obstinate than that of the Rājputs of Rājputāna, though, unfortunately, there were no bards in Bengal to enshrine the stirring events of this struggle in heroic ballads. Had not these Kāyastha Bhuiñyās of Bengal been inspired by a tradition of long independent rule, they could hardly have maintained this unequal struggle for so long. Not only the Bhuiñyās, but the minor zemindars of those days, were mostly Kāyasthas. Abul Fazl writes in his *Aīn-i-Akbari*, completed in A.D. 1594:—"The zamindars are mostly *Kāyaths*." † The establishment of the centralised Mughal imperial rule marked the beginning of the downfall of the Kāyasthas of Bengal. The Mughal viceroys replaced the turbulent Bhuiñyās by more accommodating Brāhman zemindars and thereby reduced the ruling class of Bengal to the condition of mere writers or literate serfs.

* *Ibid.*, 1873, Part I, p. 229.

† Jarrett's *Ain-i-Akbari*, Vol. II, p. 129.

CHAPTER VI.

INDO-ARYANS AND IRANIANS.

In Chapter I, I have already touched on the kinship between the Indo-Aryans and the Iranians by suggesting that the Ṛṣi clans, like the Atharvans, Aṅgirases, Bhṛgus and Vasiṣṭhas who formed the nucleus of the Brāhman caste, were akin to the Magi of Iran on the ground that the Magi also, like the Indian Brāhmans, formed a hereditary priesthood (p. 33). An eminent Iranist, Professor J. H. Moulton, recently questioned the Aryan origin of the Magi in his lectures on *Early Zoroastrianism* (London, 1913), and Dr. D. B. Spooner of the Archæological Department of India has declared that the Indo-Aryans of the Outer countries are the descendants of Magian immigrants.* In this concluding chapter I shall deal with Iranian origins and the supposed Iranian affinities of the Indo-Aryans of the Outer countries.

The very close relationship between the language and the religion of the *Veda* on the one hand, and the language and the religion of the *Avesta* on the other, has long been recognized by scholars. Geldner writes:—

"The clearest evidence of the extreme age of the language of the gāthās is its striking resemblance to the oldest Sanskrit, the language of the

* *Journal of the Royal Asiatic Society*, 1915, p. 430.

Vedic poems. The gāthā language (much more than the later Zend) and the language of the *Vedas* have a close resemblance, exceeding that of any two Romanic languages; they seem hardly more than two dialects of one tongue. Whole strophes of the gāthās can be turned into good old Sanskrit by the application of certain phonetic laws." *

Among the common elements of the Vedic and Avestic religions are a great number of gods—Asura, Mithra, the Dragon-slayer Verethragna (the Indra of the Indian), the Water-shoot Apām-napāt, etc. Eduard Meyer thus summarises the other common elements: "So, too, fire-worship, especially the sacrificial flame; the preparation of the intoxicating *soma*, which fills man with divine strength and uplifts him to the gods; the injunction to "good thoughts and good works," imposed on the pious by Veda and Avesta alike; the belief in an unwavering order (*ṛta*)—a law controlling gods and men and dominating them all; yet with this, a belief in the power of the magical formulae (*mantra*), exclamations and prayers, to whose compulsion not merely demons (the evil spirits of deception—*druh*) but even the gods (*daeva*) must submit; and, lastly, the institution of a priesthood of fire-kindlers (*āthravan*), who are at once the repositories of all sacred traditions and mediators in all intercourse between earth and heaven." †

* *Encyclopædia Britannica* (11th Edition), Vol. 21, p.247.

† *Ibid.*, p. 203.

This intimate relationship between the language and the religion of the Veda and those of the Avesta has led scholars to assume that the ancestors of the Vedic Indians and the Iranians at one time formed a single people—that of the Aryans. According to Eduard Meyer "their residence must have lain chiefly in the great steppe which stretches north of the Black Sea and the Caspian, through South Russia, to Turan (Turkestan) and the Oxus and Jaxartes. For here we continually discover traces of Iranian nationality . . . . . From the region of the steppes the Aryans must have penetrated into the cultivable land of Eastern Iran: thence one part spread over the district of the Indus, then on again to the Ganges; another moved westward to Zagros and the borders of the Semitic world." * The "undoubtedly Iranian" names borne by some of the princelings of Syria and Palestine and the Kings of Matanni named in the Tell-el-Amarna letters and other cuneiform inscriptions and the appearance of horse in Babylonia, Egypt and Greece about 1700 B.C., have led the same authority to hold "that towards the middle of the second millennium before Christ, the Iranians made a great forward movement to the West, and that certain of their princes—at first probably in the role of mercenary leaders, reached Mesopotamia and Syria and there founded principalities of their own, much as did the Germans under the

---

* *Ibid.*, p. 202.

Roman Empire, the Normans, Turks, etc." * The names of the gods invoked by a Mitanni King in a Boghaz-keui inscription of about 1400 B.C. —Indra, Varuṇa, Mitra, and the Nāsatyas—further show that there was complete agreement of the ancestors of Indians and Iranians in language and religion still in the fourteenth century B.C.† Though this theory of Eduard Meyer has been adopted by Geldner,‡ other Iranists hold divergent views. Professor Jackson considers it "premature to theorize" on Boghaz-keui inscriptions and adds: "The mention may be merely a direct reference to Indian deities without having any immediate connection with Iran." § Professor N. Söderblom of Upsala (quoted by Moulton) is of opinion that the Boghaz-keui inscription confirms the belief that the Hittites were of Aryan origin, and the names "depend perhaps on a branch of the Aryans slowly pushing their way from the Baltic coasts to their new home in the East." || Dr. B. B. Charles, a Semitist, holds that "the Hittites were a people, possibly of mixed Aryan and Caucasic elements," and the Mitannians were "apparently a Hittite people."¶ Professor Moulton writes: "Here I would only observe that we know nothing about the movements of Indian or Iranian

* *Ibid.*, p. 203.

† *Journal of the Royal Asiatic Society*, 1909, p. 1096.

‡ *Encyclopædia Britannica*, vol. 28, p. 1041.

§ *Encyclopædia of Religion and Ethics*, IV, p. 620*a*.

|| *Early Zoroastrianism*, p. 6.

¶ *Encyclopædia of Religion and Ethics*, VI. 723*a*.

tribes in the second millennium, and could postulate an ebb from India to the North-West without compromising anything that is really established." * Moulton's latest view regarding the prehistoric migration of the Aryans deserves notice. Referring to an essay of his on some points in Iranian ethnography contributed to the volume dedicated to Professor William Ridgeway, he writes in a note to his *Early Zoroastrianism* (p. 5): "I make the founders of the Aryan culture—or rather the speakers of the language in which it expressed itself—to have been a German tribe which made a very rapid trek across Russia past the north end of the Caspian, into the country north of the Punjab, into which before very long the bulk of the invading tribe passed on." This hypothesis well explains the presence of white and yellow-haired Brāhmans in India (p. 25).

But we are not here concerned with the hypothetical prehistoric Aryan movements or the Mitannian controversy, but with Aryans who settled in Iran and specially the Magi who dwelt in Western Iran or Media. According to Herodotus the Magi were one of the six tribes of Media. Herodotus writes (i. 132) that whenever a Persian offers a sacrifice, "a Magian man stands by and chants a theogony thereto, for such the Persians say the chant is. Without a Magian it is not lawful for him to offer sacrifices." We also learn from Herodotus and later classical writers that the Magi not merely played the role

* *Early Zoroastrianism*, p. 7.

of "Fire-kindlers" (*āthravan*) of the *Avesta*, but formed a hereditary sacredotal caste, acting an important part in the state—advisers and spiritual guides to the King, and so forth. Moulton writes: "From the first the Greek writers assume that the Magi were priests, with special skill in divination and oneiromancy. They were already essential for all priestly acts, and identified thoroughly with the Persian religious system. Moreover, from the fourth century [B.C.] down there are frequent allusions to Zoroaster himself as a Magus, and many of the foremost modern authorities have accepted this as probably true." * Among the foremost modern authorities Geldner writes of Zoroaster:—"Probably he emanated from the old school of Median Magi, and appeared first in Media as the prophet of a new faith, but met with sacredotal opposition, and turned his step eastward. In the east of Iran the novel creed first acquired a solid footing, and subsequently reacted with success upon the West." † In one passage of the Gāthās (Ys. 33.6) Zoroaster calls himself a priest (*Zaotar*=skt. *hotar*).

Professor Moulton endeavours "to blaze a path off the beaten track of scholarship" "through a rather difficult wood" by theorising "that the Magi were part of the indigenous population of Media" with "several remark of peculiarities of belief and habits which distinguish them sharply from Aryans and Semites alike."

* *Early Zoroastrianism*, pp. 196-197.

† *Encyclopædia Britannica*, Vol. 28, p. 1041.

Instead of dealing with the arguments of Professor Moulton in support of his hypothesis, I should first point out the consequences this hypothesis involves. According to Parsi tradition (Arda Virāf, I, 2) Zoroaster taught, in round numbers, some 300 years before the invasion of Alexander (330+300 = 630· B.C). This date is accepted by Jackson, West and a few other scholars. Eduard Meyer conjecturally puts the date of Zoroaster at 1000 B.C., which "may be too high" according to Geldner.* Moulton writes of the date of Zoroaster: "The traditional date (660-583 B.C.) is a minimum, but there are strong reasons for placing Zarathushtra and his Gāthās some generations earlier still." † The rebellion of Gaumata the Magus broke out in the reign of Cambyses (528-521 B.C.). This was not a national rising of the Magians or Medians against their Achæmenian rulers, but Gaumata, though a Magian, adopted the role of an Achæmenian (Persian) in the revolt and pretended to be Bardiya (Smerdis) the younger son of Cyrus who had been secretly slain by Cambyses. Gaumata was slain by Darius in 521. B.C. The statements of Herodotus (B.C. 484-424) about the position of the Magi in the Persian empire seem contradictory. While stating that it is not lawful for a Persian to offer sacrifices without a Magi, Herodotus gives an account of a festival called Magophonia which was a celebration of the slay-

* *Ibid.*, p. 1041. † *Early Zoroastrianism*, p. viii.

ing of the Magian Gaumata, the pseudo-Smerdis, by Darius, and then, 'no Magian may appear in the light, but the Magians keep themselves in their houses that day.' * But Dr. L. H. Gray has furnished a very satisfactory explanation of this curious festival. He writes :—

"Why the Magi, so universally honoured in Iran, were obliged to keep within doors during the Magophonia has been a hard problem on the basis of the current explanation ; but if, as Marquart holds, it was originally a New Year celebration, to be connected with the Mihrajān, which was also a New Year feast, it may probably be connected further with the Sacæa, which, from the statement of Dio Chrysostom and Berosus, was almost certainly a New Year festival, the prominent feature of which was the killing of a criminal who had for five days been permitted to wear royal robes, to sit on the royal throne, and empowered not only to issue whatsoever mandates he would, but even to consort with the royal concubines, and who, after his brief tenure of office, was scourged and hanged, so that the Sacæa probably represents, in attenuated form, the wide-spread practice (found also in Babylonia) of killing the priest-king. It would then follow that the origin of the Magophonia was the actual killing of a Magus who was at the same time both priest and king. This explains why the Magians were both reverenced and also liable to be killed, although

* *Encyclopædia of Religion and Ethics*, V, p. 374.

long before the historical period the actual killing had been abandoned, and the festival survived merely in a season of merriment, during which the Magi were perhaps the butt of practical jokes and prudently remained indoors. The success of the attack of Darius and his comrades on the pseudo-Smerdis was very likely due in great part to the fact that Gaumata was himself a Magian; and later, as already noted, the Magophonia ('Magus-slaying') was rationalised to commemorate this event, just as in Strabo's day the Sacæa itself had come to be reinterpreted as commemorating a victory over the Scythians which may, indeed, have been won at the time of the celebration of the ancient festival of the Sacæa, after it had long since lost its primal significance.''*

This theory regarding the origin of Magophonia indicates that it was celebrated by the Persians even in the time of Darius and it involved on their part the recognition of the Magi as representatives of their primitive priesthood. But even if we refuse our assent to this theory and its consequences and hold with Moulton that Magophonia was nothing but an anniversary of the slaying of Gaumata "intended to remind the subject population of the consequences that would follow if they tempted fortune again with an effort to throw off the yoke,"† it is very difficult to understand how could the Magi gain the ascendancy that they

---

* *Encyclopædia of Religion and Ethics,* V, pp. 874b-75a.

† *Early Zoroastrianism,* p. 186.

enjoyed in the Achæmenian empire in the time of Herodotus in spite of such celebrations. Professor Moulton puts his case thus briefly in his Preface (p. x):—" It is argued that the Magi were an indigenous tribe of priests or shamans, the leaders of the non-Aryan population of Media, who, after failing to gain political supremacy in the revolt of Gaumata, secured in two or three generations a religious ascendancy which compensated for any failure." History furnishes no parallel to the change of which these lines contain a hint. Darius's inscriptions show that he was an ardent devotee of the great God Auramazda "who made this earth and yon heaven, who made man and amenity (civilization) for men, who made Darius King."

According to Moulton the early Achæmenian Kings belonged to the unreformed Iranian religion and Darius was the first true Zoroastrian of the dynasty. But whether the religion professed by Cyrus, Cambyses and Darius was the reformed Iranian religion or no, the question of questions in this connection is, whether this religion required the services of priests or it was a priestless religion —a thing as yet unknown. Professor Moulton does not deny the existence of priests in the time of the early Achæmenian Kings. He writes, " The Aryan Medes and Persians had known them [Magi] for generations as skilled magicians and occultists; and when they volunteered for the work of the Persian *Āthravan* and *Zaotar*, which was confined to no special class, the people would feel that they had a special guarantee of correct and effective ritual." * If the work of the *Āthravan* and *Zaotar* was not confined to any special class, it was open to people of all classes. In the time of rulers like Cyrus and Darius when the Persians reached the height of power and prosperity, the work of *Āthravan* and *Zaotar* must have brought considerable profit, honour, and influence to those who undertook it. That Aryan Medes and Persians, after enjoying such profits and privileges from time immemorial down to the time of the early Achæmenian Kings, should then quietly surrender the right to the shamans of an inferior race in return for a guarantee of correct and effective ritual is simply incredible. Such a surrender is not only incredible but impossible If the work of *Āthravan* and *Zaotar* was confined to no special class in the time of Darius and before, it could not have gone on a-begging for so long, it must have been included among the functions of the king and must have been exercised by the king and his deputies. This conclusion is forced upon us by the history of the priesthood of almost all civilised nations, whether Aryan, Semitic or Hamitic.

Sir James Frazer writes: "The union of a royal title with priestly duties was common in ancient Italy and Greece. At Rome and in other cities of Latium there was a priest called the Sacrificial King or King of the Sacred Rites. In republican Athens the second annual-magis-

* *Ibid.*, p. 194.

trate of the State was called the King, and his wife Queen; the functions of both were religious. . . . . . . Many other Greek democracies had titular kings, whose duties, so far as they are known, seem to have been priestly, and to have centred round the Common Hearth of the State. . . . . Some Greek states had several of these titular kings, who held office simultaneously. At Rome the tradition was that the Sacrificial King had been appointed after the abolition of the monarchy in order to offer the sacrifices which before had been offered by the kings. A similar view as to the origin of priestly kings appears to have prevailed in Greece. In itself the opinion is not improbable, and it is borne out by the example of Sparta, almost the only purely Greek State which retained the kingly form of government in historical times. For in Sparta all State sacrifices were offered by the kings as descendants of the God . . . .

"This combination of priestly functions with royal authority is familiar to every one. Asia Minor, for example, was the seat of various great religious capitals peopled by thousands of sacred slaves, and ruled by pontiffs who weilded at once temporal and spiritual authority, like the popes of mediæval Rome. Such priest-ridden cities were Zela and Pessinus. Teutonic Kings, again, in the old heathen days seem to have stood in the position, and to have exercised the powers, of high priests." *

* *The Magic Art* (London, 1913), Vol. I, pp. 44-47.

In the Semitic world, among the Babylonians and the Assyrians—"At first the ruler was supreme in both the secular and the religious sides of life, but in time the priesthood developed till its help was needed for all religious actions. Yet the King remained priest in theory. . . . . The priests were always under the control of their chief, the King." * Among the Hebrews,—"The King was judge, general, and priest, the officers set apart for these duties being only his deputies. There is no clear statement of the King being the chief priest, but there are many indications that he sometimes exercised priestly functions. In Phœnicia, Tabnit styles himself 'priest of Astarte, King of the Sidonians,' like his father. His son Eshmunazar calls his mother (she was his father's sister) 'priestess of Astarte' and 'queen,' though he himself does not bear priestly title" †

In Egypt—"As son and successor of all the divinities (national or local) of the kingdom, the Pharaoh is by right the chief servitor of the Supreme God and the chief pontiff of all the priesthoods. In the bas-reliefs of the temples he is figured as the chief officiating priest, and everywhere he is represented in the dwellings of his divine fathers, celebrating sacrifice, offering incense or libations, or consecrating the offering, opening the tabernacle, adoring the divine image, and going in front of his retinue." ‡

The observation of the same phenomenon among

---

* *Encyclopædia of Religion and Ethics,* VII, p. 726b.

† *Ibid.*, p. 725b. ‡ *Ibid.*, p. 714a.

both savages and civilised peoples have led Sir James Frazer to the following generalisation as regards the evolution of kingship :—

"On the whole then we seem to be justified in concluding that in many parts of the world the King is the lineal successor of the old magician or medicine-man. When once a special class of sorcerers have been segregated from the community and entrusted by it with the discharge of duties on which the public safety and welfare are believed to depend, these men gradually rise to wealth and power, till their leaders blossom out into sacred kings. But the great social evolution which thus begins with democracy and ends in despotism is attended by an intellectual revolution which affects both the conception and the functions of royalty. For as time goes on, the fallacy becomes more and more apparent to the acuter minds and is slowly displaced by religion; in other words, the magician gives way to the priest, who, renouncing the attempt to control directly the processes of nature for the good of man, seeks to attain the same end directly by appealing to the gods to do for him what he no longer fancies he can do for himself. Hence the King, starting as a magician, tends gradually to exchange the practice of magic for the priestly functions of prayer and sacrifice."*

. Frazer's view has revolutionized our idea of the origin of kingship. Mr. A. E. Crawley writes, "Anthropological research has lately revolution-

* *Lectures on the Early History of the Kingship*, London 1905, pp. 127-28; *The Magic Art*, I. pp. 371-372.

ized opinion as to the origin of kingly office. Without excluding the elements of leadership, organization, and generalship in war, J. G. Frazer has established by a long array of facts the theory that among the primitive peoples it was the medicine-man, the shaman, or public magician who laid the foundations at least in part of the kingly office.'' * The theory explains the origin of the union of the political and sacredotal functions in the person of the King.

The *Kṣatriya* King of India and the *Khshāyathiā* (King) of Persia are the two prominent exceptions to the rule. In India, from the very dawn of history, the sacerdotal function is confined to an exclusive social class, the Brāhman caste. According to Professor Moultan's own admission the same state of things obtained in Persia two or three generations after Gaumata when the Magi gained the monopoly of priesthood. The reason why Moulton requires this interval of two or three generations between the revolt of Gaumata and the appointment of the non-Aryan Magi as the sole priests of the Aryan religion of Persia is that when Herodotus gained the opportunity of gathering first-hand information about this religion some seventy years after the failure of Gaumata during his travels in the Persian empire, he found the Magi "in undisputed possession of the priesthood.'' † If this undisputed possession had been the result of a very recent change, the historian could hardly

* *Encyclopædia of Religion and Ethics*, VII, p. 709a.

† *Early Zoroastrianism*, p. 76.

have failed to notice it. Even if we hold with Moulton that "the success of the foreign shamans (Magi) in securing a monopoly of the priesthood for a cultus wholly alien to their own is no difficulty when we consider the conditions" (p. 174), the silence of 'the father of history, about a change of so great a magnitude cannot be ignored. If in course of his travels Herodotus could meet with men who supplied him with authentic informations about the failure of the Magi two to three generations before, it is difficult to believe that there was nobody to tell him anything of the Magi's great triumph in his own generation. And if Herodotus had heard of the way in which the Magi had very lately secured the monopoly of the priesthood of the 'alien' Persian religion, he could not have passed it over in silence. Therefore, in the absence of any positive evidence to show that the early Achæmenian kings and their predecessors exercised the priestly functions, which their successors voluntarily surrended to the alien Magi, we have no other alternative but to accept as a historical fact the traditional view that the Magi were the hereditary priests of the Aryan Medes and Persians from time immemorial and that Zarathushtra himself was a Magus.

The origin of the Magian priesthood of Iran may be explained on the analogy of the Brāhman priesthood of India (*ante*, p. 33). The Magi were perhaps the most pure-blooded of Aryan settlers of Iran who elaborated the Iranian religion and gave it its peculiar shape and imposed it upon their neighbours who were mixed in origin and inferior in culture. The Magophonia indicates that the Magus was at one time both the king and the priest. He was probably deprived of his sceptre by some one of his powerful subjects who dared not deprive him of his priestly functions. In some such way the separation of the political and sacerdotal functions might have been brought about in ancient Iran. The analogous division of functions happened in India probably under similar conditions. The arguments adduced by Professor Moulton in support of his theory have been ably dealt with by Professor A. Berridale Keith in a short article on the *Magi* published in the *Journal of the Royal Asiatic Society*, 1915, pp. 790-799, which should be carefully read by every one interested in the question.

While recognising the distant kinsbip between the Vedic Indian Brāhman and the Median Magi, it is difficult to subscribe to the theories of Dr. D. B. Spooner enunciated in his second paper on the *Zoroastrian Period of India History* already referred to (*ante*, p. 155). Dr. Spooner's theories practically amount to this :—After the coming of "those Aryans who first invaded Northern India, and to whom we attribute rightly the Rigveda," there followed a series of invasions of the Magians from Persia that continued till the rise of the Maurya empire. These Persian invaders inaugurated the Zoroastrian period of Indian history that closely followed the Ṛgvedic period and bequeathed to India the Outer band of Indo-Aryan languages, the Atharvaveda among the Vedas, the Buddha and Buddhism, and the powerful empire of the Mauryas. As was to be expected, these views have already been subjected to a good deal of adverse criticism.* Dr. Spooner has restated his main theory in a somewhat modified form in a letter published in *The Bengalee* (Calcutta) of March 11th, 1916. In this letter his position is thus defined :—

"I do not say that either Chandragupta or the Buddha was a Persian in our modern sense. I say they were members of a body of Aryans who came into this country at a date subsequent to the arrival of the first Aryan immigrations, when sufficient time had elapsed for the Vedic Hindus and their Iranian cousins to have developed differences of faith."

Dr. Spooner then goes on to sum up the evidences upon which he bases his theory in this way :—

"When the Linguistic Survey of India shows us, at that time beyond all explanation, that the Aryan languages of North India fall into two groups; when the Prākṛt Grammarians assert

---

* Mr. Vincent A. Smith in the *Journal of Royal Asiatic Society*, 1915, pp. 800-802; Prof. Berridale Keith in the same Journal of 1916, pp. 138-142, and Dr. F. W. Thomas in pp. 362-365; Mr. K. P. Jayaswal in the *Journal of the Bihar and Orissa Research Society* of March, 1916; the present writer in a Calcutta lecture reported in the *Statesman* of the 11th March, 1916; "Nimrod" in the *Modern Review* of April, 1916.

that the (obviously Iranian) dialect of Balkh was integral part of Māgadhi; when the language of these Outer Band Districts display Iranian characteristics; when excavation at Pataliputra discloses pottery with the Persian fire-altar emblazoned on it, as well as a group of palaces agreeing in minute detail and even in grouping with the complex of Persipolis; when the *Prabodhacandrodaya* tells us that Magadha was a country peopled mostly by foreigners; and when the present population of Bihar shows such a number of admittedly Sākadvīpin Brāhmans, is it so wholly preposterous to suggest that this region must have been settled by an Iranian body in prehistoric times?"

(1) The classification of the Aryan languages of Northern India into two groups was never regarded as beyond all explanation. One explanation was suggested by Dr. Hœrnle, the author of this classification, and has been adopted by Sir George Grierson in whose opinion "the contention is entirely borne out by the results of ethnological enquiries" (*ante*, p. 45). The present writer put forward another explanation in a paper entitled the *Origin of the Bengalis* published in *East and West* (Bombay) of April, 1907 (noticed in *Nature*, July 25th, 1907) which is elaborated above in Chapter II. Dr. A. C. Haddon has expressed very similar views with regard to the western section of the Indo-Aryans of the Outer countries. He writes in *The Races of Man* (pp. 60-61):—

"A zone of relatively *broad-headed* people extends from the great grazing country of the Western Punjab through the Deccan to the Coorgs. Risley supports the view that this may be the track of the Scythians, who found their progress east blocked by the Indo-Aryans and so turned south, and mingled with the Dravidian population, and became the ancestors of the Marathas and Canarese. But evidence seems to be lacking that the Scythians penetrated far into the Deccan, and apart from brachycephaly there is little to associate these peoples with Scythians. It seems quite possible that these brachycephals are the result of an unrecorded migration of some members of the Alpine race from the highlands of south-west Asia in pre-historic times.''

Dr. Haddon repeats this opinion in *The Wanderings of the Peoples* (Cambridge, 1911), p. 27, where he adds that "the foreign element is certainly Alpine, not Mongolian."

(2) Dr. Spooner's linguistic arguments are not likely to commend themselves to philologists. Among the languages of the Outer Band, the modern languages of Eastern India, viz., Behāri, Bengali, Assamese and Oriya owe their origins to Māgadhi Prākṛt. According to Pischel Māgadhi Prākṛt "included all those Prākṛt dialects which had *ya* instead of *ja*, *la* for *ra*, *śa* for *sa*, and in which the nominative of nouns in *a* ended *e*." * Some of these peculiarities, the nominative of nouns in *a* terminating in *e*, and the change of *r* into *l*, are also found in all the inscriptions of Aśoka except those of Girnar and of North-West-

* *The Indian Antiquary*, XXX, p. 555.

ern India.* The latter peculiarity is found in a Mleccha word spoken by the Asuras according to the *Satapatha Brāhmaṇa* III, 2. 1. 23. The text runs—

te' surā āttavacaso he'lavo he'lava iti vadantaḥ parābabhūbuḥ.

"The Asuras, being deprived of speech, were undone, crying, 'He'lavaḥ! he'lavaḥ.'"

Patañjali in his *Vyākaraṇa Mahābhāṣya* (I. 1. 1) quotes this passage in this modified form—

te' surā helayo helaya iti kurvantaḥ parābabhūbuḥ.

"The Asuras were undone crying, 'He *alayaḥ* (=*arayaḥ*, 'enemies'); he *alayaḥ*!'"

The Mleccha speech here assigned to the Asuras which changed *r* into *l* was evidently a Prākṛt dialect with an important phonetic peculiarity that characterises the Prākṛt used in eastern part of the empire of Aśoka and the Māgadhi Prākṛt of the Grammarians. This change of *r* into *l* distinguishes the Māgadhi Prākṛt not only from Sanskrit but also from Zend and Persian. Another peculiarity that distinguishes the Māgadhi Prākṛt from Zend is the change of *s* into *ś*, while the latter changes the original *s* into *h*. Therefore it is more reasonable to trace Māgadhi to an independent source than to Zend or to Vedic Sanskrit.

(3) The pottery with the Persian altar emblazoned on it and the Persipolitan style and grouping of the Maurya palaces disclosed by the

* *Ibid.*, XXI., p. 173.

excavation of the site of Pāṭaliputra should perhaps be attributed to the Persian architects and artizans employed by the Mauryas and not to the natives of Magadha whose ancestors are supposed to have come from Iran in the prehistoric period. The style of high-class architecture cannot be recognised as an evidence of the ethnic origin of the native population among whom the buildings are erected. The buildings of Darius and Xerxes at Persepolis and Susa are not Persian in style. Eduard Meyer writes: "The royal edifices and sculptures are dependent mainly on Babylonian models, but, at the same time, we can trace in them the influence of Greece, Egypt and Asia Minor; the last in the rock-sepulchres."*

(4) The well-known Sanskrit drama *Prabodhacandrodaya* was written in the reign of King Kīrttivarmaṇ Chandel of Kālañjar who reigned from A.D. 1049 to 1100 and was performed about A.D. 1065.† The statement contained in this work that "Magadha is mostly inhabited by the Mlecchas (*mlecchaprāya*)" cannot be accepted as evidence of prehistoric Iranian immigration.

(5) The presence of the Śākadvīpī Brāhmans in Bihar throws no light on the ethnic origin of the bulk of the population of Bihar. The Śākadvīpī Brāhmans are also known as Bhojaka or Maga Brāhmans, the last designation being considered as identical with Magus and on that ground the

---

* *Encyclopædia Britannica*, vol. 21, p. 210.

† V. A. Smith's *Early History of India*, 3rd edition, pp. 392-393.

Maga Brāhmans are recognised by some scholars as the modern representatives of the Persian Magi who migrated to India in the past. The legend of the coming of the Magi as narrated in the *Bhaviṣyapurāṇa* (137) is thus summed up by Bhandarkar:—

"Sāmba, the son of Kṛṣṇa by Jāmbavatī, constructed a temple of the sun on the banks of the Candrabhāgā, the modern Chenāb in the Punjāb, and no local Brāhman would accept the office of a regular priest of the temple. He thereupon asked Gauramukha, the priest of Ugrasena. He told him to get Magas, who were special sun-worshippers, from Śākadvīpa. Then is given the history of the Magas. Sujihva was a Brāhmaṇ of the Mihira Gotra. He had a daughter of the name of Nikṣubhā, with whom the sun fell in love. The son of these two was called Jarasabda or Jarasasta [=Zarathushtra], and from him sprang all Magas. They wore a girdle round their waist, which was called Avyaṅga. Thereupon Sāmba went on the back of Garuḍa, his father's vehicle, to Śākadvīpa, brought some Magas from it and installed them into the office of priests of the temple he had constructed." *

The legend of the importation of the Magas by Sāmba is referred to in the Govindapur stone inscription of the poet Gaṅgādhara, 'dated Śāka 1059, corresponding to A.D. 1137-38, thus: †—
" Hail to that gem of the three worlds, the divine

* *Vaiṣṇavism*, etc., p. 153.

† *Epigraphia Indica*, II, p. 338.

Aruṇa, whose presence sanctifies the milk-ocean-encircled Śākadvīpa where the Brāhmans are named Magas! There a race of twice-born [sprang] from the sun's own body, grazed by the lathe, whom Sāmba himself brought hither Glorious are they honoured in the world!'' This legend cannot be as old as the other legends about Kṛṣṇa and his descendants that are narrated in the *Harivaṃsa*, the *Viṣṇupurāṇa* and the *Bhāgavatapurāna*, for in that case it would have found a place in these standard authorities. So it cannot be treated as an evidence of the early migration of the Zoroastrians to India. But this legend is probably based on a tradition that the Magas were foreigners in origin—evidently related to the race of Jarasasta or Zarathushtra—and inaugurated the Saura cult in India. In the *Viṣṇupurāṇa* II. 4. 69-70 Magāh (*variant*, Mṛgāh), Magadhāh, Mānasāḥ and Mandagāḥ are given as the names of the Brāhmans, Kṣatriyas, Vaiśyas and Śūdras respectively of Śākadvīpa. In a palm-leaf manuscript of the *Mahābhārata* in Bengali character in the collection of the Varendra Research Society, in the *Bhiṣmaparvaṇ* (11, 35-38) we read:—

tatra puṇyā janapadā ścatvāro lokasammatāḥ
magāśca masakā ścaiva mānasā mandagā stathā
magā brāhmaṇabhūisṭhāḥ svakarmmanaratā nṛpa
masakeṣu tu rājanyā dhārmmikāḥ sarvvakāmadāh

mānasāśca mahārāja vaiśyadharmmopajīvinaḥ

* * *

śūdrā śca mandagā nityaṃ puruṣā dharmmaśālinaḥ

"There (in Śākdvīpa) are four holy countries praised by men—Magā, Masakā, Mānasā and Mandagā. Magā (contains) numerous Brāhmans devoted to their own duties. In Masakā there are Rājanyas pious and munificent, O King. O Mahārāja, Mānasas earn their bread by performing the duties of the Vaiśya . . . The Mandagas are ever pious Śūdras."

In the Bombay edition of the Mahābhārata and in the new edition based on the South Indian *MSS.* (printed in Bombay) we have *maṅgāh*, and in other editions *mṛgāh*, instead of *magā*. Magadhā of the *Viṣṇupurāṇa* is evidently a misreading for *Masakā* of the *Mahābhārata* and so the Magadhā cannot be connected with Śākadvīpa. But as the *Magas* are not mentioned in any of the earlier texts, though the *Magadhas* and the *Magadhadeśīyabrāhmaṇabandhus* are (*ante*, pp. 37-38), the time of the coming of the Magi cannot be pushed very far back. According to Weber, "The Magas go back to an old mission of the Mithra-cult, the members of which, after their arrival in India (about the first two centuries A.D.), were incorporated in the Brāhman caste." * Sir R. G. Bhandarkar writes: "On the coins of Kanishka there occurs a figure

---

* *The Indian Antiquary*, XVI, p. 162.

with the name Miiro = Mihira [Persian Mihr = Mithra] by its side . . . . The cult, therefore, must have penetrated to India about the time of that Kushana prince, and the Multan [Skt. *Mūlasthāna*] temple, which was its original seat, must have been constructed about the same time.''* This supposition is, I believe, correct. The Magas, as we have already seen (*ante*, pp. 160-161), appear in Indian history in connection with the worship of the sun-image, and the appearance of the name of Miiro [Mithra] on the Indian coin may be recognized as the first indication of their advent. The Magian missionaries of Mithraism probably did not come to India alone, and were partly adopted, as Weber observes, "probably together with some members of the other stratum of the Iranian immigrants, into the ranks of the Brāhmans themselves under the name of *Śākadvīpīya Brāhmans*."† Anyhow, the immigration of a class of men whose foreign origin was remembered by a people like the Hindus usually forgetful of the past cannot be pushed back to a remote antiquity. This unique tradition further shows that the Maga Brāhmans have always been recognized as aliens in Magadha and therefore a Magian origin cannot be postulated for the non-Maga population on the strength of this tradition.

Though pottery with the Persian fire-altar emblazoned on it is said to have been unearthed at the site of Pāṭaliputra, there is nothing peculiarly

* *Vaisṇavism*, etc., p. 154.

† *The Indian Antiquary*, XXX, p. 287.

Persian in the religion of Magadha in the Maurya period as known from the *Kauṭilīya Arthaśāstra*, the edicts of Aśoka and other sources. We discern three different strata in this religion,—a higher or philosophical stratum, and a Vedic stratum side by side with another that is evidently of local origin. Kauṭilya assigns to *Ānvīkṣakī* the first place among the sciences, the three others being—*trayī* (the triple Vedas), *vārttā* (agriculture or business generally) and the science of government. In the *Arthaśātra* I, 2, Ānvīkṣakī is said to comprise Sāṃkhya, Yoga and Lokāyata. The Sāṃkhya and Yoga are the names of well-known systems of philosophy. The meaning of Lokāyata is doubtful.* Patañjali (on Pāṇini VII 3, 1) names a commentary (*varṇikā*) on Lokāyata called Bhāgurī. The reason why Ānvīkṣakī is placed above the other sciences including *trayī* is thus explained by Kauṭilya I, 2 :—

" Righteous and unrighteous acts are learnt from the triple Vedas ; wealth and non-wealth from Vārttā ; the expedient and the inexpedient, as well as potency and impotency, from the science of Government ; (Ānvīkṣakī), viewing these (sciences) in the light of reason (*hetubhiḥ*), does good to the world, keeps the mind steady in weal and woe alike, and bestows skill in knowledge, speech, and action.†

---

* For an exhaustive discussion of the meanings of the term *Lokāyatā* see Rhys David's *Dialogues of Buddha* (London, 1899), pp. 166-172.

† Mr. Shamsastry translates "एतासां हेतुभि रन्वीक्षमाणा" in

" Ānvīkṣakī is ever held to be the lamp of all branches of knowledge, the means of performing all rites, and the support of all the sacred laws."

Ānvīkṣakī is grammatically irregular and the regular form Ānvīkṣikī is used in all other texts. The characteristic of viewing all other sciences in the light of reason better suits the Nyāya philosophy than Sāṃkhya and Yoga as we now have them. Vātsyāyana, the author of the *Bhāṣya* on Nyāya Sūtras of Gautama, takes Ānvīkṣikī in the sense of Nyāya philosophy. Commenting on Sūtra I, 1. 1. Vātsyāyana writes :—

" What do you mean by this Nyāya or *reasoning*? It means the examination of things [i.e. categories] by means of proofs, that is to say, Inference based upon Perception and Verbal Testimony is called 'Nyāya' or 'Reasoning'; it is also called '*Anvīkṣā*' ('investigation'), because it consists in the *reviewiug* (*anu-īkṣaṇa*) of a thing previously *apprehended* (*īkṣita*) by Perception and Verbal Testimony; the science that proceeds by this 'investigation' is called *Ānvīkṣikī*, *Nyāyavidyā*, *Nyāyaśāstra*."*

Vātsyāyana, in the concluding portion of his commentary on I, 11, reproduces the above-

---

this original as, " when seen in the light of these sciences." But this interpretation is not in agreement with the meaning of the stanza that follows wherein Ānvīkṣaki is called प्रदीपस्सर्व-विद्यानाम्, 'the lamp of all sciences.' Therefore एतासां is taken as the object of अन्वीक्षमाणा and Anvīkṣaki as the subject (understood).

* M. M. Gaṅganāth Jhā's translation, *Indian Thought*, Vol IV, pp. 174-175.

quoted stanza of Kauṭilya with one little variation, *vidyoddeśe prakīrttitā*, 'it has been expounded at the very outset of all *vidyā* or branches of knowledge' instead of *śaşvadānvīkṣakī matā*. Vātsyāyana is traditionally identified with Kauṭilya or Chānakya. The *Bhāṣya* on the *Nyāsyasūtra* attributed to Vātsyāyana is later in date than the Arthaśāstra; but the tradition of Chānakya's authorship of the *Bhāṣya* may be taken to indicate that it is a later production of a school of philosophy founded by Kauṭilya himself that subsequently specialised in Nyāya. Kāmandaka, whose Nītisāra is professedly a summary of Kauṭilya's *Arthaśāstra*, writes of Ānvīkṣikī (II, 11), "Ānvīkṣikī is *ātmavidyā* (=*padārthasvabhāvavidyā*, 'science of the nature of categories') or metaphysics; from observing (*īkṣaṇāt*) happiness and misery and finding out (*īkṣamānaḥ*) truth by means of that (Ānvīkṣikī) (one) removes pleasure and pain." *

The *Arthaśāstra* furnishes us with considerable materials for reconstructing the popular religion of the Maurya period. In the section (II, 4) on 'Buildings within the Fort' Kauṭilya ordains:—

"To the north, the royal deity of the city (*nagararāja-devatā*). . . . .

"In the centre of the city, the apartments of gods such as Aparājita Apratihata, Jayanta, Vaijayanta, Śiva, Vaiśravaṇa, Aśvin, and the

---

* आन्वीक्षिक्यात्मविद्या स्यादीक्षणात् सुखदुःखयोः ।
ईक्षमाणस्तया तत्त्वं हर्षशोकौ व्युदस्यति ॥

glorious liquor-house (*śri-madirāgṛham*) shall be situated.''*

Deśadevatā or the guardian deity of the country is also referred to by Kauṭilya. In the chapter on Remedies against National Calamities (IV, 3) Kauṭilya provides remedial measures against fire, flood, disease, famine, rats, tigers, serpents and demons (*rakṣāṃsi*). Against fire he ordains :—

"Not only on ordinary days, but also on full-moon days Agni should be worshipped (*agnipujāḥ kārayet*) with offerings, oblations, and prayers.''

Against floods :—

" On new and full-moon days also (*parvasu ca*) shall rivers be worshipped (*nadīpujāḥ kārayet*).

" Experts in magic and yoga (*māyāyoga vidaḥ*), and persons learned in the Vedas, shall perform rites against rain (*varṣamabhicareyuḥ*).

" During drought shall the husband of Sacī (Indra), Gangā, mountain, and Mahākaccha be worshipped.''

Against epidemic (*maraka*) :—

" Sprinkling water on sacred spots (*tīrthābhiṣecanam*), performance of the ceremonial called Mahākcchavardhana, milking the cows on the cremation ground, burning the trunk of a corpse, and spending nights in devotion to gods (*devarātriḥ*) shall also be performed.

" In case of epidemic among the cattle, . . . the worship of one's own favourite god (*svadaivatapūjanam*) also shall be carried out." †

* English tr., p. 61.

† English tr., p. 262. Mr. Shamsastry renders तीर्थाभिषेचनं

Against rats :—

"Holy men and ascetics (*siddhatāpasāḥ*) may also perform propitiatory rites.

"On new and full-moon days rats may be worshipped (*mūṣikapūjāḥ kārayet*)."

Against snakes :—

"Those who are learned in the Atharvaveda may perform auspicious rites. On new and full-moon days (snakes) may be worshipped."

Against tigers :—

"On new and full-moon days mountains may be worshipped."

Against Rakṣas (demons) :—

"Persons acquainted with the rituals of the Atharvaveda, and experts in magic and yoga, shall perform such ceremonials as ward off the danger from demons.

"On new and full-moon days the worship of caityas may be performed by placing on a verandah offerings such as an umbrella, the picture of an arm, a flag and some goat's flesh." *

In the concluding stanza of IX, 7 it is enjoined :—

"Whether demoniacal (*āsurī*) troubles are absent or are too many, or normal, the rites prescribed in the Atharvaveda as well as the rites undertaken by accomplished ascetics (*siddhayaḥ*) are performed for success."

as oblations to gods; and सदैवतपूजनं as the worship of family gods.

* *Ibid.*, p. 264.

The chapter on Means to Injure Enemy (XIV. 1) concludes with these formulas :—

"Salutation to Aditi! salutation to Anumati! saluation to Sarasvati! salutation to Savitṛ! Svāhā to Agni! svāhā to Soma! svāhā to Bhūḥ! svāhā to Bhūvaḥ!"

The formulas contained in the chapter on the application of medicines and Mantras (XIV. 3) furnish us with valuable materials for reconstructing the Mauriyan pantheon. These are :—

"I bow to Bali, son of Vairocana; to Śambara acquainted with a hundred kinds of magic (*satamāyam*); to Bhaṇḍirapāka, Naraka, Nikumbha and Kumbha.

"I bow to Devala and Nārada; I bow to Sāvarṇigālava; with the permission of these I cause deep slumber to thee.

* * *

"Having bowed to Manu, and having tethered the roguish dogs, and having also bowed to those gods who are in heaven (*devalokeṣu*), to Brāhmans among men;

"to those who are well-versed in the Veda, to Siddhas (holy men), and to ascetics dwelling in the Kailāsa mountain (*Kailāsa tāpasaḥ*), to all these holy men (Siddhas), I do cause slumber to thee.

* * *

"Oblation to Manu, Aliti and Paliti.

* * *

"I bow to (the goddess) Suvarṇapuṣpī and Brahmāṇī, to (the god) Brahmā and Kuśadvaja, to serpents and goddesses; I bow to all ascetics.

"Oblation to thee, O Amili, Kimile, Vayujāre, Prayoge, Phake, Kavayuśve, Vihāle, Dantakaṭake, oblation to thee.

"I bow to Bali, the son of Vairocana, to Śambara acquainted with hundred kinds of magic, to Nikumbha, Naraka, Kumbha, Tantukaccha, the great demon (*Mahāsura*);

"to Amrālava, Pramīla, Maṇḍolūka and Ghaṭodbala; to Kṛṣṇa with Kaṃsa and to famous Paulamī."

Other supernatural beings named are, Salaka demons, Caṇḍālī, Kumbhī, Tumbu Kaṭūka and Sārigha. From this catalogue of demons it is a relief to turn back to the chapter on Punishment for violating justice (IV. 13) which is thus concluded:—

"When the King punishes an innocent man, he shall throw into water dedicating to god Varuṇa a fine equal to thirty times the unjust imposition; and this amount shall afterwards be distributed among the Brāhmans.

"By this act the King will be free from the sin of unjust imposition; for King Varuṇa is the ruler of sinners among men."

It will be observed that among gods, goddesses, Ṛṣis, heroes and demons invoked in the *Arthaśāstra* of Kauṭilya, there are some that do not belong to the Vedic pantheon. We may recognise in them the gods and demons worshipped by the early inhabitants of Magadha. The images of gods (*devapratimā*), *Caityas* and *Stupas* were regularly worshipped; for we are told (XIII. 2):—

"When the enemy is in the habit of paying frequent visits to holy men (*siddhas*), wandering mendicants (*pravrajita*), *Caityas*, *Stupas*, and images of gods (*daivata-pratimā*), spies hidden in underground chambers or in subterranean passages, or inside the walls, may strike him down."

Caitya-stupa may be a compound and mean 'a sepulchral mound.' Here we can trace the root from which the Buddhists derived their worship of *Caityas* and *Stupas*. The following extract (XIII. 2) shows that the Caityas were high mounds situated near cities and considered as the abode of evil spirits:—

"Climbing on a *Caitya* (*caitymāruhya*) at night in the vicinity of the city of the enemy and blowing through tubes or hollow reeds the fire contained in a few pots, some firey spies may speak indistinctly, 'We are going to eat the flesh of the King or his ministers, let our worship continue.'"

In the *Āśvalāyana-Gṛhya-Sūtrā* I. 12, 1-7, the following rite called the *Caitya sacrifice* is ordained:—

1. "At a Caitya sacrifice he should before the Sviṣṭakṛt (offering) offer a Bali to the Caitya.

"If, however, (the Caitya) is distant (he should send his Bali) through a leaf messenger.

*   *   *

5. "If there is anything dangerous between (them and the Caitya), (he gives him) some weapon also.

6. "If a navigable river is betweeen (them and the Caitya, he gives him) also something like a raft with (the words), 'Hereby thou shalt cross.'" *

Āśvalāyana's statement, read in the light of the *Arthaśāstra*, leaves no room for doubting that Caitya denoted a mound worshipped as a fetish. The Caitya was an object of popular worship and was borrowed both by the Brāhmans and the Buddhists from the folk religion. The author of the *Arthaśastra*, as an orthodox Brāhman, is hostile to the Buddhists. Under 'Miscellaneous offences' he ordains (III. 20): "When a person entertains, in dinner dedicated to gods or ancestors, Buddhists (Sakya), Ājīvakas, Śūdras and exiled persons (*pravrajita*), a fine of 100 paṇas shall be imposed." †

The Gayāśīrṣa hill and the Akṣaya (imperishable) Vaṭa tree of Gaya were the two very holy objects of Magadha. In the *Institutes of Viṣṇu* (LXXXV, 4-5) it is enjoined that Śrāddha (funeral oblations) offered at Gayāśīrṣa and near the Vaṭa (Akṣayavaṭa) confers eternal bliss upon the giver. In the *Mahābhārata* (III. 84, 83) we are told: "There (at Gaya) is the Akṣayavaṭa renowned in the three worlds; it is said that what is offered there to the ancestors never perishes." In the *Gṛhya Sūtras* and in the *Dharmasūtras* of Āpastamba, Gautama and Vaudhāyana Gaya is not mentioned in connection with the funeral

* *Sacred Books of the East*, XXIX, pp. 178-179.

† English tr., p. 251.

oblations. But Gautama ordains (XV. 5) that when one is near a particularly sacred place no restrictions as to time need be observed regarding funeral oblations. The holy Gayāśīrṣa hill and the Akṣayavaṭa of Gaya were chosen for funeral oblations evidently under this rule.

The edicts of Aśoka also afford us glimpses of the folk religion of the Maurya period. In the fourth rock edict Aśoka proclaims: "But now, in consequence of the adoption of the *dharma* (law of morality) by Devāṇāṃpriya Priyadarśin, the sound of the drum is, lo! but the sound of the *dharma*, the spectacle presented to the people, processional cars, elephants, bonfires and others, the representations of the *devas*." *

Here Aśoka refers to religious processions that he arranged for the edification of his subjects. In these processions images of gods riding on chariots and elephants were exhibited. The correct translation of the term *misā* in the Rūpnāth, Sahasrām and Brahmagiri edicts by M. Sylvain Levi has revealed to us another phase of Aśoka's activities in the same line. The passage in the Rūpnāth edict containing the term is thus translated by Hultzsch:—

"Those gods who up to this time had been unassociated (*with men*) in Jambudvīpa have now been made associated (*with them*)."

The corresponding passage of the Sahasrām edict is thus rendered:—

* Prof. S. K. Aiyangar's translation, *The Indian Antiquary*, Vol. XLIV, p 205.

"Men in Jambudvīpa who up to this time had been unassociated with the gods have (*now*) been made associated with the gods." *

The same fact is also stated in a passage of the newly discovered Maski rock edict of Aśoka. †

The text of the passage runs:—

pure Jaṁbu - . s [i] . . . [deva husu] te d [ā] ni misibhūtā

misibhūtā, like *misā* in the Rūpnāth and other edicts, is derived from Pāli *missa*, Sanskrit *miśra*, 'mixed,' and should be rendered as 'got mixed,' 'got associated'; and the passage should be rendered thus:—

"(*Those gods who*) were (*not*) formerly (*associated with men*) in Jambu [dvīpa] . . . have now been made associated (with them)." ‡

The most important question in this connection is, who were the gods whose cults were propagated by Aśoka all over his empire? Dr. F. W. Thomas suggests: "Are we to understand a conversion of people who previously did not recognize the Brāhmanical gods?" § This view is endorsed by Professor Hultzsch who adds, "In a slightly modified form, this suggestion finds support in many passages of the rock and pillar edicts, in which Aśoka declares that his chief

---

* *Journal of the Royal Asiatic Society*, 1911, pp. 1114-1115.

† *Hyderabad Archæological Series*, No. I, *New Asokan Edict of Maski*, p. 4.

‡ Mr. H. Krishna Sastri, the editor and translator of the edict, takes *misibhūtā* in the sense *mṛṣībhūtāḥ* (p. 5).

§ *Journal of the Royal Asiatic Society*, 1912, p. 480.

aim was to secure the 'attainment of heaven' (*svagaradhī*, Girnār, ix, l. 9) by his subjects through the practice of morality."* Perhaps this is the correct view. But I would venture to suggest that by "Brāhmanical gods" we must neither understand the ancient Brāhmanical Vedic gods, nor the Brāhmanical gods recognized by the modern Hindus, but the Brāhmanical gods recognized by the natives of Magadha. The *Arthaśāstra* of Kauṭilya affords us a glimpse of those gods.

In the religion of the Maurya period as set forth above we do not discern any element that is peculiarly Persian or Magian. Of course magic (*māyāyoga*) occupied a very prominent place in this religion. But magic was not the monopoly of the Magi, it was universal. Dr. Otto Schrader writes, "There was among the Aryans, just as among all other people, a more ancient way of bringing the supernatural within reach of the natural than sacrifice and prayer, namely, *magic*." † Other elements may be traced to the Indo-Iranian or even the Aryan period.

I shall bring this criticism of Dr. Spooner's theory to a close with a few observations on one other aspect of his theory,—his rejection of the accepted view regarding the origin of Buddhism that Gautama, "having been born a Hindu," "repudiated the teachings of Hinduism, denied the authority of its scriptures, broke from it altogether and founded a rival church which grew

* *Ibid.*, p. 1059.

† *Encyclopædia of Religion and Ethics*, II, p. 40*a*.

and flourished at the expense of the Hindu faith." Dr. Spooner defines his own view as follows:—

"I hold that Gautama broke away, not from the Hindu faith, but from the Magian, and stepped out, not away from Hinduism but towards it, and built up his following not primarily from the ranks of Hinduism but from those of the Iranian community in this country, thereby setting in motion forces which reached their culmination when at length the Buddhist community in India merged by slow degrees imperceptively into the Hindu fold and ceased to have an individual existence."

One proof of Gautama's Magian origin adduced by Dr. Spooner is the name Śākyamuni, the dictionaries asserting that this word Śākya means "descendants of the Śakas or Scythians." It is now generally held that the Scythians were Iranian in speech, but that they were also Magian in religion has not yet been seriously suggested. Whatever the dictionaries may say, the oldest Buddhist texts, the *Ambaṭṭha Sutta** and the *Mahāvastu,*† derive Śākya from *Śakya,* 'able' (see also *ante*, p. 155). In Vedic India Śāka was quite a common name among the Brāhman teachers. A Śākadāsa Bhāḍitāyana is mentioned in the Vaṃsa Brāhmaṇa. Śākāyanya, 'descendant of Śāka,' is the patronymic of one Jāta in the Kāṭhaka Saṃhitā (XXVII, 7). Śākāyanins or followers of Śākāyanya are referred to in the Śatapatha Brāh-

* Rhys David's *Dialogues of the Buddha* (I), p. 115.

† Senart's *Mahāvastu*, Vol. I, p. 351.

maṇa (X, 4. 5). In the Maitrāyani Upaniṣad one Sākāyanya is the teacher of Bṛhadratha, a king of the Ikṣvāku line.* In the dictionaries 'Śāka' is also as explained 'relating to Sāka or Indo-scythians.'

The accepted view that Gautama Buddha was born a Hindu is based on traditions and legends enshrined in such canonical works as the *Mahāvastu*, the *Diviyāvadāna*, and the *Lalita Vistara*, and non-canonical works like Aśvaghoṣa's *Buddhacarita* and the Pali *Nidānakathā*. These works agree in representing Suddhodana as a Brāhmanist. A Brāhman named Udayana was his *Purohita* (domestic priest).† Ten days after the birth of the future Buddha, we are told in the *Buddhacarita* I, 88-89, Suddhodana "offered for his son most elaborate sacrifices to the gods with muttered prayers, oblations" and gave to the Brāhmans cows full of milk. When the child first entered Kapilavastu with his mother, he was taken to the temple named *Śākyavardhana* for bowing to the feet of the image of the goddess *Abhayā*, according to the *Mahāvastu*.‡ Abhayā was probably a form of Durgā In the *Divyāvadāna* the temple (*devakula*) is called *Śākyavardha*, but the presiding deity is not named.§ In the *Lalita Vistara* the name of the temple is omitted, but it is said that the temple

* *Vedic Index*, II, pp. 368-369.

† *Lalita Vistara* (Lefmann), p. 121.

‡ राज्ञा शुद्धोदनेन अमात्या आज्ञप्ता। इम एवं कुमारं शाक्यवर्धनं देवकुलं नेथ अभयाये देवीये पादवन्दनं। *Mahāvastu* (Senart) II, p. 26.

§ *Divyāvadāna* (Cowell and Neil), p. 391.

contained the images of the following gods—Śiva, Skanda, Nārāyaṇa, Moon, Sun, Vaiśravaṇa, Śakra, Brahmā and the Lokapālas (viz., Dhṛtarāṣṭra, Viruḍhaka, Virupākṣa and Vaiśravaṇa).* If one chooses to ignore these traditions, while crediting others like the next-of-kin marriage practised by Gautama Buddha's remote ancestors, anything can be proved about him.

Traditional evidences are also not wanting to show that Gautama Buddha deliberately repudiated Brāhmanism. The great renunciation of Sarvārthsiddha took place in the dead of night. Leaving Kapilavastu he rode southward. We are told in the *Mahāvastu* that after riding on Kanṭhaka for twelve *yojanas* the prince reached a place (*adhisṭhāna*) called Anomiya in the Malla country not far from the hermitage of the Ṛṣi Vasiṣṭha (i.e., of the Vasiṣṭha clan). After assuming the garb of a monk Gautama entered the hermitage of the old Ṛṣi and was cordially welcomed there. The Ṛṣi asked the prince, "Who are you, and why have you come to this hermitage?" Gautama said that he came of the Ikṣvāku line (*vāṃśa*) and was the son of King Suddhodana; he had renounced the world to seek liberation from birth, disease, old age, and death. The Ṛṣi replied that nothing was unattainable for one like him. Nothing more is said in the *Mahāvastu* about Gautama's doings in the hermitage, and the narrative is abruptly cut off with the statement that the Bodhisattva ('future Buddha') went to

* *Lalita Vistara* (Lefmann), pp. 119-120.

Vaiśāli, and sought instructions from Ārāḍa Kālāma.* In the *Divyāvadānā* it is said that the sage to whose hermitage the Bodhisattva went after donning the yellow robe of a monk was Bhārgava (son of Bhṛgu).† In the *Buddhacarita* also the same tradition is preserved. "Then when the sun, the eye of the world, was just risen, he, the noblest of men, beheld the hermitage of the son of Bhṛgu" (VI. 1).‡ In this hermitage of the son of Bhṛgu the prince met with Brāhman ascetics who, desirous of heaven, were performing different kinds of penance. "He spent several nights there, himself like the moon, examining their penances; and he departed from that penance field, feeling that he comprehended the whole nature of penance" (VII, 34). As Gautama was leaving the hermitage, the chief of the ascetics implored him to stay in the hermitage. Gautama replied, "But this devotion of yours is for the sake of heaven,—while my desire is that there may be no fresh birth; therefore I wish not to dwell in this wood; the nature of cessation is different from that of activity" (VII. 48). Leaving the hermitage of the Brāhman ascetics, the Bodhisattva sought the help of the Śramaṇas Arāḍa Kālāma of Vaiśāli and Udraka Rāmaputra of Rajagṛha in succession. Dissatisfied with their teachings, the Bodisattva retired to the forest of Uruvilva near Gaya and

* Senart's *Mahāvastu*, II, pp. 164, 195-198.

† *Divyāvadāna*, p. 391. See also *Lalita Vistara* (Lefmann), p. 238.

‡ *Mahāvastu* II, pp. 124-130.

there performed for six years penances practised by the Śramaṇas and the Brāhmans of those days.* After practising severe penances for six years he discovered that "this is not the way to enlightenment" (*nāyam mārga bodhāva*), "this is not the way to liberation" (*nāyam mārga mokṣāye*). Thus was Hinduism repudiated by Gautama the Bodhisattva. But it was not a complete repudiation of Hinduism. One aspect of Hinduism, faith in the doctrine of transmigration, led this Kṣatriya monk to repudiate another aspect—the practices leading to heaven.

---

* Cowell's translation, *Sacred Books of the East*, XLIX.

NOTES.

A. Ārya and Śūdra (p. 2).

In the early Ṛgvedic age, before there were Vaiśyas and Śūdras, the 'noseless' aborigines who opposed the Āryas were called Dasyus or Dāsas. In the later Vedic literature, the Śūdra, instead of the Dasyu or Dāsa, is contrasted with the Ārya. It is usually assumed that the term Ārya is used in the ethnic sense in the Ṛgveda as well as in the later Vedas. But such a view is opposed to tradition which should not be ignored in the interpretation of texts like the Yajurveda wherein not only the four castes, but also some of the so-called mixed castes find mention, and the Atharvaveda which is even later in form. According to Pāṇini (III. 1. 103) Ārya means 'master' (*svāmī*) as well as 'Vaiśya.' So when Ārya is not used in the sense of 'Vaiśya,' it denotes the first three castes—Brāhman, Kṣatriya, and Vaiśya—not because they are Aryan in blood, but because they are 'masters,' that is to say, freemen, and not slaves. This is evident from the following passages of Kauṭilya's *Arthaśāstra* (III. 13) wherein even a Sūdra freeman is classed as an Ārya:—

"The selling or mortgaging by kinsmen of the life of a Śūdra, who is not a born slave, and has not attained majority, but is an Ārya in birth, shall be punished with a fine of 12 paṇas; of a Vaiśya, 24 paṇas; of a Kṣatriya, 36 paṇas; and of a Brāhman, 48 paṇas.

* * * *

"It is no crime for Mlecchas to sell or mortgage the life of their own offspring. But never shall an Ārya be subjected to slavery.

* * * *

"Deceiving a slave of his money or depriving him of the privileges he can exercise as an Ārya (*Āryabhāva*) shall be punished with half the fine (levied for enslaving the life of an Ārya). * * * *

"The offspring of a man who has sold off himself as a slave shall be an Ārya. A slave shall be entitled to enjoy not only whatever he has earned without prejudice to his master's work, but also the inheritance he has received from his father.

"On paying the value (for which one is enslaved), a slave shall regain his Āryahood (*āryatvam*). The same rule shall apply either to born or pledged slaves." *

To attach any ethnic significance to the term Śūdra and also to the term Ārya as used in the later Vedic and Sanskrit literature is, therefore, misleading.

B. The Piśāca Affinities of Lahndā, Sindhī and Kashmirī.

In a paper on *The North-Western group of the Indo-Aryan Vernaculars* (*Indian Antiquary*, XLIV, p. 226) Sir George Grierson writes:—

"The position of Lahndā in regard to Pañjābī is altogether peculiar. The whole Pañjāb is the meeting ground of two entirely distinct languages, *viz.* the Piśācha parent of Lahndā which expanded from the Indus Valley eastwards, and the old Midland language, the parent of the modern Western Hindī, which expanded from the Jamna Valley westwards. In the Pañjab they overlapped. In the Eastern Pañjāb, the wave of old Lahndā had nearly exhausted itself, and old Western Hindī had the mastery, the resulting language being Pañjābī. In the Western Pañjāb, the old Western Hindī had nearly exhausted itself, and old Lahndā had the mastery, the resulting language being modern Lahndā. The latter language is therefore in the main of Pīśācha origin but bears traces of the old Western Hindī. Such traces are much more numerous, and of much greater importance in Pañjābī. Lahndā may be described as a Pīśācha language

* English translation, pp. 230-232.

infected by Western Hindī, while Pañjābī is a form of Western Hindī infected by Piśācha.

"Sindhī, on the contrary, shows a much more clear relationship to the Piśācha languages, being protected from invasion from the East by the desert of Western Rajputānā. While modern Lahndā, from its origin, merges imperceptively into Pañjābī, Sindhī does not merge into Rājasthānī, but remains quite distinct from it. Such border dialects as exist are mere mechanical mixtures, not stages in a gradual linguistic change.

"On the South the case of Sindhī and Gujarātī is nearly the same; but there is a certain amount of real change from one language to another in the border dialect of Kachchhī owing to the fact that Gujarātī, although now, like Rājasthānī, a member of the Central Group of Indo-Aryan Vernaculars, has at its base remnants of some north-western language."

Sir George Grierson writes about Kāshmīrī:—"Kāshmīrī is a mixed language, having as its basis a language of the Dard group of the Piśācha family allied to Shiṇā. It has been powerfully influenced by Indian culture and Indian literature. and the greater part of its vocabulary is now of Indian origin and is allied to that of the Sanskritic Indo-Aryan languages of Northern India. As, however, its basis—in other words. its phonetic system, its accidence, its syntax, its prosody—is Piśācha, it must be classed as such, and not as a Sanskritic form of speech." (*Indian Antiquary*. XLIV, p. 270).

The place of the so-called Piśācha languages in the Aryan family is thus defined by the same authority:—"It has been previously pointed out that the Piśācha languages, which include the Shiṇā-khōwār group, occupy a position intermediate between the Sanskritic languages of India proper and the Eranian languages further to their West. They thus possess many features that are common to them and to the Sanskritic languages, But they also possess features peculiar to themselves. and others in which they agree rather with the languages of the Eranian family." (Ibid.. p. 257).

C. Sound Changes in Bengali.

Speaking of Kāshmīrī phonetics, Sir George Grierson writes in the second article quoted in the last note: "In none of the modern Piśācha languages, except in the case of a few borrowed words, are there any sonant aspirates. When such letters originally formed part of a word, the aspiration is dropped, so that *gh* becomes *g*, *jh* becomes *j* or *z*, *ḍh* becomes *ḍ* or *r*, *dh* becomes *d*, and *bh* becomes *g*. There is nothing like this in India proper, but it is a universal rule in Kāshmīrī" (p. 258).

Sir George Grierson has already noted in his *Linguistic Survey of India*, Vol. V, Part I (Specimens of the Bengali and Assamese Languages) that in the dialects of Eastern Bengal aspiration is often omitted from soft consonants, *gh*, *jh*, *ḍh*, *dh*, and *bh*. The present writer can speak from personal knowledge about the dialect spoken by the common people of Vikrampur (Munshigunge Subdivision), Dacca District. In this dialect sonant consonants *gh*, *jh*, *ḍh*, *dh* and *bh* have no place.

1. (*a*) *ghar*, 'house,' is pronounced as *gar*: *ghoḍā* is *gorā*.
   (*b*) *aghor* is pronounced as *agor*.
   (*c*) *bāgh*, 'tiger,' is pronounced as *bāg*.
2. (*a*) *jhaḍ*, 'storm,' is pronounced as *jar* or *zar* and *jhāṁṭā* is pronounced as *jāṭā* or *zālā*.
   (*b*) *bujhilām*, 'I understand,' is pronounced as *bujilām*.
   (*c*) *bojhā* is pronounced as *bojā*, *sojhā* is pronounced as *sojā*. Medial and terminal *jh* is pronounced *j* even in the spoken language of Calcutta.
3. (*a*) *dhūti*, 'loin-cloth,' is pronounced as *duti*,
   (*b*) *adhar* is pronounced as *adar*.
   (*c*) *kāṁdh* is pronounced as *kānd*, *bāṁdh* as *bānd*.
4. (*a*) *ḍhāk*, 'drum,' is pronounced as *dāk*, *dhākā* as *dākā*, 'covered' (hence Dacca).
5. (*a*) *bhāvanā*, 'anxiety,' is pronounced as *bāb'na*, *bhāri*, 'heavy,' as *bāri*.
   (*b*) *abhay* is pronounced as *abay*.
   (*c*) *ābh*, 'mica,' is pronounced as *āb*.

While Sir George Grierson traces the Bengali pronunciation of *kṣ* as *kkha*, *hy* as *jjh*, *kt* as *t*, and *sāgara* as *śāgara* or śāyara to the influence of Māgadhī Prākṛt as illustrated by the grammarian Hemacandra,* he lays no stress on the absence of sonant aspirates in the spoken language of Eastern Bengal. This cannot be a mere accident, but an heirloom from the non-Sanskritic predecessor of the present Sanskritic Bengali. In Eastern Bengal the Sanskritic Bengali of our day is pronounced not with genuine Sanskritic sounds, but with the sounds of its predecessor or parent as far as the sonant aspirates are concerned. This non-Sanskritic parent of modern Bengali was akin to the parent language of Kāshmīrī and other languages spoken in the North-West of India and named Piśāca languages by Sir George Grierson. Another phonetic peculiarity of the spoken language of the illiterate classes of Eastern Bengal which points to the same conclusion is the pronunciation of the initial sibilant *ś* as *h*. Thus, *śvaśur*, 'father-in-law,' is pronounced as *haśur* or *haur*; *ṣām̐ḍ*, 'bull,' as *hār*; and *sāp*, 'serpent,' as *hāp*, and *sakal*, 'all,' as *hagal* or *haggal*. Though in the written Bengali *ś*, *ṣ*, and *s* find place, yet in the spoken Bengali there is only one sibilant *ś*, a legacy from the Māgadhī Prākṛt and in Eastern Bengal, as in Kashmir, this initial ś is pronounced as *h*.

D. Un-Vedic Pañcarātra (Chapter III, p. 108).

The orthodox view regarding the un-Vedic phase of the Pāñcarātra is thus stated by Mitra Miśra in his *Vīramitrodaya*:—

"Further, the *Pāśupata* scriptures have to be divided into the 'Vedic' and the 'Non-Vedic': in view of what the *Kūrmapurāṇa* says in regard to it......

* * * *

In the *Vāyusaṃhitā* also we find the following:—'The Śaiva (*Pāśupata*) scripture also is of two kinds—Vedic and non-

* *Linguistic Survey of India*, Vol. V, Part I, p. 15.

Vedic; the Vedic is that which contains the essence of the Veda, and the non-Vedic is that which is independent. The independent one is of ten kinds: .... that which contains the essence of the Veda extends a millionfold. The highest Pāśupata is that which lays down observances and right knowledge.

Here also the distinction between the 'Vedic' and the 'non-Vedic' is made quite clear. We find above the phrase 'the Śaiva scripture *also*', the 'also' of which indicates the other cognate scriptures of the *Vaiṣṇava*. the *Pāñcarātra* and the like—the activities and results connected wherewith are similar to those of the *Pāśupata*, and which also are of two kinds, *Vedic and non-Vedic*.

That the *Pāñcarātra* and other scriptures are *Vedic* in their character is thus declared in the *Viṣṇudharmottara* as quoted in the *Hemādri* :—

'The Sāṃkhya, the Yoga, the Pāñcarātra, the Vedas and the Pāśupata—these constitute the five doctrines in the seeking of Brahman. These are the road to the ending of birth and rebirth, and also to the bringing about of the sovereignty of Heaven. That which extends up to the Vaiṣṇavadharma has been described as the very essence. Such is the entire Vedic path, as described by you.'

The term '*bhāva*' here stands for *sovereignty*; and '*setu*' for *road*. In the *Kūrmapurāṇa* we read :—

'The Kāpāla. the Pāñcarātra, the Yāmala, the Vāma, the Ārhata—these and several other systems are for the purpose of deluding people.'

But the 'delusive' character here attributed to the *Pāñcarātra* refers to the *non-Vedic* Pāñcarātra; because in the same Purāṇa we find the passage—'The several scriptures that are found in this world to be contrary to the Veda and the Smṛtis, the foundation of all these is purely delusive';—where what are referred to are clearly only those that are contrary to the Veda.

*   *   *   *

In the Sāmba-Purāṇa we find the passage—'A man who has fallen off from the Veda, and is afraid of having to perform the expiatory rites laid down in the Veda, should, in due course, have recourse to the *Tantra*, for the purpose of accomplishing Vedic knowledge.' Again in the *Kūrma-purāṇa* we read:—'Aṃśu, the high-souled Sātvata, the great devotee of Viṣṇu, was addicted to charity, he was the best of archers, was engaged, by Nārada's advice, in the worshipping of Vāsudeva; he propounded the scripture which is followed by lower born persons: the excellent scripture came to be known by his name, as Sātvata; and this scripture, duly propounded, became conducive to the welfare of the low-born.' The *Śrī Bhāgavata* also says as follows:—'The Sātvata Tantra was propounded by him, knowing which one becomes a participator in Final Release; it is in accordance with this Tantra that women and Śūdras are entitled to the Vaiṣṇava rites.' On the basis of these passages some people have asserted that, inasmuch as these texts lay down that only such people as have fallen off from the Veda are entitled to the Āgama-scriptures, it means that persons not so fallen have nothing to do with them. But this is not a statement by persons acquainted with logic. Because the texts speaking of those 'fallen off from the Veda' do not lay down such people as the 'Agents' in connection with *Tantra*,—in the way in which the King is laid down as the Agent in regard to the Rājasūya sacrifice: and inasmuch as the texts do not lay down any such Agents, it cannot follow that people other than those mentioned are not entitled to the performance of the acts laid down in the Tantra. What the passages do is to assert that the *Tantra* is for the people mentioned (i.e., those who have fallen from the Veda). So that, just as in the case of the text—'inasmuch as the Veda is not heard by women, Śudras and low Brāhmans, the Bhārata has been put forward—even though the *Bhārata* is spoken of as propounded for the sake of women and Śūdras, yet that does not preclude the title of other persons also to that work,—in the same manner, even in the face of the aforesaid passages, the title of others (i.e., those *not* fallen from the Veda) also to the Āgama scriptures remains unshaken (*Indian Thought*, VII, pp. 387-390)."

APPENDIX.

Anthropometric Data.

To supplement the data of anthropometry published in the *Ethnographical Appendices* to Census of India, 1901, Report, and to test the historical value of the tradition that Rāḍhīya and Vārendra Brāhmans of Bengal are the descendants of five Brāhmans imported by King Ādiśūra from Kanauj. Mr. Sasadhar Ray, M.A., B.L., and myself measured, in 1909 the head form of 35 Rāḍhīya and 76 Vārendra Brāhmans of Bengal and Rao Sahib Pundit Matadin Sukul, M.A., B.E., then Executive Engineer, Rajshahi Division, measured on our behalf 63 Kanaujia (Kānyakubjīya) Brāhmans of the Cawnpore district (U. P. and Oudh). Unfortunately the papers containing the figures relating to head length and head breadth are lost and the indices that were recorded in a separate note-book are tabulated below :—

	Rāḍhīya Brāhmans.		Vārendra Brāhmans.		Kanaujia Brāhmans	
	No.	Percentage.	No.	Percentage.	No.	Percentage.
Cephalic indices under 70.	..	..	..	..	3	5
Cephalic indices from 70 to 72·4.	1	2·9	3	4	16	25
Cephalic indices from 72·5 to 74·9.	6	17·2	9	12	21	33
Cephalic indices from 75 to 77·9.	10	28·6	20	26	14	23
Cephalic indices from from 78 to 79·9.	5	14·3	16	21	5	8
Cephalic indices of 80 and over.	13	37	28	37	4	6

In 1910 I was placed on special duty for ethnological researches for three months by the Government of Eastern Bengal and Assam and measured the head form, nose form and stature of the male members of the following castes and sub-castes of Bengal and Bihar with anthrometrical instruments lent by the Ethnographical Survey of India.

Santāls.

(Settled near Ghoraghat in the District of Dinajpur.)

1	2	3	4	5	6	7	8	9	10
Serial No.	District of birth.	Age.	Head length.	Head breadth.	Cephalic index.	Nasal height.	Nasal breadth.	Nasal index.	Stature.
1	Santāl Parganas	35	176	135	76·7	43	42	97·6	165·4
2	,, ..	33	185	143	77·3	43	40	90·9	154·0
3	,, ..	25	196	135	68·8	46	37	80·4	165·0
4	,, ..	45	172	140	81·4	43	44	102·0	158·0
5	,, ..	43	183	141	77·0	40	38	95·0	156·0
6	,, .	32	181	137	75·6	47	36	76·6	157·0
7	,, ..	40	180	137	76·1	38	39	102 6	158·0
8	,, ..	42	177	138	77·9	38	44	115·7	158·0
9	,, ..	31	188	131	69·1	39	36	92·3	157·2
10	,, .	36	170	139	81·7	44	30	68·1	156·0
11	,, ..	40	186	144	77·4	37	36	97·2	160·0
12	,, ..	44	181	136	75·1	48	39	81·2	157 0
13	,, ..	26	180	132	73·3	37	39	105·4	162·0
14	,, ..	45	195	143	73·7	38	45	118·4	164·0
15	,, ..	38	176	133	75·5	42	36	85·7	156·2
16	,, ..	32	183	127	69·4	42	37	88·0	160·0
17	,, ..	27	189	130	68·7	43	40	93·0	164·2
18	,, ..	38	177	125	70·6	46	41	89·1	161·0
19	,, ..	29	171	132	77·1	45	39	86·6	159·0
20	,, ..	26	192	135	70·3	43	40	93·0	157·0
21	,, ..	33	173	133	76·8	42	46	109·0	162·0
22	,, ..	36	192	133	69·2	43	36	83·7	144 0
23	,, ..	27	169	13	76·9	41	36	87·8	170·2
24	,, ..	30	195	139	71·2	41	36	87·8	159·6
25	,, ..	44	183	138	76·6	45	40	88·8	163·0
26	,, ..	42	192	135	70·3	40	43	107·5	164·4
27	,, ..	40	187	135	72·1	46	38	82·6	161·0
28	,, ..	28	184	125	67·9	38	38	100·0	163·0
29	,, ..	38	189	140	74·0	41	39	95·1	162·0

Brāhman (Bengal).

1	2	3	4	5	6	7	8	9	10	
Serial No.	District of birth.	Age.	Head length.	Head breadth.	Cephalic index.	Nasal height.	Nasal breadth.	Nasal index.	Stature.	Sub-Caste.
1	Pubna ..	29	183	145	79·2	54	38	70·3	165·8	Vārendra.
2	Murshidabad	25	185	157	84·9	51	37	72·5	172·1	,,
3	Pubna ..	35	182	151	82·9	45	36	80·0	157·3	,,
4	,, ..	33	180	146	81·1	50	33	66·0	168·2	,,
5	Mymensingh	36	192	145	75·5	50	32	64·0	182·6	,,
6	Rajshahi ..	41	178	144	80·8	45	35	77·7	161·2	,,
7	,, ..	25	180	140	77·7	50	36	72·0	175·4	,,
8	,, ..	38	183	141	77·0	47	39	82·9	169·6	,,
9	,, ..	42	184	133	72 2	45	31	68·8	162·2	,,
10	,, ..	35	190	151	79·4	56	34	60·7	168·4	,,
11	Faridpur ..	48	195	143	73·3	53	35	66·0	176 0	,,
12	Rajshahi ..	30	178	148	83·1	51	30	58·8	162·6	,,
13	Mymensingh	24	185	149	80·5	48	37	77·0	173·9	,,
14	Dacca ..	29	180	142	78·8	44	32	72·7	173·2	Rāḍhīya
15	,, ..	36	188	140	74·7	50	37	74·0	170·4	,,
16	Hughli ..	34	181	146	80·6	46	36	78·2	174·6	,,
17	Burdwan ..	30	177	138	77 9	43	31	72·0	154·0	,,
18	Calcutta ..	42	18[illegible]	146	81·1	47	36	76·5	171·4	,,
19	Nadia ..	31	167	140	83·8	44	37	84·0	169·0	,,
20	,, ..	25	177	138	77·9	47	34	72·3	166·4	,,
21	Rungpur ..	31	187	136	72·7	45	38	84·4	162·0	,,
22	Murshidabad	26	198	16	80·8	46	40	86·9	176·0	,,
23	Hughli ..	26	175	141	80·5	56	34	60·7	164·6	,,
24	Murshidabad	26	188	140	74·4	48	40	83·3	163·9	,,
25	Jessore ..	38	199	155	79·3	51	36	70·5	165·6	,,
26	Khulna ..	37	180	155	86·1	50	31	62·0	164·4	,,
27	Jessore ..	30	191	146	76·4	45	37	82·2	166·0	,,
28	Dacca ..	33	195	140	71·8	43	41	97·7	167·0	,,
29	,, ..	32	175	143	81·7	44	37	84·1	163·0	,,
30	Faridpur ..	24	178	142	79·7	48	37	77·0	162·2	,,
31	24-Parganas	44	184	148	80·4	40	42	105·0	167·2	,,

Pāścātya Vaidik Brāhman (Bengal).

1	2	3	4	5	6	7	8	9	10
Serial No.	District of birth.	Age.	Head length.	Head breadth.	Cephalic index.	Nasal height.	Nasal breadth.	Nasal index.	Stature.
1	24-Parganas (Bhatpāḍā).	26	190	148	76·3	56	34	60·7	178·0
2	,, ..	24	181	150	82·8	46	38	82·6	170·6
3	,, ..	21	170	142	83·5	44	33	75 0	165·0
4	,, ..	41	174	140	80·4	46	35	76·0	159·2
5	,, ..	34	174	145	83·3	50	35	70·0	157·2
6	,, ..	40	178	137	76·9	47	36	76·6	156·2
7	,, ..	42	188	150	79·7	49	37	75·5	165·2
8	,, ..	25	181	139	79·7	51	33	64·7	165·2
9	,, ..	52	171	141	82·4	53	38	71·7	163·0
10	,, ..	37	182	148	81·3	50	30	60·[illegible]	169·7
11	,, ..	23	181	142	78·4	44	32	72·7	167·5
12	,, ..	47	185	145	78·3	44	35	79·5	152·7
13	,, ..	32	195	154	78·9	47	36	76·6	174·6
14	,, ..	23	165	148	89·6	47	35	74·4	172·7
15	,, ..	30	181	144	79·5	41	30	73·1	162·8
16	,, ..	25	191	131	68·6	50	34	68·0	170·5
17	,, ..	23	174	140	80·4	51	30	58·8	173·7
18	,, ..	50	174	144	82·7	49	38	77·5	159·6
19	,, ..	40	185	143	77·3	47	39	82·9	162·6
20	,, ..	37	180	145	80·0	52	31	59·6	159·2
21	,, ..	24	184	144	78·2	47	30	63·9	168·2
22	,, ..	53	183	144	78·7	46	37	80 4	173·5
23	,, ..	23	180	147	81·5	51	31	60·8	174·0
24	,, ..	31	190	147	77·6	51	35	68·6	165·0
25	,, ..	45	178	135	75·8	52	31	59·6	165·2
26	,, ..	25	175	139	79·4	50	39	78·0	174·0
27	,, ..	25	175	150	85·7	55	31	56·3	169·7
28	,, ..	22	175	144	82·2	47	30	63·8	168·2
29	,, ..	28	184	146	79·3	49	31	63·2	167·4
30	,, ..	32	192	147	76·5	48	32	66·6	162·2
31	,, ..	41	176	150	85·2	50	33	66·0	162·2
32	,, ..	34	183	153	83·6	53	33	62·2	156·8
33	,, ..	32	183	149	81·4	48	32	66·6	159·2
34	,, ..	35	174	143	82·1	45	36	80·0	159·8
35	,, ..	25	172	145	84·3	49	35	71·4	168·2
36	,, ..	35	190	156	82·1	48	36	75·0	170·0
37	,, ..	35	171	138	80·7	43	33	76·6	156·2
38	,, ..	45	190	151	79·4	48	39	81·2	161·5
39	,, ..	49	188	145	77·1	43	41	95·3	166·2
40	,, ..	49	181	140	77·3	43	39	90·7	164·5
41	,, ..	29	181	142	78·3	52	35	67·3	169·5

Pāścātya Vaidik Brāhman (*Bengal*)—concluded.

1	2	3	4	5	6	7	8	9	10
Serial No.	District of birth	Age	Head length	Head breadth	Cephalic index.	Nasal height.	Nasa breadth.	Nasal index	Stature
42	24-Parganas (Bhatpaḍa)	34	191	140	73·3	45	38	84·4	169·0
43	,, ..	36	175	130	74·3	46	32	69·5	161·0
44	,, ..	25	193	156	80·8	46	39	84·8	171·8
45	,, .	22	175	143	81·7	48	35	72·9	164·0
46	,, ..	34	188	144	76·6	53	37	69·8	179·2
47	,, ..	26	189	145	76·7	44	33	75·0	172·5
48	,, ..	25	183	145	79·2	46	35	76·0	172·0
49	,, ..	45	176	137	77·8	49	30	61·2	162·5
50	,, ..	52	186	160	86·0	50	37	74·0	173·2

Uttararāḍhīya Kāyastha.

1	2	3	4	5	6	7	8	9	10
Serial No.	District of birth.	Age.	Head length.	Head breadth.	Cephalic index.	Nasal height.	Nasal breadth.	Nasal index.	Stature.
1	Murshidabad ..	28	187	144	77·0	49	37	75·9	165·2
2	Burdwan ..	33	182	136	74·6	47	32	68·0	165·3
3	,, ..	34	173	145	83·8	48	43	89.6	162·1
4	Dinajpur ..	32	196	145	73·9	51	34	64·7	167·3
5	Murshidabad ..	38	181	141	77·9	45	43	95·5	165·2
6	,, ..	27	181	143	79·0	49	45	91·8	171·0
7	,, ..	25	178	139	78·0	47	36	76·6	170·0
8	Burdwan ..	41	180	138	76·6	46	37	80·4	171·0
9	Murshidabad ..	34	191	145	75·9	47	38	80·8	172·3
10	Dinajpur ..	25	183	152	83·0	47	36	76·6	169·0
11	Murshidabad ..	31	183	138	75·4	41	33	80·4	170 0
12	Dinajpur ..	28	185	145	78·4	48	33	68·8	161·3
13	,, ..	30	171	130	76·0	42	33	78·6	155·2
14	Murshidabad ..	44	185	136	73·5	44	34	77·3	164·2
15	Dinajpur .	27	180	150	83·3	53	36	67·9	172·0
16	Burdwan ..	36	195	141	72·3	54	34	63·1	179·0
17	Murshidabad ..	29	175	140	80·0	44	37	84·0	155·0
18	,, ..	42	183	130	71·0	50	40	80·0	161 0
19	Dinajpur ..	26	190	139	73·1	47	33	70·2	170·0
20	Murshidabad ..	47	186	140	75·2	46	36	78·2	171·0
21	Dinajpur ..	53	177	132	74·5	46	35	76·0	164·0
22	Murshidabad ..	25	180	139	77·2	40	35	87·5	162·4
23	Burdwan ..	53	204	145	71·0	46	35	76·0	171·0
24	,, ..	30	188	149	79·2	41	34	82·9	170·2
25	,, ..	27	190	142	74·7	50	36	72·0	169·4
26	Birbhum ..	33	188	136	72·3	47	32	68·0	171·6
27	Murshidabad ..	53	180	135	75·0	50	36	72·0	175·0
28	,, ..	49	189	134	70·8	45	37	82·2	166·8
29	Bhagalpur ..	26	187	149	79·6	44	38	86·3	169·0
30	Murshidabad ..	51	173	142	82·0	55	37	67·2	162·0
31	,, ..	33	185	140	75·6	44	34	77·2	159·4
32	Birbhum ..	24	185	140	75·6	48	33	68·7	171·4
33	,, ..	45	194	143	73·7	45	36	75·5	168·0
34	Hughly ..	23	190	145	76·3	44	38	86·3	167·0
35	Burdwan ..	30	182	141	77·4	43	33	76·7	168·6
36	,, ..	30	180	140	77·7	47	38	80·8	165·0
37	Jessore ..	33	185	154	80·3	42	31	73·8	181·0
38	Burdwan ..	34	176	145	82·3	45	37	82·2	161·4
39	Jessore ..	42	181	144	79·5	46	34	73·9	174·0
40	Murshidabad ..	29	190	141	74·2	44	38	86·3	173·0
41	Birbhum ..	39	180	137	76·1	52	36	69·2	179·2
42	Murshidabad ..	29	184	139	75·5	43	33	76·7	169·0

Uttara Rāḍhīya Kāyastha—continued.

1	2	3	4	5	6	7	8	9	10
Serial No.	District of birth.	Age.	Head length.	Head breadth.	Cephalic index.	Nasal height.	Nasal breadth.	Nasal index.	Stature.
43	Murshidabad ..	26	189	145	76·7	45	38	84·4	165·2
44	,, ..	38	185	143	77·2	37	37	100	162·4
45	,, ..	39	179	142	79·3	51	38	74·5	165·0
46	,, ..	39	195	140	71·8	40	36	90·0	161·7
47	Hughly ..	45	184	140	76·0	51	37	72·5	169·8
48	Murshidabad ..	42	192	149	77·6	50	36	72.0	161·6
49	,, ..	30	180	142	78·8	52	34	65·4	162·0
50	Hughly ..	31	190	142	74·7	46	41	89·1	164·0

Kāyastha (Bengal).

1	2	3	4	5	6	7	8	9	10	
Serial No.	District of birth.	Age.	Head length.	Head breadth.	Cephalic index.	Nasal height.	Nasal breadth.	Nasal index.	Stature.	Sub-caste.
1	Faridpur ..	38	175	139	79·4	44	35	79·5	163·0	Vaṅgaja.
2	Dacca ..	37	181	133	73·4	44	30	68·1	159·6	,,
3	,, ..	33	175	142	81·1	47	33	72·1	162·0	,,
4	Faridpur ..	33	181	143	79·0	50	33	66·0	182·0	,,
5	Dacca ..	39	181	143	79·0	48	43	89·5	164·0	,,
6	Mymensingh	25	173	136	78·6	45	36	80·2	161·0	,,
7	Faridpur ..	36	198	144	72·7	45	37	82·2	175·2	,,
8	,, ..	33	186	141	75·8	47	35	74·5	164·0	,,
9	,, ..	27	181	131	72·3	50	30	60·0	169·2	,,
10	24-Parganas	48	194	145	74·7	46	39	84·8	172·6	,,
11	,, ..	43	186	155	83·3	50	41	82·0	178·6	,,
12	Faridpur ..	35	175	139	79·4	45	37	82·2	161·1	,,
13	Khulna ..	37	192	142	73·9	43	37	86·0	169·0	,,
14	Murshidabad	41	185	148	80·0	45	36	80·0	171·6	,,
15	,, ..	41	176	154	87·5	49	34	69·4	168·4	,,
16	Dacca ..	27	168	145	86·3	48	37	77·0	167 8	,,
17	,, ..	36	188	145	77·1	41	35	85·4	174·0	,,
18	Howrah ..	40	186	158	85·1	47	40	84·9	165·0	Dakṣiṇa Rāḍhīya.
19	Hughly ..	32	185	136	73·5	45	37	82·2	161·0	,,
20	,, ..	37	186	145	77·9	46	41	89·1	172·2	,,
21	Calcutta ..	43	194	150	77·3	43	38	88·4	169·0	,,
22	Burdwan ..	32	188	136	72·3	46	34	73·9	163·0	,,
23	,, ..	30	193	143	74·0	50	34	68·0	163·6	,,
24	Calcutta : ..	45	177	149	84·2	49	38	77·5	166·4	,,
25	Hughly ..	40	179	137	76·5	46	38	82·6	167·4	,,
26	24-Parganas	46	177	152	85·8	52	36	69·2	172·4	,,
27	Khulna ..	30	177	141	79·6	49	36	73·4	163·0	,,
28	Pubna ..	27	165	145	87·8	43	34	79·0	142·8	Vārendra
29	Rajshahi ..	42	185	150	81·0	50	37	74·0.	174·6	,,
30	,, ..	31	182	147	80·0	49	30	61·2	166·0	,,

Tili or Taulika (Bengal).

1	2	3	4	5	6	7	8	9	10
Serial No.	District of birth.	Age.	Head length.	Head breadth.	Cephalic index.	Nasal height.	Nasal breadth.	Nasal index.	Stature.
1	Rajshahi ..	35	188	158	84·0	50	38	76·0	169·2
2	,, ..	36	188	157	83·5	50	36	72·0	163·4
3	,, ..	32	185	142	76·6	53	37	69·8	170·6
4	,, ..	38	185	140	75·6	47	37	78·7	153·6
5	,, ..	26	190	149	78·4	45	38	84·4	155·8
6	,, ..	25	185	145	78·3	46	37	80·4	158·0
7	,, ..	45	177	137	77·4	48	34	70·8	167 0
8	,, ..	32	180	144	80·0	42	35	83·3	167 6
9	,, ..	45	170	131	77·0	45	37	82·2	158·4
10	,, ..	38	177	135	76·2	47	36	76·6	162·0
11	,, ..	26	185	135	72·9	45	34	75·5	169·8
12	,, ..	45	180	145	80·5	45	35	77·7	160·4
13	,, ..	30	196	150	76 5	50	39	78·0	169·6
14	,, ..	34	186	143	76·8	47	37	78·7	161 0
15	,, ..	38	184	140	76·0	48	37	77·0	162·0
16	,, ..	42	185	148	80 0	50	42	84·0	170·0
17	,, ..	45	184	138	75·0	42	35	83·3	162·0
18	,, ..	29	186	148	79·6	43	39	90·7	166·0
19	,, ..	45	183	143	78 1	43	38	88·3	160·0
20	,, ..	30	175	142	81·1	40	32	80·0	163·0
21	,, ..	33	183	135	73·7	42	35	83·3	158·0
22	,, ..	32	182	143	78·5	37	36	97·3	158·2
23	,, ..	44	193	137	70·9	42	40	95·2	169·4
24	,, ..	32	175	137	78·2	38	35	92·1	151·4
25	,, ..	42	183	140	76·5	40	39	97·5	154·2

Vaidya (Bengal).

1	2	3	4	5	6	7	8	9	10	
Serial No.	District of birth.	Age.	Head length.	Head breadth.	Cephalic index.	Nasal height.	Nasal breadth.	Nasal index.	Stature.	Sub-caste.
1	Dinajpur ..	39	180	139	77·2	37	35	94·5	161·4	Rāḍhīya.
2	Burdwan ..	33	200	146	73·0	45	38	84·4	168·8	,,
3	,, ..	25	186	141	75·8	45	33	73·3	159·0	,,
4	,, ..	31	181	145	80·1	48	38	79·1	168·0	,,
5	Hughli ..	36	183	150	81·9	46	38	82·6	168·6	,,
6	,, ..	29	176	147	83·5	51	39	76·5	172·6	,,
7	Calcutta ..	38	182	144	79·1	48	37	77·0	163·7	,,
8	Hughli ..	23	189	140	74·0	45	38	84·4	162·6	,,
9	Calcutta ..	26	180	145	80·5	52	29	55·7	179·4	,,
10	Dacca ..	34	195	152	77·9	47	41	87·2	159·4	Vaṅgaja.
11	Calcutta ..	26	200	158	79·0	45	40	88·8	178·6	,,
12	Dacca ..	51	198	145	73·2	49	41	83·6	168·8	,,
13	Jessore ..	34	189	141	74·6	45	38	84·4	157·2	,,
14	Dacca ..	23	198	146	73·7	51	38	74·5	179·0	,,

Chāsī Kaivarta or Māhiṣya (Bengal).

1	2	3	4	5	6	7	8	9	10
Serial No.	District of birth.	Age.	Head length.	Head breadth.	Cephalic index.	Nasal height.	Nasal breadth.	Nasal index.	Stature.
1	Rajshahi ..	45	185	144	77·8	52	36	69·2	165·2
2	,, ..	26	180	144	80·0	45	39	86·6	163·0
3	Nadia ..	35	183	147	80·3	49	35	71·4	173·8
4	Rajshahi ..	30	182	132	72·5	50	38	76·0	161·4
5	Nadia ..	25	186	143	76·8	46	39	84·7	170·8
6	Rajshahi ..	25	180	130	72·2	48	34	70·8	164·6
7	,, ..	30	184	138	75·0	46	36	78·2	169·0
8	,, ..	32	181	136	75·1	47	35	74·4	161·4
9	,, ..	30	182	135	74·1	40	39	97·5	171·2
10	,, ..	35	177	136	76·8	45	41	91·1	160·6
11	Nadia ..	44	183	150	81·9	43	36	83·7	164·2
12	Faridpur ..	30	182	139	76·3	45	38	84·4	166·2
13	Rajshahi ..	25	180	129	71·6	45	33	73·3	159·0
14	,, ..	25	167	133	79·6	40	34	85·0	158·7
15	,, ..	32	182	137	75·2	47	31	65·9	174·8
16	Nadia ..	33	187	134	71·6	48	34	70·8	169·4

Bhuiṁhār Brāhman or Bābhan (Bihar).

1	2	3	4	5	6	7	8	9	10
Serial No.	District of birth.	Age.	Head length.	Head breadth.	Cephalic index.	Nasal height.	Nasal breadth.	Nasal index.	Stature.
1	Arrah ..	30	193	136	70·4	51	34	66·6	166·0
2	Patna ..	24	185	143	77·3	48	40	83·3	172·0
3	Gaya ..	24	183	140	76·5	51	35	68·6	174·0
4	Arrah ..	23	186	140	75·2	48	37	77·0	171·8
5	Muzaffarpur .	24	182	148	81·3	48	36	75·0	169·0
6	Chapra ..	24	185	140	75·7	43	42	98·6	176·0
7	Gaya ..	23	182	141	77·4	42	35	83 3	165 0
8	Patna ..	24	195	153	77·3	43	41	95·3	163·2
9	,, ..	26	190	136	71·6	40	33	82·5	176·4
10	Gaya .	28	184	142	77·1	46	38	82·5	174·0
11	,, .	23	189	139	73·5	45	38	84·2	168·0
12	Arrah	24	194	144	74·2	40	38	95·0	180·4
13	Patna ..	26	192	140	72·9	47	36	76·6	175·2
14	Champaran ..	25	177	143	80·8	48	36	75·0	178·2
15	Gaya ..	24	194	135	69·6	44	37	84·0	168·0
16	Champaran ..	23	184	144	78·3	45	37	82·0	171·6
17	Gaya ..	24	192	140	72·9	48	33	68·7	165·8
18	,, ..	25	182	134	73·6	43	39	86·0	169·2
19	Patna ..	25	188	138	73·4	43	38	88 6	170·0
20	Muzaffarpur ..	24	183	146	79·7	43	39	86·0	176·6
21	Gaya ..	26	199	145	72·9	43	37	86·0	173.0
22	,, ..	24	183	147	80·3	45	32	71·1	167·0
23	,, ..	24	196	141	71·9	49	37	75·5	178·6
24	Patna ..	24	190	143	75·2	43	40	93·0	167·0
25	,, ..	25	190	135	71·1	42	36	85·7	168 6

Maithiḷa Brāhman (Bihar).

1	2	3	4	5	6	7	8	9	10
Serial No.	District of birth.	Age.	Head length.	Head breadth.	Cephalic index.	Nasal height.	Nasal breadth.	Nasal index.	Stature.
1	Bhagalpur ..	25	191	134	70·1	43	36	83·7	163·8
2	,, ..	24	186	131	70·4	40	35	87·5	165·2
3	,, ..	26	194	132	68·0	48	36	75·0	164·2
4	,, ..	23	194	139	71·6	44	31	70·4	168·0
5	,, ..	24	180	130	72·2	42	33	78·5	155·6
6	,, ..	23	186	130	69·8	45	32	71·1	171·8
7	,, ..	40	185	145	78·3	44	31	70·4	158·8
8	,, ..	60	192	135	70·3	46	35	76·1	163·2
9	,, ..	32	184	138	75·0	46	35	76·1	169·0
10	,, ..	25	184	140	76·1	44	39	88·6	160·6
11	,, ..	50	190	138	72·6	43	34	79·5	156·0
12	,, ..	27	198	138	69·6	43	38	88·3	167·4
13	,, ..	50	183	137	74·8	47	38	80·8	162·6
14	,, ..	37	177	142	80·2	41	35	85·3	169·8
15	,, ..	55	194	131	67·5	36	38	105·5	165·8
16	,, ..	34	182	135	74·1	36	38	105·5	153·4
17	,, ..	40	182	145	79·6	48	35	72·9	155·6
18	,, ..	35	191	139	72·7	43	38	88·3	169·0
19	,, ..	25	194	142	73·2	46	35	76·0	166·6
20	,, ..	27	190	142	74·8	47	35	74·4	173·2
21	,, ..	29	182	144	79·1	45	36	80·0	166·0
22	,, ..	27	185	145	78·3	44	38	86·0	169·0
23	,, ..	27	191	135	70·6	44	36	81·8	159·0
24	,, ..	24	183	136	74·3	47	35	74·4	174·2
25	,, ..	37	190	132	69·4	45	37	82·2	165·8
26	,, ..	34	195	139	71·2	45	35	77·7	169·0
27	,, ..	55	203	143	70·4	51	36	70·5	171·2
28	,, ..	52	204	150	78·4	54	35	64·8	172·8
29	,, ..	27	183	147	80·3	43	35	81·4	169·2
30	,, ..	32	186	145	77·9	51	35	68·6	163·8
31	,, ..	25	186	144	77·3	48	34	70·8	157·0
32	,, ..	40	179	131	73·1	48	36	75·0	157·0
33	,, ..	28	192	140	72·9	42	37	88·0	162·0
34	,, ..	28	189	147	77·8	44	36	81·8	150·6
35	,, ..	39	193	135	69·9	41	36	87·8	164·0
36	,, ..	48	185	140	75·7	42	34	80·9	167·0
37	,, ..	50	190	141	74·2	41	38	92·7	164·0
38	,, ..	35	192	151	78·6	55	35	63·6	170·2
39	,, ..	23	189	134	70·9	46	37	80·4	160·4
40	,, ..	25	195	137	70·2	41	38	92·7	170·0
41	,, ..	28	200	139	69·5	45	36	80·0	171·0
42	,, ..	22	204	135	66·6	43	39	92·0	160·8
43	,, ..	55	190	143	75·2	49	38	77·5	161·8

Maithila Brāhman (*Bihar*)—continued.

1	2	3	4	5	6	7	8	9	10
Serial No.	District of birth.	Age.	Head length.	Head breadth.	Cephalic index.	Nasal height.	Nasal breadth.	Nasal index.	Stature.
44	Bhagalpur ..	45	200	142	71·0	46	37	80·4	164·2
45	,, ..	36	187	135	72·2	48	38	79·1	165·6
46	,, ..	50	190	138	72·6	46	40	86·9	176·6
47	,, ..	50	196	140	71·4	43	38	88·3	170·4
48	,, ..	30	193	144	74·6	48	38	79·1	171·8
49	,, ..	35	202	136	67·3	53	38	71·7	165·6
50	,, ..	34	190	135	71·0	44	37	84·1	164·2

Rājput or Chatri (Bihar).

1	2	3	4	5	6	7	8	9	10
Serial No.	District of birth.	Age.	Head length.	Head breadth.	Cephalic Index.	Nasal height.	Nasal breadth.	Nasal Index.	Stature.
1	Muzaffarpur ..	23	191	145	75·9	39	35	89·7	175·4
2	,, ..	24	199	140	70·3	41	36	87·9	166·3
3	,, ..	23	189	138	73·0	39	32	82·0	160·2
4	,, ..	23	181	145	80·0	43	38	88·3	162·0
5	Arrah ..	35	165	138	83·6	48	37	77·0	170·8
6	,, ..	28	194	134	69·0	49	35	71·4	165·2
7	Muzaffarpur ..	32	176	146	82·9	45	32	71·1	177·4
8	Arrah ..	35	195	143	73·3	46	43	93·4	169·4
9	,, ..	23	181	143	79·0	45	35	77·7	162·6
10	,, ..	24	186	138	74·1	42	37	88·7	169·8
11	,, ..	23	191	137	71·7	41	33	80·4	170·0
12	,, ..	30	191	139	72·7	43	38	88·3	174·4
13	,, ..	27	188	150	79·7	42	35	83·3	174·8
14	Gaya ..	22	190	142	74·7	47	42	89·3	165·5
15	Chapra ..	32	191	135	70·6	52	34	65·3	166·8
16	Arrah ..	30	194	135	69·5	42	39	92·8	164·0
17	,, ..	37	192	137	71·3	48	35	72·9	172·8
18	,, ..	25	181	140	77·1	51	35	68·6	168·8
19	,, ..	45	186	134	72·0	44	31	70·4	161·8
20	,, ..	45	192	151	78·6	46	43	93·4	170·8
21	Chapra ..	45	181	153	84·5	45	38	84·2	169·6
22	Arrah ..	24	190	145	76·3	45	39	86·6	170·6
23	,, ..	24	202	137	67·8	40	39	97·5	167·4
24	,, ..	22	190	143	75·2	43	39	92·0	166·8
25	,, ..	24	191	144	75·4	44	34	77·2	170·0
26	Chapra ..	23	196	139	70·9	41	35	85·3	170·4
27	Arrah ..	25	178	138	77·5	40	37	92·5	164·0
28	Chapra ..	23	185	146	78·9	44	33	75·0	168·0
29	Muzaffarpur ..	22	193	142	73·5	45	39	86·6	169·2
30	Arrah ..	23	185	140	75·6	47	37	78·7	171·0
31	,, ..	24	190	136	71·5	48	37	77·0	167·2
32	,, ..	25	191	135	70·6	43	33	76·7	167·8
33	Chapra ..	23	188	135	71·8	47	35	74·4	170·0
34	,, ..	23	173	151	87·3	40	35	87·5	165·2
35	Arrah ..	26	198	142	71·7	51	38	74·5	183·2
36	,, ..	25	189	139	73·6	41	35	85·3	171·0
37	,, ..	22	188	139	73·9	44	37	84·0	165·0
38	,, ..	23	185	146	78·9	43	40	93·0	175·0
39	,, ..	24	183	148	80·8	50	36	72·0	170·0
40	Bhagalpur ..	22	190	135	71·0	46	39	84·7	168·2
41	,, ..	23	190	141	74·2	47	37	78·7	165·0
42	Chapra ..	24	186	141	75·8	44	38	86·3	166·0
43	,, ..	23	189	137	72·4	41	35	85·3	165·0
44	,, ..	40	195	142	72·8	45	37	82·2	176·0

Kanaujiya Brāhman (Bihar).

1	2	3	4	5	6	7	8	9	10
Serial No.	District of birth.	Age.	Head length.	Head breadth.	Cephalic index.	Nasal height.	Nasal breadth.	Nasal index.	Stature.
1	Muzaffarpur ..	35	192	136	70·8	42	37	88·0	172·0
2	" ..	32	180	135	75·0	48	29	60·4	170·0
3	Arrah ..	36	192	139	72·3	44	40	90·9	169·4
4	" ..	24	186	136	73·1	44	36	81·8	174·2
5	Chapra ..	26	191	135	70·6	54	37	68·5	166·6
6	Arrah ..	25	180	146	81·1	46	36	78·2	165·4
7	Chapra ..	24	191	143	74·8	47	36	76·5	165·4
8	Arrah ..	36	199	142	71·3	50	35	70·0	172·8
9	Bhagalpur ..	24	198	142	71·7	44	38	86·3	165·4
10	Arrah ..	24	186	135	72·5	46	36	78·2	163·0
11	Chapra ..	26	173	142	82·0	48	32	66·6	171·0
12	" ..	23	187	139	74·3	44	32	72·7	165·8
13	Arrah ..	45	183	142	77·5	48	35	72·9	162·2
14	" ..	24	183	140	76·5	50	37	74·0	160·0
15	" ..	23	193	136	70·4	42	38	90·4	169·8
16	" ..	22	190	139	73·1	45	35	77·7	173·2
17	" ..	24	173	143	82·6	44	35	79·5	163·2
18	" ..	25	185	140	75·6	43	35	81·4	165·4
19	Chapra ..	30	188	140	74·5	41	36	87.8	173·0
20	" ..	..	177	142	80·2	43	38	88·3	175·6
21	Arrah ..	26	187	142	75·9	49	39	79·5	170·8
22	Palamau ..	30	195	135	69·2	45	34	77·2	173·0
23	Arrah ..	27	197	140	71·0	40	33	82·5	174·0
24	" ..	28	187	139	74·3	42	36	85·7	168·0
25	" ..	26	190	136	71·5	44	34	77·2	163·2

Summary of Head Measurements.

Name of caste and tribe.	Province of birth.	Percentage of Cephalic Indices.					
		Under 70.	70 and under 72·5.	72·5 and under 75.	75 and under 77·5.	77·5 and under 80.	80 and over.
29 Santals. ..	Santal Parganas	20·7	17·2	10·3	44·8	0	7
31 Brahmans ..	Bengal ..	0	6·5	13	19·5	16	45·5
50 Pāścātya Vaidik Brāhmans ..	,, ..	2	0	4	22	26	46
50 Uttara Rāḍhīya Kāyasthas ..	,, ..	0	10	18	40	16	14
30 Kāyasthas ..	,, ..	0	6·6	20	17	20	36·6
25 Tilis or *Taulikas*..	,, ..	0	4	4	8	40	24
14 Vaidyas ..	,, ..	0	0	35·7	21·8	14·3	28·6
16 Chāsi Kaivartas..	,, ..	0	18·7	12·6	44	6	18·7
25 *Bhuṁhār* Brāhmans (*Bābhan*)	Bihar ..	4	16	28	32	8	12
50 Maithila Brāhmans	,, ..	18	26	26	14	12	4
44 Rājputs or Chatris	,, ..	6·8	25	22·7	20·4	11·3	13·6
25 Kanaujiya Brāhmans	,, ..	4	32	28	20	0	16

Seriations (Risley).

Name of caste or tribe.	Province of birth.	Percentage of Cephalic Indices.					
		Under 70.	70 and under 72·5.	72·5 and under 75.	75 and under 77·5.	77·5 and under 80.	80 and over.
100 Santals ..	Chota Nagpur	1	11	25	28	21	13
420 Rājputs ..	Rajputana ..	17	36	26	15	5	1
100 Brāhmans ..	United Provinces ..	16	24	34	15	9	2
68 Brāhmans ..	East Bengal ..	0	1	12	21	31	35

ADDITIONS AND CORRECTIONS.

Page 6, line 8, *for* Śabara *read* Śavara.

,, ,, ,, 22, *for* -ecting *read* -jecting.

,, 9, ,, 23, *omit* Semangs who are now differentiated from the Sakai as a separate and independent type probably most closely connected with the Andamanese (Nigrito).

,, 13, ,, 25, *for* reign *read* rain.

,, 19, ,, 17, *for* Atharvanas *read* Atharvans

,, 22, ,, 19. The Visvâmitras avenged themselves by casting Śakti into fire. "Śakti is said in the *Jaiminīya Brāhmaṇa* to have been the son of Vasiṣṭha, and to have been cast into the fire by the Viśvāmitras. According to Saḍguruśiṣya, who appears to follow the Śātyayanaka, the story of Śakti is as follows: Visvāmitra, being defeated in a contest by Śakti, had recourse to Jamadagni, who taught him the *Sasarparī*, later he revenged himself on Śakti by having him burnt in the forest. The *Bṛhaddevatā* relates the first part of the tale only." (*Vedic Index*, II, pp. 348-349.)

,, 23, ,, 9, *for* Sudāsa *read* Sudās.

,, ,, ,, ,, *for* Paijavana *read* Pijavana

,, 24, ,, 8, *for* Brahman *read* Brāhman.

,, 37, ,, 15, *for* Vāhika *read* Vāhīka

,, 38, ,, 21, *for* Ghanntas *read* Ghnantaś.

,, 39, ,, 12, *for* or one *read* or upon one.

,, 40, ,, 1, *for* Aṇga *read* Anga.

,, ,, ,, 8, *for* Ānarṭṭa *read* Ānartta.

,, 43, ,, ,, *for* representations *read* representatives.

,, 48, lines 14-18. This passage is quoted from Oldenberg's *Buddha*, English tr. (London, 1882), p. 392 note.

,, ,, line 21, *for* Kanśāmb *read* Kauśāmb.

,, 49, ,, 29, *for* Brahman *read* Brāhman.

,, 53, lines 3-6. According to the *Lalita Vistara* (Lefmann, p. 21) there was no king in Vaiśālī. "Every one thinks, 'I am king, I am king'" (एकैक एव मन्यते । अहं राजा अहं राजेति). But in the city of Mithilā, the capital of the kingdom of Videha, a king named Sumitra reigned (p. 22) at the time of the Buddha's descent from the Tuṣita heaven

Page 61, line 18, *for* Chola *read* Cola.
,, ,, ,, 19, *for* Pāndyas *read* Pāṇḍyas.
,, 62, ,, 17, *for* on indices *read* of indices
,, 70, ,, 29, *for* Turkistan *read* Turkestan
,, 76, ,, 1, *for* Rudra *read* Agni
,, 82, lines 4-5, *for* Ramskṛṣṇa *read* Ramkṛṣṇa.
,, 86, line 11, *for* Bālcaritā *read* Bālacarita.
Pages 96-99, *for* Bhâgavadgītā *read* Bhagavadgītā.
Page 97. Garbe's interpretation of Gitā vii. 4-6 is very instructive. "When it is asserted in vii. 4-6 that God has two natures, one a higher spiritual nature, by which the universe is sustained, and a second, a lower and material nature, consisting of all that, according to the Sāṅkhya, belongs to *prakṛti* or matter, this statement is not to be construed in the sense that a half of the Divine essence is composed of matter, the meaning is rather that matter is not itself independent, following its own blind impulses, but that its evolution is under the control of God, in other words, that God works in matter, and acts through it. This is clearly expressed in other passages of the Bhagavadgitā. God deposits in matter the germ from which development takes place (xiv. 3, 4) He is therefore the father of all creatures, while matter may be compared to the mother's womb" (*Encyclopaedia of Religion and Ethics*, II, p. 536*b*)
,, 99, line 16, *for* Nigrantha *read* Nirgrantha.
,, ,, ,, 19, *for bhāśya read bhāṣya.*
,, ,, ,, 24, *for* Śāndilya *read* Śāṇḍilya.
,, 100, ,, 15, *for* Laksmi *read* Lakṣmi .
,, 101, ,, 8, *for* Bhāgavadgītā *read* Bhagavadgītā.
,, 116, ,, 5, *for* authors *read* author.
,, 119. ,, 2, *for* and " have *read* and who " have.
,, 124, ,, 31, *for* in the epithets younger, &c., *read* in the epithets, " younger, &c.
,, 126, ,, 3, *for supujitā read supūjitā.*
,, ,, ,, 4, *for* Prākṛtā *read* Prākṛt.
,, 129, ,, 14, *for Mārkandeya read Mārkaṇḍeya.*
,, 142, ,, 16, *for bhiksukī read bhikṣukī.*
,, 145, ,, 9, *for* Nāgabhata *read* Nāgabhaṭa.
,, 148, ,, 24, *for sāmsāra read saṃsāra.*
,, 152, ,, 3, *for* perference *read* preference.
,, 157, ,, 11, *for* Bhagdatta *read* Bhagadatta.
,, 159, ,, 19, *for* Chaldeean *read* Chaldean.
,, 164, ,, 3, *for* Sarsvatī *read* Sarasvatī.
,, 165, , 16, *for* inscription *read* inscriptions.
,, 168, ,, 27, *omit* Vilāsadevi.